THE FALCON AND THE SERPENT

THE FALCON AND THE SERPENT

Cheryl A. Smith

CROSSWAY BOOKS • WESTCHESTER, ILLINOIS
A DIVISION OF GOOD NEWS PUBLISHERS

The Falcon and the Serpent.

Published by Crossway Books, a division of
Good News Publishers, Westchester, Illinois 60154.

First printing, 1990

Cover illustration: David Yorke

Printed in the United States of America

Library of Congress Catalog Card Number 89-81262

ISBN 0-89107-556-9

To Stephen
who first showed me
the love of the
Redeemer God

. . . you have been born again not of seed which is perishable but imperishable . . . through the living and abiding word of God.

(1 Peter 1:23, NASB)

. . . He, . . . because He abides forever, holds His priesthood permanently.

(Hebrews 7:24, NASB)

One

The air shimmered with a barely suppressed excitement. Sunlight filtered down through the trees like golden honey dripping from the branches. The air was filled with the sound of insects as they darted through the sunlight, their bright-colored wings patterning the blue, cloudless sky. The villagers could feel that something was coming and many sought out the priests wanting to know if it would be good or bad. The priests comforted the people, giving them news of good things to come; the very air foretold it.

Cand-hoen had received few visions from the gods in his lifetime, even though he was the high priest. He had received one when he was a small boy that even now haunted his waking moments. But as frightful as that vision of the destruction of his god had been, it was not as awful as the vision he had received last night. It was terrifying if only for the reason that he did not understand it.

He poked at the remembrance of it, sifting through the images, trying to glean the meaning from it. But it still eluded him this morning. He did not give the people meaningless words of comfort when they came to him, for he did not feel that the wind bore good tidings. As beautiful as the summer day was, and he had seen no better, there was an underlying current of tension or dread, something evil.

He looked out the window upon the village: the people scurrying about their business, animals always under foot and wagon wheel, shouts filling the air. He searched the faces of the people he knew, scanning their activities, hoping to find the cause of his unrest. His gaze at last rested on a young boy, and Cand-hoen could not stop the smile that spread over his face at the sight of him. He was perhaps a little dirtier than the rest of the boys, his hair maybe less brushed. His face, although unremarkable in its composition, was filled with an awe for life which transformed his face into something wonderfully beautiful. As Cand-hoen gazed and marveled, his heart filled with love for the boy, and for a time he forgot the distress his omen had placed in him.

Cand-hoen did not have long to wait before the knock came at his door. He turned and watched as the boy entered, unhesitant about his reception, the wonder in his face a marvelous window into his soul. *Ah*, thought Cand-hoen, *was my delight ever that high?* He smiled at the boy. "What brings the prince to the temple today?"

"You know why I have come, Uncle Candy."

"Why should I know something like that?"

"Did you get it?"

"Did I get what?"

"Uncle Candy . . . my birthday is less than two days away!"

"Is it now? What do you want me to do about it, boy?"

"You know! You promised me a god! Did you get me one?"

"A god? I promised? I don't remember. It was a long time ago."

Prince Temrane threw his arms around the priest. "I know you did! You wouldn't forget."

"Temrane, your father would not be happy if I got you a god."

"We won't tell him then, Uncle Candy. Oh, please." His voice and face pleaded; the dark eyes shone with the very thought of it. "In two days I become a man. What is a man without a god?"

Sometimes a king, Cand-hoen thought bitterly, but said nothing. If his relationship with his brother, the king, was a little on the cool side, at least it did not extend to his brother's son. The relationship between the prince and the priest, between nephew and uncle, was as close—closer—than that between father and son. Cand-hoen could ask little else of the gods.

To Temrane he said, "A good question, that. What is a man without a god?"

Temrane took the stance of a pupil before his master. "A man without a god is a drifter. He is one who takes from the land and returns nothing. When he is dead, the land will take him and return nothing."

"Very good, young prince."

Temrane's eyes sparkled, the pleasure of pleasing the high priest greater than anything else he could have asked. "Tell me again, Uncle Candy, about your father and how he became a priest."

Cand-hoen settled back in his chair, preparing to indulge the nephew he could never refuse. "Your grandfather's name was Moc. As a young man of five and twenty, he used to walk through the fields day after day, hour after hour. He loved the fields. He loved the feel of the wheat brushing against his bare legs, the smell of the wet earth after the rains fell, the feel of the fruit as it dropped in his hands. And as he walked day by day, hour by hour, he asked, 'Where does the fruit come from? Why does the rain fall on the earth? Why does wheat grow?' One day as he walked in the wheat, the rain began to fall. The wind also began to blow, and it blew so hard that Moc was thrown to the ground. He picked up handfuls of damp earth, and he heard these words from the heavens: 'I am the earth god, Hoen. I give life to the crops . . . I make the rain fruitful . . . I give life to man, for man is but earth. Serve me.' Moc stood up, still with the earth in his hands, and he vowed to be a priest. In honor of the god, he changed his name from Moc to Moc-hoen and . . ."

". . . he raised his children . . ." Cand-hoen and Temrane turned at the unexpected voice of the king. ". . . Cand-hoen and Fel-hoen to serve the earth god as priests. So it has been, so shall it always be." King Fel-hoen looked at his son. "It is a story for little children, not men." Temrane dropped his eyes in shame. "Come . . . a dark, stale temple is no place for a man on a summer's day such as this."

Temrane stood, and though he did not say anything to his uncle, Cand-hoen could read the volumes written in his sorrowful eyes.

As he watched man and boy mount their horses, a wave of desperation flooded over Cand-hoen, and he relived again the frightful confusion of his vision.

• • •

Fel-hoen tried to shake off the mood he had created in his son when they left the temple. He cursed himself for it, knowing that was not the way to turn his son away from service to a god. As he had rebelled against his father and left the priesthood, so now his son would undoubtedly rebel against him, and Moc-hoen would indeed be vindicated.

"So," he began, forcing cheerfulness back into his voice, "the celebration is in two days' time. Are you excited?"

"Yes, Father."

"The whole realm will celebrate the day you become a man. There will be feasts and drink and singing. I had wanted that minstrel—what is his name? . . . Batakis!—to come and play. But unfortunately the realm of Paduan has some sort of feast in Beren on that day and he cannot come. Is there another minstrel other than your favorite?"

"The court minstrels are very good," Temrane said dutifully. Then, knowing it would anger his father, but being unable to contain himself any longer, he said, "Will I have the Calli-kor, Father?"

Fel-hoen's anger threatened to rise and choke his forced cheerfulness. He had done so much to prepare for this birthday, so much revelry and merrymaking—and all his son could think of was the religious rite! This was the doing of Cand-hoen . . . the king was sure of it! He smiled tightly. "Of course . . . Every man goes through the Calli-kor. You will be no different because you are a king's son."

Temrane's heart leapt. His father would let him go through the Calli-kor, even though it was a temple rite. His father could not risk the anger of the people he ruled; though he had strayed far from the gods' ways, his people had not.

"I will not disappoint you, Father."

You already have, my son, Fel-hoen thought. *You already have.*

• • •

"He hates me, Kenda."

"He doesn't hate you. You're his father."

"He respects me because I am his father. But he loves Cand-hoen. He always has."

"He and Cand-hoen are very special to each other. Why can you not be glad for that?"

"How can I be glad of anything that concerns Cand-hoen? He is taking my son from me."

"No . . . You, my husband, are giving him to Cand-hoen by driving your son away from you."

Fel-hoen looked at his wife and was once again amazed at her beauty. Kenda's dark hair surrounded the fair oval face like a picture frame. Her eyes were splashes of blue color, snapping at him now because the argument was an old one. Their daughter, Merry, had taken after her in the way she looked and in her personality. Temrane looked more like the father, with dark skin and eyes and yet hair that was strangely gold. Temrane had also inherited his stubbornness, though as of yet he had not acquired his love for the throne.

"How am I driving him away?"

"You refuse him the thing he loves, and so he searches for it elsewhere."

"You mean, of course, the gods?"

"I do. I knew when I married you that the gods were not important to you, and I married you anyway because you were more important to me than the gods were. Perhaps that was my mistake. But I think the gods are punishing you with a son who loves the gods and temple worship. He is bound to be a priest, Fel-hoen, whether you approve of it or not. The gods have marked him."

"You are a fool, woman! Do not speak to me this way! He is a prince first and last. He is not marked to be a priest. He is a king's son, and a king's son he shall remain!" Fel-hoen strode out of his wife's bedchamber, raging at her, his son, and the gods.

He entered his own chambers, sending away with a glare the servants who came to attend him. How dare she speak to him as if he were a servant and not the king! He put up with her only because she was as beautiful as the summer day that had just finished.

Kenda has no idea how close she came to the mark, the king thought to himself. Fel-hoen closed his eyes as he thought of what was to take place immediately after the birthday celebration and after the Calli-kor. Temrane would indeed become a priest, but he would be a priest to the old wizard Crotalus. Even the name caused Fel-hoen to shudder as his mind recalled the scaly skin and the grizzled hair that hung to the waist. In two days' time . . . Fel-hoen sighed. What had begun sixteen years ago was now about to reach its terrible conclusion.

It had seemed back then like the world stretched out in front of him in an endless number of eternities. Sixteen years. What appeared so interminable at the beginning now in reality was ending. In two days' time, it would be over.

• • •

Cand-hoen lay on his straw pallet and tried to sleep, but it eluded him as surely as seeking to grasp clouds in the hand. He remembered the fear that had swept over him as he watched Fel-hoen and Temrane ride away from the temple. His vision had something to do with them, but he didn't know what.

Often in his role of priest, people came to him with dreams they wished him to interpret. Most of the time Cand-hoen was surprised that the dreamer couldn't come up with his own explanation, because it seemed so simple, so clear. At other times he had to work harder, but knowing the person involved usually gave him a clue as to what the dream meant. Never had anyone come to him with a vision. Oh, they all thought their dreams were visions, but none had that sparkling clarity of a vision. They were dreams, and he interpreted their dreams as though to delight little children.

He reflected now on the two times in his life he had received a true vision. The first came when he was Temrane's age and had been serving his father, the high priest, in the temple. Cand-hoen had never thought of a life beyond the temple, and he never wanted to be anything but a priest, as his father had been. The temple that day was filled with smoke from the incense, but the sweet smell could not remove the stench of dead animals from his nostrils, which this day seemed particularly strong. He watched as his father, never so big and powerful as on this day, raised the knife above the struggling form of a young lamb. As Moc-hoen's knife descended into the lamb, and Cand-hoen watched the blood spurting over the knife and the hands of his father, Cand-hoen was suddenly removed from the temple.

He stood on a high and grassy hill in Corigo overlooking the village of Zopel. He could identify even now what hill it was. The temple he served in, the temple his father had raised to Hoen, was no longer standing. But in its place, larger than anything Cand-hoen had before seen, stood the god. He was massive in grandeur, and the bronze muscles stood out starkly. Although he wore no clothing, vines covered him, vines bursting with life. This was Hoen himself, the god of earth and of all earthly existence. Cand-hoen stood straighter as he looked upon him, for he was proud to serve such a wonderful god as this.

And then he noticed the lamb standing next to him on the hill, looking at him with dark, liquid eyes. He stared at the lamb for a long time before the lamb spoke. And when the lamb did speak, all he said was "Look!" Cand-hoen did look, and the sight amazed him. A large knife was descending from the skies, a priest's knife. It struck the image of Hoen on the head, and the god split in two and crumbled to the ground.

The next thing Cand-hoen remembered was his father gently slapping his face, trying to get him to wake up. His father said later that as he was coming around, he kept muttering over and over, "No blood . . .

No blood," but his father could make nothing of it. Moc-hoen recognized the signs of a vision and tried to get his son to disclose it to him and the other servants in the temple. Cand-hoen steadfastly refused. To tell what he had seen was impossible.

The vision even now sometimes frightened him. Yet, the one he had yesterday was worse in a way because it was so confusing. Cand-hoen had at last come to some sort of conclusion about that first vision. The god was not a sacrifice . . . of course not . . . how could he be? Cand-hoen decided the meaning of it was to make sure god and sacrifice were always separated.

But this new vision he had no answer for. Again he stood on the grassy knoll overlooking Zopel. In the middle of the village was the temple, but it was much larger in the vision than in real life. It filled the village, and everyone came to it. There were other temples, other gods: Lanyi, the sun god; Kurelo, the moon god; Velad, the goddess of the sea. But none of these gods or temples compared with that of Hoen.

The lamb again stood at Cand-hoen's side. It opened its mouth, but instead of the bleat of a lamb the roar of a lion filled the air. Leaves danced to the sound of that roar, and the air trembled with joy. Cand-hoen looked, and the lamb had changed. The white fleece was replaced with a coat of tawny gold. The black mane framed a face that was at once horrible and beautiful. Velvet paws rested on the ground for only a moment before springing forward from the hill. Cand-hoen watched as the lion landed in the middle of the temple, and the temple suddenly was no more. The lion too was gone.

Cand-hoen watched silently, grieving, but whether he grieved over the loss of the lion or the temple he could not tell. People wept with him, crying in an anguish he could scarcely bear. People around him were dying, starving, murdering, fighting, whipping, lashing, hating. Cand-hoen stood in the middle of them. All of them touched him, and yet he alone remained whole. Fel-hoen crawled to him on the ground, his king's crown askew and dented, his royal robes torn and soiled. Then Cand-hoen was wearing both the crown and the robes, whole and beautiful. And still the people died . . .

At first, upon awakening, Cand-hoen thought the vision was an old dream he had once had about taking the kingship away from Fel-hoen. But those days were long gone. He no longer raged, even silently, about Fel-hoen's betrayal. It still grieved him, as only the betrayal of a brother could. But he was no longer jealous . . . He was sure of that! Why then a vision in which amid thousands of people suffering, he rose victorious—amid loss, he alone gained?

Cand-hoen shivered in his bed though the night was warm. He felt as though he had looked into a pit as dark as midnight and had seen his own soul.

Two

The summer night of Corigo masked the landscape. The air was warm; a slight breeze dancing with the trees cooled the air only momentarily. Clouds, surprisingly bright in the dark sky, covered the full moon, throwing long shadows on the paved road, called The King's Highway, between the cities of Zopel and Beren.

Merry rode through the velvety summer night toward the realm of Paduan. Her maid, Elenu, rode silently beside her, her only companion. Merry knew that her father, the king, would be furious with her were he to know of this midnight ride to Paduan. Hopefully he would not find out. She would be in Paduan by morning and back in Zopel by nightfall. She did not want to go into the capital city, or any of the cities of Paduan for that matter; she just wanted to cross the border.

Twenty miles off the main road between Zopel and Beren ran the South Conmia River. Between the South and North Conmia Rivers, it was said, lay some of the most fertile and beautiful land Hoen had ever given to his people. Merry thought this talk was foolishness. If it was the most beautiful land, why didn't Hoen give it to the people who worshiped him, rather than to the strange people of Paduan who were said to worship only one god and none of the common ones? And why didn't Cand-hoen build the temple there between the rivers? Possibly because he was afraid of water. Was Hoen also fearful of running water?

But no matter what her feelings were on the subject of the gods and their dealings with men, her brother, Temrane, was one of the most loyal followers of Hoen she had ever known. And his birthday was in two days. He wanted something from the earth god, and Merry could think of nothing better for him than something taken from this blossoming valley.

Merry, only two years older than Temrane,was already a woman; yet there was also much of the child in her. Temrane and Merry could not have been more dissimilar if they had been born of separate parents and lived separate lives in different places. Temrane was serious, striving always to please Hoen, most happy when he spent time in the temple with Uncle Candy. Merry was just what her name implied. She lacked the purposefulness of Temrane, she rarely gave thought to the gods, and though she loved Uncle Candy she much preferred her friends or her horse to sitting in a dark, cold, smelly temple. Temrane would no doubt have been shocked to hear such sentiments, but they got along as well as two diverse people who are brother and sister can.

The clouds which had covered the moon dissipated, and in moments the landscape was lit with an eerie silver light. In this light there was no color except black and silver. Stars on the edge of the sky blinked in the bright moonlight, beckoning to the two travelers. Merry watched as the things she knew melted away in the silver light and new things took shape. Trees grew taller here and filled the land. She could smell the ground, could almost sense its rich darkness with her nose. The more they descended, the softer the ground became. Trees grew more thickly, and grasses sprouted everywhere. She could feel the greenness with her body, though her eyes could not see it. They had crossed over into Paduan.

Merry knew that to the south, if she followed this road, lay Beren, the capital city. The peoples of Beren and Zopel often traded, and this road was heavily traveled between the two. But Beren, though she would like to go there someday, was not her destination tonight.

"Elenu," she spoke, breaking the long silence, "tell me where Eschay is."

"Oh, my lady, it is much too far to think of traveling there without a coach. We would have to go another hundred miles. It is on the near bank of the North Conmia."

"I don't want to travel there, certainly not this morning. But I have heard much of the people there."

"My grandmother's people were from there, my lady, before the thought of mining precious jewels brought them to Andurin."

"The people of Eschay are farmers, are they not?"

"They are. The Fertile Valley would be put to waste if it were not farmed. The people of Beren are farmers also, but it is a different farming. They have the sea, while Eschay has the river."

"What is farmed in the valley?"

"Every kind of fruit you can think of . . . vegetables . . . wheats for bread."

Merry was again silent, wondering what she could possibly take from this valley that would be worth anything to Temrane. She wished he could be here. She was sure that he would find the worship of Hoen more meaningful in this place of dark soil and rich-smelling loam. Surely the god himself resided here.

They crossed the South Conmia River at daybreak, and Merry was overcome with the beauty of the place. The red sun gently kissed the white clouds hovering over the valley, turning them a magnificent pink and then gold. The water of the river rushed by in a dazzling display of purple, white, and gold. Merry watched the sun play on the water, casting sparkling diamond drops before her, and she almost wished, for half a second, that her family truly worshiped Velad, the sea goddess, rather than Hoen. Of course, they paid homage to all the gods and goddesses. To not do so was foolishness. But every family had their own special god, and Hoen was theirs. *It is a pity though*, she thought, *because the water is so much more beautiful than the land.*

They found a broad, shallow place in the river and there crossed with their horses. Merry delighted in the water kicked up on her legs by the horse, and if Elenu would not have been with her, she would have splashed in the water herself, as happy as the fish she saw swimming by.

After crossing the river, Merry slipped from her horse and just stood a moment, aware with every part of her being that she stood in The Fertile Valley, Hoen's Valley. She could see the trees heavy with fruit still, even though it was summer. She could almost feel the earth pushing up the grains and grasses, offerings to the god. *How strange*, she thought, *that with so much life here in this valley, the people do not worship the god.*

"Let's leave the horses here by the river," she said to Elenu. "They will be safe. I wish to walk among those trees."

Elenu did as her mistress wished, and the two walked across the field until they came to a line of dark green trees, bearing a fruit that seemed to be made of temple gold. Merry reached forward and grasped one in her hand. It came away readily. The fruit was smooth and smelled of the earth. She was getting ready to bite into the wonderful fruit from Hoen's Valley when she heard a rustling behind her. She turned hurriedly, half-aware of Elenu's frightened look. Someone was coming quickly through the bushes.

"Into the trees," she whispered urgently to Elenu as she shimmied up the tree from which she had just taken the fruit. She watched as Elenu did the same. Merry knew that neither of them were covered very well by the branches; she only hoped that whoever was coming would be in such a hurry, he would not pay attention to the trees. In a sudden rush of panic, she remembered the horses. Whoever was coming would certainly see the horses and would most probably steal them, and she could do nothing about it.

She watched in wretched silence, impatient for the owner of the footsteps to come into view. At last he did, and Merry almost laughed, for he was a boy, not much older than herself, possibly seventeen. He had pale gold hair and fair skin. The clothes he wore were the clothes of a hunter. He strode through the trees easily, as though he had been through them many times. His gait had a naturalness about it that said he was at home in the woods.

Merry was sure neither she nor Elenu made any noise, but he suddenly whirled around and looked directly into the tree in which she perched uncomfortably. He walked beneath the tree, his eyes never leaving her, as if he had come across a rare species of bird. "What are you doing up there?" he asked.

Merry looked down into a face that was wholly kind. He was not angry, just inquisitive. "I didn't know who was coming through the woods. There could be robbers in these woods."

He laughed. "There are no robbers in these woods. Only farmers. The robbers are all in the city."

He helped her down from the tree and then turned to help Elenu. "I am Kreith . . . at your service." He bowed low, sweeping from his head an imaginary hat, and though his voice was half-mocking, Merry was delighted.

"I am Princess Merry, daughter of King Fel-hoen from the realm of Corigo. This is my maid Elenu."

"A princess! I had no idea I was entertaining such royalty. But you are far from home, your highness."

"I have come to Hoen's Valley to find a gift from the earth for my brother."

"Hoen's Valley? I have never heard it referred to as such. We call it The Fertile Valley."

"But Hoen is the god of the earth, and if this valley be more fertile than others, it is truly his valley." She heard a horn sound far off, a low, lonely sound. "What is that?"

"That is the king's horn. Today is the king's hunt. The realm of Paduan will be holding its annual feast in Beren tomorrow. We hunt now as a beginning of that feast."

"Are you a hunter then?"

"Yes, your highness."

"Are you not then of the royal family or the son of his knights?"

Kreith smiled at the disappointment in her voice. "I am but a simple man," he said laughingly. "Come, I will help you find a gift worthy for your brother, the prince."

"I think I have found one," she said holding the fruit out to him.

Kreith took the fruit and with his other hand took a knife from his belt. He sliced the fruit and handed both halves to Merry.

"Why, it's hollow!"

"This fruit is only good to look at, Princess Merry. It contains nothing on the inside to merit its beauty. Come further in the woods. I know just the fruit you wish."

They followed him in, walking among tall trees that bent down to shelter them from the rising heat of the sun. Soon they came to a sort of clearing. The trees thinned out and became shorter. Finally they came to a grove of trees that were only as tall as Merry. Its branches spread out several feet in all directions. There was not much fruit on these branches; most of it had been harvested. Kreith reached deeply into one, and though he came away with several scratches on his arm, he also came away with a beautiful fruit of dusky purple. He cut it open and again handed it to Merry. She looked at it for a moment, enchanted by its loveliness. The inside flesh of the fruit was a delicate pink, like the sunrise she had seen that morning over the valley. Moisture trickled through her fingers, sweet and sticky. She bit into the soft fruit, and her whole mouth awakened with its juice.

"This is a mevone tree. It is said that one will never die as long as one has the fruit of the mevone tree."

She finished the fruit and held the pit in her hand. It too was purple and smooth, almost like a nut. "The pit," Kreith said, "can be sliced and eaten like a meat, or it can be replanted to grow another tree."

"This is wonderful!" Merry exclaimed. "What a perfect gift for Temrane! Thank you, Kreith, for showing it to me."

Kreith only smiled at her and after obtaining more of the fruit led them back to where their horses quietly grazed on the dark green grass of The Fertile Valley.

He helped them mount the horses and watched as they rode off across the river, heading for Corigo. A horse's footfall sounded behind him.

"Kreith! I wondered where you had gone!"

"Hello, Falcon," he said to the king's knight, sitting astride a dark brown steed.

"Who was the girl I saw you with?"

"Princess Merry, from Corigo."

"She was very pretty."

"She was beautiful, Falcon. I have never seen a lovelier vision than she. I am in love."

Falcon did not laugh, as one might at such a sentiment from one so young. He knew that love, whenever it came and whether it was a first or last love, was special, a heartbreaking, sleepless, wondering special.

"Will you see her again?"

"I hope so, Falcon. I intend to spend much time in this valley to see if she will return."

"Does she know who you are?"

Kreith smiled a little sadly. "No. She thinks I am a farmer."

Falcon did laugh this time and was glad to see Kreith's wistful smile broaden.

"Come, your majesty," Falcon said. "We must be getting back to Beren."

Three

Zopel, the crown city of the realm of Corigo, lay at the base of the towering, cold Amil Mountains. Because the land was not friendly to farmers, animal husbandry was heavy in Zopel. Walking the streets of the city one could see large sows with piglets following close behind, chickens pecking the ground, goats sniffing anxiously at the large pockets of peasant boys, hoping for a tasty morsel, but settling for shirttails to chew on if there was nothing else. Sounds of neighing, braying, baaing, clucking, cooing mingled with the cries and laughter of the children, settling on the ears of all who lived in Zopel like snow settles on the dry, thirsty ground, for these were the sounds of life.

The cloud of doom that Cand-hoen had burdened under had not touched the village people. Life went on as normal during these fine summer days. Lomeli, the leatherworker, sold as much leather goods as he usually did in the Summer. Drucker's pigs grew nicely fat, and he and his wife looked forward to the slaughter in the Autumn harvest. He sought the gods daily to thank them for their providence and to petition further blessings. Anson, the blacksmith, shoed more horses than he had in a long time, hammer on anvil constantly ringing through the hot days and warm nights. The King's Highway connecting Zopel and Beren was traveled frequently, the trade being good between the animal community and the farming community. Apparently the gods had smiled on Beren also, though the people there did worship a god that no other god recognized.

Merry sat on the hill overlooking Zopel, feeling the contentedness of her life. Elenu sat with her, silent on her horse, waiting for her mistress to make a move toward the castle. Merry often chattered easily to Elenu, as though they were the best of friends rather than servant and royalty, but she had said little to Elenu on the ride back into Zopel. Elenu felt the change. She had always enjoyed the friendship with Merry, even though she knew that it would someday end and would become what it was meant to be from the beginning.

Though Merry did not say anything, Elenu could tell from the look on her face that she was thinking of the man she had met, Kreith. As if Elenu's thinking his name brought remembrance to Merry's mind, she sighed deeply. She looked to Elenu, who inadvertently smiled. Merry smiled back. "He was the most handsome man I have ever seen."

"He was that, my lady."

"His gold hair was even more beautiful than Temrane's, and his skin was light rather than dark. And his eyes! The Conmia River did not look as blue." She remembered his look as he watched her, his laugh, the sound of his voice.

"I could tell he liked you too," Elenu said timidly, for she was not sure that the friendship was restored yet. Her fears were put to rest by Merry's glance. Merry turned to her friend with a conspiratorial laugh.

"Do you think so? Oh, but it is no matter. He is a peasant."

"Many a royal person has fallen in love with a peasant."

"That is true, but my father would never consent to it. If I know my father, he already has a royal husband picked out for me . . . maybe the prince of another realm, so he can unite the realms . . . maybe a knight who would brave many fierce contenders for my hand."

"So . . . you will never see Kreith again?"

A slight shadow passed over Merry's face, blotting out the sunshine there, as if his very name were a delicious pain. "I will see him again, Elenu. Will you help me?"

"You know I will."

"On Temrane's birthday the whole realm will be celebrating. I will give Temrane his gift and then I will get sick. You must see me to my room. As soon as I am away from them, I will ride back to Hoen's Valley."

"My lady, you cannot ride alone!"

"Oh, I must, Elenu! You must stay behind in case someone asks for me. You can tell them I am still not well and need my rest. Oh, please, Elenu. You are the only one I can trust."

Merry had appealed to Elenu's weak point, their friendship. "I will help. But please be careful. Ride swiftly and return quickly."

Merry smiled, the sunshine dispelling all clouds. "Come . . . we must get to the castle now. We have already been away far too long."

Merry spurred her horse, and together they rode to the castle where they left their mounts with the stable boys. Merry then left Elenu to prepare her bath and clean clothes while she went in to her mother.

Queen Kenda was with her personal maid, Niccola, when Merry burst into the room. Niccola had the expensive brushes in her hands and was working magic with the long brown hair of her mistress. Merry stopped a moment, watching. Niccola had always fascinated her. The woman was beautiful. Her hair was a shiny black that caught at the lights when she passed by them. The thickness was luxuriant, and Merry knew that she perfumed it. Her skin was dark, her eyes almost black. She carried herself with a royal air and if Merry hadn't known Niccola she would have said she was a queen or a lady, and not the queen's servant. But the beauty stopped with her skin, for she was a sullen woman, and Merry had never known her to say much. She almost seemed to resent being the queen's personal maid, although it was a high position for any peasant to attain.

Kenda looked at her daughter with a fond smile, but did not say anything until Niccola had finished her hair. She then nodded to Niccola. "That will be all for now. Please prepare the blue dress for me for dinner tonight."

"Yes, Your Highness," she said stiffly and glided out of the room like a defeated princess.

Kenda turned in her chair to her daughter, and Merry rushed into her arms. "You look wonderful, Mother."

"Do not try to please me, child," she chided. "You have been missed since yesterday."

"Don't scold me, Mother. I had to go."

"I should have that maid of yours whipped for letting you go."

"Elenu's my friend. She accompanied me."

"Ah, Merry, when are you to learn that your servants are servants and not friends? They are to serve you."

"She does serve me, and I like her. She is much better than Niccola."

"Niccola is a wonderful maid. She does her work well without being chatty. Elenu would do well to look to that example. You are not a child anymore, my dear; you are the princess, and it is time you acted like one. Your father will be very displeased when he hears of this."

Merry smiled. "You mean he doesn't know yet? Oh, Mother, please don't tell him! I was getting a present for Temrane, something really wonderful. Please don't spoil it!"

Kenda stroked her daughter's lovely hair and delighted in the twinkle in her blue eyes. She could not refuse anything to her daughter for very long, even though she knew it would not be the last time; the twinkle told her that.

Something is different, Kenda thought as she watched Merry flitting around the room like a butterfly, lighting on this and that, not able to be still. *She is in love. It shows in her smile, her eyes, the way she carries herself.* Kenda could not help but wonder who the man was, sighing that it should come so soon.

• • •

Niccola sat in the servants' quarters that she shared with her husband, Lomeli. The grate was cold, and she did not light any lamps. She hated the small apartment and wanted to see as little of it as possible: the tiny kitchen in one corner of the room, a bed in another corner. She clenched and unclenched her fists. She had known that the queen would be with the princess for a time, so Niccola had at least an hour free before she would have to prepare the queen's dress and toilet for dinner. She should have gone to the castle library; no one would be using it this time of day, and she could easily slip in and out.

She grunted in disgust and kicked at the small table at her feet. She had been in that library for months now and had not found anything in the history of the family that she could use. The closest thing to a scandal the family had ever seen was Fel-hoen leaving the priesthood and becoming king. But the whole realm knew about that; it was not a secret.

Her heart yearned to find something she could use against him, some way to attain the royalty she deserved. She had been betrayed . . . horribly, wickedly betrayed. And now, instead of ruling she submitted, instead of ordering she served. And instead of living with a king, she lived with Lomeli.

The bitterness rose in her until it almost choked her with its hotness. Lomeli, the plodding, unimaginative, unintelligent leatherworker. She couldn't bear his presence, his leather smell, his rough touch. She had borne him a son, Caldon, five years ago. Why couldn't Lomeli leave her alone now? Caldon already followed him around like a loyal worshiper. He had eyes only for his father.

She stood suddenly, upsetting the table, the lamp crashing to the floor. *Let them live in squalor*, she thought viciously, *I refuse*. She stormed out of the small living quarters and headed surreptitiously to the castle library.

• • •

Lomeli ran his hand over the finished piece of leather. Its smoothness caressed his fingertips, and the smell of newly worked leather rose up in his nostrils, making him tingle with pleasure. It was always this way when he completed a task. The smell and excitement were always new to him, always a joy. This piece was for Malcolm, the king's knight, and Lomeli swelled with pride. There were other leatherworkers in the realm of Corigo, a few of them in Zopel, but *he* had been chosen to serve the king, his knights, and his nobles. He wondered sometimes if that could have been because Niccola was the personal maid to Queen Kenda (what an honor that was!), but he preferred to think that it was his love for the leather, which made his workmanship superior.

His round apple-face beamed as Caldon rushed in the door. He was teaching the love of leather to his son early in life, as his father had him, and Caldon was responding much the same as he had, with wide-eyed wonder. But Caldon barely paid attention today to the jerkin his father had just finished, his mind filled with good news that wanted to burst from him at the first sight of his father.

Lomeli swept him into his large, sinewy arms. "What is the rush, Caldon?"

"It is Aunt Freyda, Papa. Devona is with her now. Uncle Farni sent me to say that it is time and that we must offer a prayer to the gods." Caldon smiled deliriously when he finished, not only because of the news, but because he had been commissioned to send it.

Although Lomeli's sister, Freyda, and her husband served Velad, the sea goddess, and he served the mountain god, Anok, he still respected all the gods and did as Farni asked. He and Caldon bowed in front of the god Lomeli kept in the workroom, and together they asked for the blessing of all the gods on the small child about to make his passage into the world of men, leaving the world of the gods.

• • •

Farni stood outside the small cottage he and Freyda shared with their daughter Lis. He could hear Freyda's moans from inside, escalating into screams when the pain gripped her. He could feel his own heart speed up as her pains got worse. He had been through this before, when Lis was born. He felt he shouldn't be afraid, and yet he was. His palms were sweaty, his heart pounding, his ears straining at each sound, but trying to shut out the sounds of labor nonetheless.

He peeked through the open window of the cottage where he could see Freyda lying on the bed, covered with the white down comforter that had been part of her dowry. Devona, the midwife, was bustling around the room, preparing blankets, water, a place to lay the babe.

He considered Devona as she hurried by, effectively taking his mind off his fear for Freyda. Devona had been midwife as long as he could remember. She could be anywhere from fifty to seventy years old. No one really knew except Devona herself, and she wasn't telling. Farni was thirty, and he knew that Devona had delivered him to his parents.

Her looks didn't betray her age either. The hair, though gray, was piled softly and gently on her head, falling now and then around the nape of her neck, as it did now in the heat of the summer night. Her blue eyes were as clear as a child's, sparkling with secret knowledge. Wrinkles touched her eyes lightly with laughter. She had never had a husband, although she often joked that her beaus had been plenty. Her heart was as good as the sunshine, for though she lived in Beren and worshiped a different god, she never stayed away from Zopel because of it. In fact, her work brought her often into Zopel, and she had delivered most of Zopel's children and their children after them. There were other midwives, but everyone wanted Devona because of the laughter in her eyes and her love for children.

She rushed past the window again at a particularly piercing scream from Freyda. "You mustn't scream, Freyda. Push! Use that energy to push the child into the world!"

Farni looked to his wife, focusing on her sweat-streaked face. To him she was as beautiful now as on the day he married her, even though her hair had begun to show a little gray. She had a hard life, one that told on women. Her hands, which had once teased him with their softness, were now red and rough, the hands of a fisherman. They had worked together for the ten years of their marriage, hauling and mending nets, repairing boats, cleaning fish. There was nothing Freyda could not do as she worked willingly alongside him. It was a good life, for it brought food to the table and clothes for their backs.

Then came Lis, a beautiful girl with the kiss of the gods on her face. Food became harder to put on the table, for Lis was sickly and was not able to work with them in the boats.

Farni closed his eyes and offered a silent prayer to Velad for a son who could help them in the business.

"Farni?" He opened his eyes to see Devona summoning him through the window. He entered the cottage. Freyda's face was averted, but Devona was smiling. She held a bundle of blankets out to him. He took it and looked at his second child. The face was red and scrunched up, as though it hated being in this cold and bright world. He pulled down the blankets a little to see the tiny fist curled lightly around the blanket. He slipped his finger inside, wondering, as he always did, about this small life.

"You have another daughter," Devona said. Farni looked to Freyda, and she was watching him, a tear silently coursing its way down her face.

"It doesn't matter," he said, although his heart ached. "We shall call her Anne, because Freyda's mother's name was Anne."

Devona took the babe from him and gently laid it in Freyda's arms. Farni watched as Freyda's eyes cleared and she stroked her baby's face and fuzzy head. Devona touched his arm. "Come . . . Let us walk a moment before you return to Freyda. Let her rest a moment before you talk."

They walked along the edge of the yard. "I know you are disappointed with having another girl, Farni. So is Freyda, a little. But she is a woman, and a woman always loves her child. She will love this child unless she does not see the love in you. The Redeemer God gives only good gifts. They do not always seem such, but the Redeemer God has His purposes. Take this as a gift from His hand and love her."

He could not speak because the tears had welled in his eyes and in his throat. He was deeply touched by her concern, and he squeezed her hand to show that he understood her.

He went back to the cottage alone, for Devona had to return to Beren. Farni stood looking at the new member of his family a moment before going in to Freyda. The reddish face was becoming a more natural color, the brown fuzz on her head stood straight up, her lips were pursed in the whistle of sleep. He could not help but love her.

"I'm sorry, Farni," Freyda whispered softly from the bed. He instantly went to her, took the hand she held out, and sat on the edge of the small cot they shared. "I know we wanted a boy. We can't afford a girl. Perhaps we should give her to the temple."

He had often thought this while Freyda was with child. The priests of Velad did not like to take a child for a sacrifice, but Hoen would. Farni had considered this, knowing it would be pleasing to the god and perhaps they would then be blessed with a son. But now such thoughts seemed barbarous. He could not countenance taking that small, wondrous baby to the temple.

"No," he said at last. "She is ours. As Devona said, the gods have their purposes. Who are we to question the ways of the gods?"

A tear slowly slid down Freyda's face to dampen the pillow. "Devona says many strange things and worships an even stranger god. Velad, and indeed all the gods I know of, say to serve well and be blessed well. I did something wrong, Farni. I am being punished for something. I will go to the temple tomorrow and make sacrifice for my wrong. We shall try again and this time I shall not fail. The gods will be pleased with me, Farni . . . I promise."

He stroked her damp face lovingly with his fingers until she had again fallen asleep. What could he say? This was the way of their gods. Freyda was right. They had not done enough. That was why Lis was sickly and why their second child had been born a girl. He would also go to the temple and make it right. The gods would be pleased with them both.

• • •

Cand-hoen waved the incense solemnly through the temple, cleansing it, making a pleasing smell to Hoen. Drucker still lay prostrate before the god, and Cand-hoen wished for a moment that Drucker would leave so he could go to bed. But it was a fleeting thought. He often yearned for the townspeople to be more like Drucker and his wife, Winni. Drucker was in the temple every night, Winni every morning. If their animals grew fat and harvest looked good, they thanked Hoen for his faithfulness. If things went wrong, they made sacrifice for their sins. They had one son, Jasper, who was eight, and a sunbeam of a daughter named Kalei, who was three. They longed to have more children as proof of the god's favor, and Cand-hoen suspected that might be the nature of the prayers tonight. The hoped-for pregnancy had not materialized, and that meant more money to the temple, more sacrifices, more pigs to the priest. They were holy people, and this was proved by their success in life.

At last Drucker rose to his feet. "The fertile time is upon Winni," he said to Cand-hoen. "Perhaps I have done enough this time. Do you think I should purchase another god, just in case?"

"No. You already have four for the four in your family. And you come to the temple twice a day. I shall petition for you also."

Drucker grasped his hand tightly, gratefully, knowing that the priests did not often petition for specific townspeople. Hoen would certainly hear the prayers of his own priest—he would have to. Drucker went home to Winni joyful and expectant.

Four

Devona sang a song to the Redeemer God as she walked along the road to Beren. Her heart was light and full of love, as it always was when she helped bring a child into the world. She only hoped that Freyda and Farni would love the girl. She knew why people wanted boys, but a girl could offer much to a family like that. With Freyda working alongside Farni in the fishing boat, a girl would be able to take care of the family and the house the way Freyda would have liked to. She would be able to work with Lis, as her parents did not have the time to do.

Devona heard a cry behind her as a wagon approached, and she turned to see Batakis, the minstrel, waving to her. She waited for the two-horse wagon to pull beside her.

"Devona, I thought that was you! Why do you walk? Where is your wagon?"

"A rim broke from the wheel. It is being repaired, but will not be ready until next week. So I walk. It is good for these old bones."

"Come, ride with me."

Batakis jumped from the wagon and helped Devona into the small seat next to his. "I've always liked to have company with me on the road, and your company is more welcome than most."

Devona laughed at his gallantry. As he hopped back into the wagon, he looked very like a flame with his red shirt and bright blue pants. The sight of him was enough to make anyone smile, any blue spirits rise.

"Whose baby did you deliver in Zopel? I know quite a few of the ladies are with child."

"The fisherman and his wife, Farni and Freyda. Do you know them?"

Batakis screwed up his brow in thought. "They have a daughter? Lis?"

"Yes . . . the one with the twisted leg."

"Ah," he said with emotion clouding his face, "I would give just about anything to make her whole. She is a delightful child. I don't know the parents."

"They are good enough people. But they believe that Lis is a punishment for something they did that did not please their goddess. Freyda just now gave birth to another girl, even after sacrificing and praying for a boy, and they believe the new one is another punishment. I fear they labor under a very heavy burden."

Batakis had seen it often in his travels to Zopel. He and Devona were perhaps the only two people from Beren who were trusted enough to share their lives, to know of the gods of Zopel, to talk of the Redeemer God. He had seen the burden Devona spoke of and knew it was indeed a heavy one.

"Why were you in Zopel?" Devona asked.

"I have a new stock of toys that I took around to the families."

"And how many did you sell?" she asked, for Batakis was well-known for his soft heart and easy generosity.

"Enough," he replied. "Don't chide me, Devona. I make enough money when I entertain to keep me fed. I have never made much money from the toys anyway."

She didn't doubt that was true, but he spent so much time making the toys, and she knew that a piece of his heart went into each one. There wasn't a child in Beren or Zopel who didn't have a toy made by Batakis—and not one child in Beren or Zopel who didn't love him fiercely and loyally.

Batakis winked at Devona. "I make enough money to take a wife and keep her fed as well."

She slapped playfully at his arm. "Don't start that again, young man. I'm old enough to be your grandmother."

"Not my grandmother . . . Maybe my mother, but not my grandmother."

"You are right. I didn't deliver your mother, but I did deliver you and watched you grow up. That was thirty years ago, Batakis, and my courting days are done."

"But you never married and therefore they aren't finished."

She slapped at him again. "That will be enough talk like that, Batakis. Any more of it and I shall leap out of the wagon and walk."

"All right, I shall be silent for now. What would you like me to speak about instead?"

"Tell me your plans for the feast."

"I have nothing planned beyond walking the streets and entertaining. I will take part in some of the games, but not in the hunt. I never could ride a horse. What will you do?"

"Like you, I have no plans except to be with my many children. Bria has offered me a part of their meal, and I shall likely take it."

"I was hoping you would share the meal with me."

Devona laughed, and the sound jingled with the bells on the minstrel's wagon. "People would begin to talk if we spent too much time together, Batakis."

They rode down the road to Beren pleasantly, and it was hours later when Kerrin, the only daughter and youngest child of the king's horse trainer, ran from the village excitedly to meet them, shouting to the other children that "Batakis is back!"

He smiled and shrugged to Devona, but she knew that he was highly gratified and that this was his real reward for what he did in life. He handed her the reins and jumped from the wagon, sweeping Kerrin into his arms almost instantly. Soon the blue pants and red shirt were lost in a sea of laughing and hugging children, and all Devona could see of Batakis was the curly dark head rising above the rest. His face could well have been that of a child. He had never grown a beard like most of the men in Beren, and his face with bright blue eyes staring out of it was as guileless as a babe's. She watched as he reached into the back of the wagon, uncovered his wooden wares, and handed out toys all around. As he showed how each one of them worked, some of them climbed into the wagon and onto Devona's lap.

We are quite a pair, she thought. *He is their favorite uncle, and I am their favorite grandmother.*

The children scattered soon, playing with their new toys, shouting for parents to come and see. Batakis leaped back into the wagon, and Devona for an instant wondered if he ever got in and out of a wagon in a normal manner. "Where can this handsome coach and coachman drop your ladyship?" he asked as he took the reins from her hands.

"I should like to see Bria for a moment to discuss with her the plans for the feast."

He drove her to the bakery where Bria and her husband, Alde, made the best pastries that ever tantalized a nose. He helped her out of the wagon and waved to her as he drove off, promising to see her during the feast.

Inside the bakery, her nose delighted in the mingling smells, and her eyes feasted on the flaky wonders. Bria and Alde had been baking for two days in order to have enough for the feast. Tarts, scones, and waffled cookies invited the mouth to taste just a little. Devona wound her way past these delicacies to the back of the shop where the baking was done. Both Bria and Alde were there, rolling out the dough that would become the top crust of a berry pie bursting with red juice.

Alde did nothing more than nod at her and went back to work. Devona, although she tried hard to see good in everyone, had trouble seeing it in Alde. He was an angry, jealous man who found some piece of gossip to spread about everyone in Beren. Devona reflected that as bitter as Alde was, he had a wife whose disposition was as sweet as the good things she baked.

"Devona! It's good to see you!"

"I came by to see if you needed any help with anything for the feast."

"How thoughtful of you! No . . . Alde and I have things working just fine now. The ovens were not heating properly yesterday, but they have been fixed, thank goodness! Oh, here comes Constance! I must get back to the oven. Devona, will you give her what she needs? Thank you so much. And I shall see you early tomorrow. We shall go to the grounds together."

Constance was Queen Alexandria's maid. Devona had not seen much of her, for she was a loyal servant and did not leave the queen's side unless on a special errand.

Devona wrapped her order for her, and they chatted about the goings-on at the castle. Everyone in the castle, indeed the entire realm of Paduan, was preparing for the annual feast tomorrow. The games, the fights, the food, the hunt – each person had some duty to perform to be in readiness. "Prince Kreith is even more excited about this feast than the last," said Constance. "I believe that the more of a man he becomes, the more he realizes the feast's importance to the realm."

Devona nodded in agreement. "He is becoming a fine man and in time will become a fine king."

• • •

But Kreith on that fine summer's day, with the smell of the feast in the air and Batakis' songs on the wind, was not thinking of the day he would become king. He was not thinking of anything in Paduan at all. His thoughts lay to the northwest, in Corigo and more specifically, in Zopel. The vision of Merry with the silken dark hair and enchanting eyes stayed with him, teasing him with its nearness, tugging at his heart.

"You still think of the lady," Falcon commented when he noticed that his talk of the feast was not being listened to.

"Yes . . . She is the most lovely woman I have ever seen." Kreith dismounted his horse and sat against a tree. Falcon waited a moment and then did the same, knowing that Kreith's lesson in weaponry would be useless today. As the king's knight, Falcon was entrusted with teaching the prince the ways of war in preparation for the throne. It was a high honor, one that Falcon took seriously, but he also knew when to cease the lessons and be a friend to the young prince, who naturally was sometimes a little lonely.

"Have you ever been in love, Falcon?"

Falcon sometimes went for months without thinking of Rafaela, but occasionally something would intrude into his inner world, thrusting a dagger of pain deep within him. This happened now, and for a moment he could not speak. With years of practice behind him, he hardened his heart and spoke flippantly. "Yes . . . once."

"What was she like?"

"She was short and fat and had a wart on her nose and chin. Oh, yes, and she was bald besides. She died of ugliness."

Kreith laughed. "What was she really like?"

Falcon sighed, wishing he could forget, knowing that he could not. "She was beautiful. But then, the woman that you're in love with is always beautiful."

"I am going to The Fertile Valley tomorrow."

"You don't know that she will be there."

"I will go there every day until I see her."

"You cannot go tomorrow. Tomorrow is the feast."

"I can do both. I will be at the feast in the early part of the day and then ride to The Fertile Valley."

"Your majesty," Falcon said gently, but using the more formal title as if to remind him of his post, "you will be wanted during the day at the games and the hunt."

"Falcon, don't deny me this. She is loveliness itself, and I shall die of a broken heart if I don't see her. Let's not do any more lessons today. I know you have things to ready for the feast, and so do I. Grant me this one thing, Falcon, and I promise that the day after the feast I shall work twice as hard."

Falcon laughed. "I have never been able to deny you anything for long, and you're already an excellent horseman, as well as swordsman. Go . . . prepare for the feast."

Kreith jumped onto his horse and looked at Falcon once more, still lying in the grass beneath the tree. His look was one of excited boyishness, even though he was seventeen. Falcon recognized the look of hero-worship on his young face and wished that Kreith had bestowed it on someone more able to carry the responsibilities of being a hero.

"Come early tomorrow, Falcon, please."

"I'll be there early. We must make sure that everything is ready because you will ride out with the knights tomorrow."

Kreith nodded and with the swiftness of rushing water rode toward the castle.

Falcon remained there only a moment before mounting his own horse and riding for the small hut he shared with his sister, Ivy, and their father. He knew when he arrived he would feel the warmth of their love, even in their bustle to prepare for the feast. He hoped their love would drive from his heart the pain that still hung like a heavy fog around the name Rafaela.

• • •

Bustle was the right word to use about Ivy. She flew around the house as though she had wings—cleaning, baking, sewing. Queen Alexandria needed the new dress by tonight, and Ivy almost had it finished. She stepped back and looked with a critical eye at her work. The dress beautifully draped the model in a shimmering blue silk. The dress puffed at the shoulders, gave way to a moderately low neckline and tight waist, then opened again at the hips to the fullness of a royal feast gown. Blue bows gathered material at the calf, revealing lace underneath. Blue was the color that seemed almost magical on Queen Alexandria. Ivy knew the queen would be pleased.

She smiled like a child when Falcon walked in the door. She stood in awe of her brother, a brother who was thirteen years older than herself. Although he had had to take on much of her raising since their mother died when she was three, he had never been harsh or resentful of her. It was he who had taught her how to sew and finally obtained her the job of seamstress. She loved him with the fierce and jealous love of a younger sister.

He pecked her on the cheek and looked at the dress for the queen with an eye almost as acute as her own. He had always judged her work, making sure everything was right, and it was a source of pride to her that he had not found anything wrong in the last three years. "It is very beautiful," he said at last. "Did you finish the dress you said you were going to make new for yourself?"

"Almost. I wanted to finish this one first. I only have a few last stitches on mine."

"May I see it?"

"You can see it tomorrow along with everyone else."

He saw her blush, and the color was very becoming on her fair skin. "Did you make it with someone special in mind?"

The blush deepened, and she would not look at him. "Who could be more special than my brother and father?"

Falcon smiled. "Who indeed?"

Ivy looked at him, saw the bantering smile, and laughed.

Most of the time Falcon still treated her like a young girl, forgetting that she was a woman of twenty-five. But on occasion, and this was one such, he was impressed by her womanliness. Her brown hair had long been piled on her head in an attractive bun, and the deep brown eyes held a liveliness and intensity that was foreign to children. He was grateful to her for not marrying and leaving the care of their father to him alone. But he felt a stab of guilt as he remembered the blush that was so beautiful on her. She should be married. It was not right for her to forsake marriage because of their father. He made a vow to watch her carefully tomorrow and find out which man it was that interested her. As the responsible party in the family, it was his duty to make sure the man she was in love with was honorable and a loyal servant to the Redeemer God.

"Stop teasing me. I can tell you are wondering who this man is in my life. Well, I have none. I just wanted to look nice for the feast. Now go in and see your father. He has asked for you."

"How is he today?"

"He is in much pain, but at least his mind is clear today."

Farrel Jaqeth had been a hero in the early wars of Paduan, when Jerome was still a prince fighting the evil king of Beren—Jerome's own father—in order to free the people from the opulence and greed that kept them poor and oppressed. Farrel had taken a poison arrow in his leg, and he lost all use of it. But he was a brave knight and one who was rewarded handsomely by Jerome when he finally took the throne. He was given land, a house on the land, and a wife. Falcon was glad that his mother, the wife of Farrel Jaqeth, had died before she could see the slow ravages of the poison. It had started very inconspicuously as Farrel forgot where he left his shoes or that he had already eaten breakfast. Falcon began to worry in earnest when he did not remember Ivy. He had summoned Devona, knowing that if anyone could help, it would be she. She could do nothing. His mind would slowly weaken until there was nothing left. He was already confined to bed except on those rare days when his mind was clear enough to be able to get into a chair.

Falcon knew that his father would attend the feast tomorrow in a coach sent especially for him from King Jerome, for Jerome had never forgotten, even though he was now king, the knights who had been his friends and who had fought so loyally at his side.

"Falcon, you are home early today."

"Prince Kreith could not keep his mind on lessons. He is in love, and it occupies every waking moment."

"Ah, yes, I remember. How wonderful it is to be young." Farrel's eyes became misty with remembering, and in a moment he was talking about the loves of his past and the one great love he had lost when Falcon's mother died.

Falcon held the old, gnarled hand as he spoke and half-listened to the voice that had once been so strong. But in his heart a prayer was forming: "Redeemer God, let him die soon. He is in pain. Let him come to You soon."

Five

Crotalus strode through the small castle in the Amil Mountains seeking a release for the energy inside him. He was not a patient man. He had not become the powerful sorcerer he was through patience. Intelligence, yes . . . cunning, certainly . . . but not patience. He had waited with pent-up energy for sixteen years, and tomorrow his waiting and longing would come to fruition. Tomorrow would begin the true reign of his power.

He had given orders for his army to stand down until tomorrow. He didn't know if they would be needed then or not, but he wanted to be prepared in case of treachery on Fel-hoen's part. Fel-hoen was a crawling, cowardly slug of a man. Crotalus remembered when he had come to him sixteen years ago wanting to be a king. The priesthood was disgusting to him, he had forsaken the gods, he wanted to rule. After Crotalus had made that possible, Fel-hoen seemed to renounce all knowledge of Crotalus. But Crotalus had made it very plain over the years what the penalty would be if he reneged on their bargain.

Crotalus grabbed a chair and flung it across the room, shattering it like glass against the wall. This was no good. He could not pace in this room until tomorrow. He forced himself to walk slowly, as the great sorcerer he was, and walked out of the room. He would check on his army, perhaps talk with the captain.

He found twenty of the men in the dining hall, mugs of ale in front of them, ribald jokes and coarse laughter filling the air. Crotalus gave them a cursory glance before turning toward the door, but their conversation arrested him.

"I heard he lives in Paduan. He's the king's knight."

"I wouldn't be surprised. Even when I knew him, and that was twenty years ago, he was a fiery fighter. He was only eighteen then, but I knew he would be fierce."

An older, grizzled soldier by the name of Alane joined the conversation. "Anyone could see that Falcon would be a great warrior because of his father. I knew Farrel Jaqeth, fought under him in the great wars of freedom for Paduan."

Crotalus had turned, and his eyes narrowed to slits. A few of the men saw his look and went pale at the sight of it. Alane did not notice and settled back further into his chair, his mug of ale resting comfortably on his belly as though he were preparing to tell a great tale.

"I remember when dragons walked the land . . . Oh, not the kind of dragons we have now that the circus takes around, but real dragons that could rip you open from chin to crotch with their claws and then cook you well-done before they ate you. Men ran in fear from those dragons, and well they should. Farrel, in the three years I served under him, killed five of those dragons with nothing more than his sword and shield. He had no men helping him because everyone was too afraid.

But not Farrel. That is where he earned the name Jaqeth, which means 'Dragon Slayer.' It's because of him that the dragons now are so tame. They remember his deeds and tell their young, much as we ourselves do. So it is no wonder that Falcon . . ."

He never finished his sentence, for Crotalus bounded across the room and grabbed Alane by the throat. He lifted him from his comfortable position as easily as if he were a kitten. Crotalus' yellow eyes flamed in terrible rage. The men watched in horror as Alane's life was squeezed out by the left hand of Crotalus. None dared speak against him.

"Never," Crotalus said, each word distinct and slow—and with every word he shook Alane's body—"never mention Falcon Jaqeth in my castle again." He gave one last twist to Alane's neck and tossed the lifeless body onto the table, sending ale flying in all directions. He then stalked from the room.

In an instant Crotalus was back in the tower, pacing with a fury that could have brought down mountains if he so desired. He instead turned the rage inside and heaped it upon the burning coals of an anger that he would never allow to die. *Falcon Jaqeth.* He let tendrils of flame leap around the name. He brought to mind the picture of Falcon and let it burn itself into his heart. The wavy dark brown hair, the green eyes, the straight nose and square chin. How he despised the man! Oh, the fantasies of horrible death he had created for Falcon Jaqeth!

He withdrew from his robe an image of a girl. She was no more than twenty years, with dark tresses that cascaded to her slender waist. The eyes, warm and brown, flashed with life; the mouth smiled with mirth, the gently rounded chin lifted in stubbornness. The lovely arms should have held him tenderly; the graceful legs should have carried her to him where she would have remained at his side for all time. He would have made her immortal. *Rafaela.*

• • •

The old man went about his prayers in a faithful fashion, even though he sensed an evil presence hovering near him. He unconcernedly turned even this over to the Redeemer God and went on with his worship.

The candles on the tables of his library burned low, barely illuminating the hundreds of books that filled every shelf, every table, every horizontal plane in the room.

At last the old man opened his eyes, his prayers finished for another hour, and he turned solemnly and yet eagerly to the pile of books resting on the table nearest his right hand. What had he been reading that sparked the call to worship? Ah yes, he had been reading one of the old books, older perhaps than even he knew. It had been written by a human (not all of them were), but oh, the insights this mortal had had! The old man opened the book to where he had left off and began reading about this man's knowledge of the Redeemer God.

Duncan had known, of course, that the men of long ago did worship the Redeemer God, but it was still a wonder and amazement to find new things about Him. His musings on the men of old brought to his mind the sword that was held in another part of the Forgotten City.

He stood decisively and found his way through the beautiful ruins of the city to the Home of Weaponry. This building was much larger than his own library and bedroom. He could hear his footsteps upon the stone floor echo through empty rooms. He passed through maces and lances, chain-mail armor and common swords. He gazed on short daggers, shields, and crests. These caught his attention for only a moment, but he went on, intent upon the one sword.

As he stood before it, his heart beat a little faster. It was a sword of gold, gleaming and strong. but it was not the value of it which made his heart race. He had found a picture of this very sword in one of his books about the people who had worshiped the Redeemer God long ago. This sword was not only older than anything he had known except for the Forgotten City itself, but it was the exact sword that had been used to send so many of the Redeemer's people to Him.

Duncan felt again the evil pressing around him, ominous and frightening. He stared at the sword that glistened even in the dark room.

"Is it coming then, Menon?" he asked, using the old, familiar name for the Redeemer. "Do great destinies hang upon the use of this sword? Only You know. Blessed be the Redeemer God."

• • •

So Falcon Jaqeth still resided in Paduan. Crotalus knew Falcon could not have fled far from his wrath, but he had never dreamed that Falcon would not have left at all. Crotalus had not seen Falcon in thirteen years. Yet the knight was never far from the thoughts of Crotalus or his insatiable desire for revenge that drove him on through the days and nights of his existence.

Crotalus bounded to the door of his room, flung it open, and yelled for the captain of his army. In minutes Captain Hirsch stood before him, and Crotalus could see the fear in his eyes. He had heard of the death of Alane, had seen the body with its horribly mottled face. He knew that the master he served was as volatile as some of the potions he mixed.

It is good, Crotalus thought. *He should fear me. They should all fear me.*

"I want all the information you can give me about Paduan."

"Paduan, sir? I don't understand."

"I want maps drawn, not only of Paduan, but detailed maps of each city in Paduan. I want to know the principals of each city . . . the knights . . . the size of each army, especially the king's. I don't care if you have to send a scout, but do it immediately! I want the information in my hand by sundown tomorrow or my wrath shall be visited upon you, captain. Is that understood?"

Hirsch nodded briefly. "It is understood."

Six

The Feast of the Redeemed had always been held in midsummer. Days were hot then, nights cool. Rains gently kissed the ground to bring forth fruit. Harvest approached. The people of Beren, indeed all of Paduan, celebrated many feasts to the Redeemer God: the Feast of Remembrance, the Celebration of Light, Harvest Feast. But the Feast of the Redeemed was the most joyous, the most solemn, the most looked forward to of them all. On this day they celebrated their release from captivity by their God, whom they called Menon.

The weather on this day this year was no different from the ones preceding it. Sunlight poured in through the windows of the castle, heralding a breeze that was sweet and warm. It caused the heart to yearn with things long forgotten, made it ache with things remembered.

King Jerome sat at his window in peace. His window overlooked the garden with its half-tame wildness. The smell of the trees wafted upward, settling in his heart like an old friend one has not seen in a long time.

Jerome turned as the door connecting his room with the queen's opened and Alexandria walked in. What a vision of loveliness she was!

Even though she was forty-five, her hair was as sparkling golden as the sunlight, her eyes bluer than the sky. Life had touched her gently, making her more beautiful in her maturity. He almost envied her youthfulness. He, at fifty-eight, had much silver in his black hair, and though his features were still strong, his eyes sharp, his mind clear, he sometimes felt a winter chill on his heart. Hopefully, having a queen thirteen years his junior and a son who was only seventeen would keep him younger than his years.

She smiled at him as she came to his window and sat opposite him. She took a deep breath of the air coming through the window. "What a lovely day for the feast!"

"Is Kreith awake?"

"Awake and gone long ago."

"Where did he go? He is supposed to ride out with the knights this year."

"He is so excited about that. He has been working very hard with Falcon. Constance told me that Kreith left early this morning for the stables, to speak with Jeffen about the decorations for his horse."

"Are you excited about this year's feast also?"

"I look forward to each feast more than the last, but this one in particular. This is my favorite feast, Jerome."

"In which games shall you partake?"

"I'm getting too old to partake in the games. The children looked at me strangely last year. I have consented to be the judge for the ring toss."

"Shall we eat breakfast before going to the parade grounds?"

"Of course," Alexandria said with laughter on her lips. "It would not do to have the king arrive before his subjects."

They walked leisurely down to the dining room, hand in hand as though they were Kreith's age, without a care or worry to cast a shadow over the sun. Could anything ever disrupt such serenity?

• • •

Temrane threw himself from side to side in the bed, unable to sleep for the excitement that built in him. As the sun's rays finally shot through the darkness he leapt out of bed, hurriedly threw on his clothes, and made his way to the stable where he quietly saddled his horse. In minutes he was headed toward the temple, where he knew his Uncle Candy would be starting the morning prayers.

He arrived just as the incense was lit, and he joined the solemn priest as he bowed in front of the large image of Hoen that blocked out the sun rising in the east.

Temrane waited patiently until the prayers were over, then could no longer contain himself. "Did you get it, Uncle Candy?"

"Well, good morning to you too!" Cand-hoen's eyes laughed as he watched his young nephew on his first day of manhood. "You are taking a risk being here, you know. You should be at home in your room preparing for the Calli-kor."

"But morning prayers can never hurt," he replied mischievously.

"You are right, young priest. Your present is on my table. Go get it."

Temrane forgot about the temple being a solemn place and ran to Cand-hoen's room. He was back in seconds bearing a gift wrapped in white wool, about one foot long. Temrane's eyes shone with love for his uncle as he unwrapped the present for which he had long awaited.

The god was carved out of the wood from the minu tree, the only tree that could be used for such a high purpose. Tradition said that the minu tree was the first created by Hoen and was the tree that gave him the most pleasure, for it rose straight out of the earth that bore his name. The god was dark, almost black, and was smooth with many sandings. The head was fearsome in its countenance, its body unyielding. There were no eyes in the face, for it was death to look into the eyes of a god. Its feet were embedded in dirt to signify his lordship over the earth. This was Hoen, god of the earth, giver of life.

Temrane threw his arms around Cand-hoen. "Thank you, Uncle Candy. I knew you would get me a god of my very own."

Cand-hoen let the boy hold him a minute more and then gently disengaged himself. He looked seriously into eyes that were still so childlike. "Temrane, today if you pass the test of Calli-kor you will become a man. I am no longer your Uncle Candy." He smiled as he saw the boy's face grow solemn. "You can still call me that if we are alone, but in the presence of other people and particularly here, in the presence of the god, I am Cand-hoen, priest to Hoen. When you become a priest, you shall be to me Tem-hoen and we shall be equals."

Temrane stood tall and proud. "I shall be honored, Cand-hoen, to be considered your equal. I will go now and prepare for the Calli-kor."

Cand-hoen watched him go, the boy-man, the prince-priest, and then returned to his morning prayers.

• • •

Falcon watched bemusedly as Kreith fussed with the decorations for his horse. He had ridden decorated horses before, but this was to be the first time he would ride with the knights. It was an honor – not only to Kreith, but to Falcon who had trained him – especially because he had learned so well and so quickly.

"Your banner is slipping a bit on this side," the knight said quietly.

"Falcon! You startled me! I know it's slipping, but I raise it and then it's too high."

Falcon stepped over to the horse and helped Kreith straighten the banner. The young prince nervously fiddled with the bows and bells on the banner. "Does he look all right?"

"He looks fine, a fitting mount for a prince. Why are you so nervous?"

"It is my first time out with the knights. I want to make you proud."

"You have already made me proud."

"Do you think my father will be also?"

"King Jerome can't help but be pleased. He has raised a fine prince and son."

Kreith warmed under Falcon's praise, knowing it was not lightly earned. He would have done anything for Falcon, and part of his quick learning had come from wanting to earn the praise of his father's most trusted knight. Jerome, although a good king and loving father, was almost ancient to Kreith's young eyes, and the twenty years difference between him and Falcon did not seem as large as the forty between him and his father. He had no siblings and no close friends. Falcon filled the need in his heart for someone to look up to and someone to befriend him. Kreith could never have told his father about the princess of Corigo. He just would not understand.

"What should I wear?"

"I don't think there's any need for full armor. You can wear chain mail."

"Won't I need armor to take part in the contest of strength and the mock battle?"

Falcon sighed. "Yes, but I thought we had discussed waiting until next year."

"But I am ready this year, Falcon. I know I am."

"What about the hunt?"

"The hunt is for children!"

"It is for young men. My last hunt was when I was twenty-one."

"I know, and I know it is an important part of the feast, but I was hoping . . ." He broke off, but Falcon did not miss the slight coloring of the cheeks nor the pleading eyes.

"What were you hoping?" he asked, though he knew the answer.

"I was hoping to go to The Fertile Valley."

"All right. I shall make a compromise with you. Will you abide by it?"

"Yes."

"You can take part in either the battle or the contest, not both. You will lead the hunt as you did last year, and when it breaks up into parties you may leave. Is that agreeable?"

Kreith grinned. "Yes. Thank you, Falcon." He suddenly stopped grinning and ran for the stable door. "I have to prepare my armor!"

Falcon shrugged as Jeffen, the horse trainer, came over. "I have never seen him so excited as he is about this feast."

"I don't know which is worse, the feast or the girl," Falcon wondered.

"Shall I finish with the horse, sir?"

"Yes. Thank you, Jeffen."

Falcon checked on a few of the other horses and then left to find Palmer, another of the king's knights and his best friend. They were to escort the king and queen. His thoughts returned again to Kreith. What would he tell Jerome about Kreith?

• • •

Temrane placed the god on his bedroom floor near the eastern wall. He wished that he occupied one of the bedrooms that had an east window—his faced west. But this would have to do. The god faced the center of the room, to watch over Temrane.

Temrane knew that to prepare for Calli-kor, everything had to be done in a certain sequence, with nothing out of place, or it would prove that he was unworthy of the Calli-kor. He sat on the edge of his bed and went over the steps in his mind, carefully expounding on every detail. When he knew he was ready, he stepped over to his basin and removed his clothes. He threw them out of the room. He then walked to his dressing room and removed the priest's robe that had hung there since the day of his birth thirteen years ago. This was the robe of Calli-kor, the robe every boy wore on his entrance into manhood. He laid it gently on the bed. The washing came next, and after he washed he was not allowed to touch anything that might defile his body, such as his dirty clothes, a woman, or food.

He washed in the prescribed manner, feet first with a cloth, then moving upward until he came to his head. Then he washed again, this time with his hands, head first until he reached his feet. Each time he dipped his hand into the cool water, he recited the story Cand-hoen had told him many times, the story that would be passed on from priest to priest, of how the god, Hoen, first revealed himself to Moc-hoen. "My grandfather's name was Moc," he intoned solemnly. "As a young man of five and twenty, he used to walk through the fields day after day, hour after hour. He loved the fields. He loved the feel of the wheat brushing against his bare legs, the smell of the wet earth after the rains fell, the feel of the fruit as it dropped in his hands. And as he walked day by day, hour by hour, he asked, 'Where does the fruit come from? Why does the rain fall on the earth? Why does wheat grow?' One day as he walked in the wheat, the rain began to fall. The wind began to blow, and it blew so hard that Moc was thrown to the ground. He picked up handfuls of damp earth, and he heard these words from the heavens: 'I am the earth god, Hoen. I give life to the crops . . . I make the rain fruitful . . . I give life to man, for man is but earth. Serve me.' Moc stood up, still with the earth in his hands, and he vowed to be a priest. In honor of the god, he changed his name from Moc to Moc-hoen and he raised his children, Cand-hoen and Fel-hoen, to serve the earth god as priests. So it has been, so it shall always be."

When he finished the ritual washing, he remained in the humility of his nakedness and lay on his face before the god. His arms stretched over his head until his fingertips rested lightly on the feet of the god. He remained in this position until his arms ached and his body begged for movement. When he felt he couldn't stand it any longer, he began reciting the catalogue of his sins in preparation for the prayer of Calli-kor. He racked his memory to recall every gross deed, and he listed these first. Lesser sins of attitude or anger or unkind words came after.

When he was sure he had remembered all his sins, great and small, he began emptying his mind, focusing all his thoughts into the fingertips that touched Hoen. As every thought was brought under dominion to Hoen, Temranc started the prayer of Calli-kor. When this was done, he would be able to don the priest's robe and then prove himself by deeds to be worthy of manhood. Not completing the deeds or failing in the execution of any of them would invalidate his claim to manhood. Such would demonstrate that his sins had not been forgiven. He would be unworthy.

For a moment, this thought worked its way into his mind and grabbed hold, causing a ripple of fear to start in his midsection and travel to his heart. He must not be found unworthy. Being a priest of Hoen had been his heart's desire since he was small. He could not become a priest if he did not first become a man.

He forced the thoughts of his worth out of his mind. He *would* be found worthy. There was nothing he hadn't done, or wouldn't do, for Hoen.

• • •

Falcon found Palmer finishing his breakfast in the knights' room. It was almost like seeing his mirror image sitting there, a mug of cream by his elbow, fresh goose eggs on his plate. His brown hair was a little curlier than Falcon's, but it was just as dark. The eyes were green, but where Falcon had flecks of blue in his, Palmer had bits of brown. He was as tall as Falcon and as broad through the shoulders. Growing up, they had pretended to be brothers. The relationship was now as close as though they were.

Falcon swung into the chair next to Palmer. "Still eating? I finished long ago."

Palmer grunted. "Not all of us were up at dawn. Have you seen the prince?"

"I just did. He was checking his horse. Where did you get goose eggs?"

"The cook just gave them to me. I think she likes me."

Falcon laughed. "Well, why not? What's not to like? It's time you were married."

"Just because the cook likes me doesn't mean I'm going to marry her. She's old enough to be my mother, and though my mother was a good woman I was hoping for someone a little younger. I might want children."

Falcon shrugged. "I just wanted to see you happy."

Palmer finished the eggs and picked up the mug of cream. "What is happening to you, Falcon? Are you turning into a matchmaker? Ivy told me about your attempts with her."

"What attempts? She blushed when I mentioned a man. She's in love."

"What man?"

"I don't know. She won't tell me. I just want her to be happy too."

"Do you think she would make a good wife?"

"I don't know. I'm not very objective. She has a personality that any man would love, she's loyal, she's a great cook."

"And she's very pretty."

"Yes, but she's very young."

"It only seems that way because of how old you are. She is twenty-five. Most women are married long before then."

"Then she's an old maid."

Palmer laughed. "A very pretty old maid. Is your father going to attend the feast today?"

"I hope so. It may be his last. He was still sleeping when I left. King Jerome is planning to send his carriage for him."

"Speaking of the king, are we going to escort him and the queen to the feast?"

"Yes, as soon as the summons comes from his manservant."

"And Kreith is to ride out with the knights. Do you think he'll do well?"

"Yes. He'll do very well."

"You smile as if he were your own son."

"I am old enough to be his father. What a horrible thought!"

Palmer smiled and stood up. "Come on, old man. Let us make sure everything is ready before the summons comes."

• • •

Fel-hoen stood as still as a statue outside his son's door, conflicting emotions warring within him. He wanted this day to be a joyous occasion with song and dance and laughter. He wanted the minstrels to make jokes, to cause mirth to overflow in the people. Assuredly, all this would happen in time, but first must come the serious rite of Calli-kor. Fel-hoen remembered his own Calli-kor and how he had hated it. The ritual of cleansing, the hunt for sacrifice, the bloodletting. And of course, the constant reminder from Moc-hoen of his much older brother, the one who received visions, the one whose Calli-kor had been marveled at because of its purity.

He cursed under his breath. Why couldn't his son break from the stranglehold of the gods as he had done? Ah well, after tonight it would no longer be his concern.

Kenda found him standing there with his hand on the doorknob moments later as he prepared to enter the room whether his son was ready or not. She angrily, almost fearfully pulled him away. "Don't do this to him! This is more important to him than anything else, and I won't have you ruin it for him!"

"Kenda, this is foolishness!"

"It is not foolishness to him. Let him have a few more minutes . . . please. Is that so much to ask on such a day as this?"

At that moment the door opened, and Fel-hoen looked on his son.

Temrane wore the seamless white robe that brushed the tops of his feet. The hood covered his blond hair completely and hid most of his lowered face. His arms were folded across his chest with his hands in the voluminous sleeves of the robe.

He raised his head and looked at his father. Fel-hoen almost staggered from the look. Temrane's eyes were bright and intelligent, too much so for a boy of thirteen. They seemed to hold the knowledge of what Fel-hoen had been, what he was now, and what things he had done in secret.

"I am ready, my father," he said softly.

"I have hired the minstrels to play, and they await only my command. Would you have them play a song for you first?"

"No. I am in readiness and want nothing but to please Hoen. They will play when I am a man."

Fel-hoen reined in his impatience and fury. "As you wish it, my son. We will go shortly to the temple to begin your Calli-kor. First, Merry has something she would like to give you that she says cannot wait until the later gift-giving. She is ill today and will not be attending the celebration, but she says you must have it before commencing the hunt for sacrifice."

They walked silently down the corridors of the castle in the manner prescribed by the priests long ago, the man leading, the son following, the mother behind both, until they reached Merry's room. "Go in," Fel-hoen said. "She will see you alone. We shall wait for you here."

Merry stood as Temrane entered the room, and the thought flitted through her mind that he was not a boy any longer. He did not even look like a boy. He was so serious, so grave on this public occasion. She remembered her own bloodletting into womanhood a few years before, and wondered why hers had been covered with shame and his with glory and honor.

She took the fruit from its leather pouch and handed it, almost shyly, to him. He took it from her hand, being careful not to touch her, and looked at her uncomprehendingly.

"It is called mevone," she stated. "It is from a tree which grows in Hoen's Valley. I was told that one will never die as long as one has the mevone tree."

Temrane smiled. He was touched at his sister's sensitivity to his needs and desires. Because of her, he was actually holding something from Hoen's Valley. He wanted to ask her how she had gotten it, for it was a long distance from Zopel, but it was not important. She had done it, and she had done it for him. That was what mattered.

"It has a seed inside it, after you have eaten the fruit. You can either eat the seed like meat, or replant it."

"Thank you, Merry. This means so much to me. I shall replant it and grow a mevone tree for Hoen. We must give back to the earth when we take. Thank you." He turned toward the door, carrying the small fruit close to his heart. He looked at her before he left. "Sometimes I think you are the only one who understands me."

She looked at his back as he walked out, the young prince who carried himself like a priest. *I don't understand you*, she thought but not unkindly. *I don't think anyone understands you.*

• • •

Kreith sat stiffly and proudly on his horse. The noise of the feast was about him as he rode in the pageantry of the parade. The guard had gone first, carrying the standard and colors of Paduan and King Jerome. The king and queen had ridden out next, followed by Falcon and Palmer. Kreith was behind Falcon's horse. The rest of the knights fell in behind Kreith in the order of their service. The people cheered for him as he rode past them. He felt, perhaps for the first time, the wonder of being a ruler, and he knew that he would have loyal subjects whenever he ascended to the throne.

Kreith could already see the lords of the other cities of Paduan gathered on the field to greet the king. The one he knew best was Lord McIlree, lord of the castle at Eschay in The Fertile Valley. He was a small man, but his father had said that Lord McIlree was one of the fiercest fighters he had ever known.

The parade marched around the game fields and separated into companies. Each company then performed part of the dance that was the beginning of the feast. Kreith remembered from past festivals the color that dazzled his eyes as he watched horse after horse put through exacting routines, the rider in perfect control over the beast. The color of the banners flashed in the sun, then blurred and ran together into one glorious array of color.

He could not see the color as well today, sitting astride his mount, partaking himself in the movements, but the color was in his memory, and his heart was dazzled.

As each horse came to a standstill on the outer edges of the field, surrounding the villagers, King Jerome and Queen Alexandria faced the people from the center. Never had King Jerome looked fiercer than now as he sat astride his black steed in full armor, and Alexandria was a fitting queen for him on a blonde horse, her beauty smiling down on the people.

King Jerome held up his hand for silence, and Kreith always wondered how he could command it by just lifting his hand. He did not have to raise his voice or blow a trumpet. Just a simple hand in the air. How much authority he had! Kreith was overwhelmed with love for his country, his king, and his father.

When the people grew silent Jerome began to speak, and though he did not shout, his resonant voice was heard by all. "Welcome, friends! Welcome to Beren! Welcome to my lords, Lord Sipple, Lord McIlree, Lord Diones, Lord Ulster, Lord Thomas. Welcome to the Feast of the Redeemed! Let the feast begin!"

The noise which had been loud before now burst out in joyous cheers for the king and queen. Kreith watched as groups of people broke off from the main circle. Children with their mothers headed for the games. There were ring tosses, puppet shows, and rides. Batakis, as always, had children surrounding him as he performed magic and illusions for them, juggling anything that was handed to him, playing songs on his stringed instrument.

Falcon broke into the lad's gentle reverie. "Come . . . we draw lots to see who will go against the king."

"You mean I get to draw a lot also?"

"Of course! You wanted to be in the battle."

Kreith spurred his horse to keep up with Falcon. He would have a part! He knew from watching past battles that lots were drawn to pick the enemy of the king. This enemy was allowed the choice of attacking or defending. If he attacked, he received his choice of knights and guards. If he defended, the choice of field on which to fight was his. For as many feasts as Kreith could remember, King Jerome had never lost either attacking or defending.

A barrel had been set up on the edge of the main field, and each knight, each guard, each villager who wanted to partake in the battle walked to the barrel and drew a tiny ball from it. All the balls were white but one. Whoever drew the black ball would be the king's enemy.

As Kreith approached the barrel, he didn't know whether to hope for white or black. He closed his eyes, stuck his hand in, and drew one out.

Each man drew a ball and when the barrel was empty, King Jerome looked around the circle of men. "Who has drawn the black ball?"

Kreith opened his eyes, stepped forward, and held the ball aloft for everyone to see. "I, Your Majesty."

Seven

Temrane sat on the warm ground, his back straight, legs bent underneath him, eyes closed in prayer. It was said that in the Calli-kor one's worthiness was measured by the time it took to find the sacrifice. Cand-hoen's sacrifice had been waiting for him as soon as he walked into the woods. Temrane knew the people must have gasped when Cand-hoen walked out of the forest almost as soon as he walked in. He was truly a godly man. Temrane took a deep breath. *Let me be as holy.*

The day was balmy, a good omen; no clouds colored the blue sky. Lanyi, the sun god, wished him well in his service of Hoen.

His prayers finished, he stood and, without looking at the people gathered around the edge of the forest, walked forward. He vaguely heard the laments of the women, signifying the loss of a child as that child becomes a man. More clearly, he heard the prayers of the priests, especially Cand-hoen's, resonating through the still air.

The sounds of Corigo faded quickly as he went deeper into the forest. So, his worthiness did not match that of Cand-hoen's. He let the pang of disappointment abate. It was not to be expected, but only something to hope and work for. If Cand-hoen was once blessed, Temrane was twice blessed by Hoen: once in having Cand for a blood uncle and twice in serving under him and learning from him.

He had not gone far into the woods when he spotted a buck. The great animal stood proud and unafraid on the far side of a small stream. Antlers raised high above his head, his nose lifted, he sniffed the earthy-smelling air as though he sensed the presence of man. The running water had masked any slight sounds Temrane had made, but nothing could disguise his scent.

Temrane stepped out from the small bush that had covered him. The buck stared at him with warm, brown, fearless eyes. He did not run, but awaited whatever came as though he knew the boy in front of him was holy.

Temrane reached into the quiver on his back and drew out an arrow. He dipped the tip of it into a bottle of mild poison. The poison would put the buck to sleep, but not kill it. The sacrifice must be made with a living animal.

The arrow whistled through the air and found its home in the fleshy hind part of the buck. He did not bound away as Temrane expected, but stood with intelligent eyes fixed upon the boy. In moments, the buck lay sleeping on the bank of the laughing stream, its nose gently resting in the water.

Temrane hurried across the stream and said a prayer over the animal, thanking Hoen for the sacrifice, thanking the buck for giving himself to such a high calling, asking forgiveness for whatever unworthiness still remained in him. Then, in the manner prescribed by the priests, he heaved the buck onto his shoulders. Water from its body cascaded down Temrane's back, chilling him.

It took him much longer to walk out of the forest than it did to walk into it. The buck was a heavy burden, awkward to carry. Temrane kept wondering if he had used enough poison. What would happen if the buck awoke while he still carried it? As his steps brought him closer to home and there was no sign of movement from the buck, he began to wonder if he had used too much poison. It would not fare well for him to bring back a sacrifice that had already died. Temrane would then be disgraced and banished from the temple.

As he stepped from the thicket of trees, he heard people gasp. *What is it?* he thought? Had he perhaps been too long in the forest? Was he disgraced? His mind quickly ran over the steps of the Calli-kor. No, he had forgotten nothing. Hoen had to bless him and make him a man. He had proved himself worthy.

Temrane's eye caught the eye of Cand-hoen and the beaming, proud face. Doubts melted away like snow before a warm, Spring sun. Perhaps he had been quicker than he realized. He walked over to the priest and looked him in the eye. "I offer this buck as a sacrifice to the great and glorious god, Hoen, and as a sign to the people who worship him. By this blood, and mine, I shall become a man."

Cand-hoen took the incense burner and swung it back and forth three times in front of Temrane. This would clear away any evil gods that might surround him, wanting to sabotage the ceremony. Turning, Cand-hoen led a procession to the temple where Temrane would offer the sacrifice.

The temple on this day seemed darker than usual. Holiness and death hung in the air, the smell of burning animal flesh and blood working its way into the nostrils and under the skin of the young boy who stood trembling at the mission that was placed before him. This was the only day a boy was given the chance to offer sacrifice. Any other day he would be struck dead if he attempted it. Only a priest could dare approach the gods with blood. But the Calli-kor was different, and Temrane knew that for him this was only the first sacrifice. He was destined for the priesthood. He would serve the gods here, in this holy, dark, and cold temple, offering sacrifices, making petitions for the people, granting forgiveness, interpreting and proclaiming visions.

Cand-hoen pressed the cold knife that was used solely for Calli-kor into Temrane's hands. The boy becoming a man felt the chill of it enter his body, turning his blood to ice and his heart to stone. He placed his hands on the warm, breathing body of the buck, letting himself get into the mind of this servant of Hoen. There was no fear there, only yielding. In a flash, Temrane knew this was the way he was to live his life. He was to yield to Hoen's will whether he understood it or not. The gods could sometimes be fickle and playful, even cruel at times. But they were still gods, and Temrane was still a servant, as was this buck.

He kept this in mind as he slit the buck's throat and drained the blood into a cup. He could feel the eyes of the people upon him as he did this, making sure he did not spill any of the precious blood. Cand-hoen was at his side, and though Temrane did not look at him, he sensed his approval. He searched for his father, but did not find him. Disappointment at his father's lack of interest, not only in the Calli-kor, but in his son, stabbed through him.

No, he thought, riveting his eyes again to the cup of blood in front of him, *I will not think of him. I will think only of Hoen and pleasing him by becoming a man. There will be time to please my father later.*

Another knife was handed to him, this one also cold, but longer, curved. He turned to Cand-hoen, who took the boy's robe in both hands, said a prayer of worthiness to Hoen, and rent the seamless robe down the middle, exposing the youthful chest. Temrane repeated the prayer of worthiness three times and then, in the manner of his fathers, cut the skin of his chest, over his left breast, from the armpit to the center. Blood immediately welled and ran. As he finished cutting, he laid aside the knife and picked up the cup with the sacrificial blood in it. He leaned over it and let his blood mingle with the blood of the buck. He closed his eyes and said the prayer of death, the prayer of unity with the buck and with all things. He had become one with the buck and one in his death. His soul merged with the other, and they entered into the god together.

Opening his eyes, he saw Cand-hoen standing where his father should have been. The father always stood with the son to pour the blood on the altar. The son's hands needed to be steady so as not to splash any of the blood. The blood was sacred; to spill it meant to remain a boy.

It was the father's duty to help the son into manhood. So it has been, so shall it always be. But his father was not there. His eyes scanned the company, but could not find him. Cand-hoen recognized the look and whispered briefly to him, "Do not concern yourself with that now. He has gone to tend to the musicians. I shall be your father."

How appropriate it was for him to say that. Cand-hoen had always been his father—spiritually, emotionally, in every way except the physical, and what did that really matter? Temrane hung his head in shame, for it *did* matter. What was Hoen except the physical expression of life?

Temrane took the cup of blood and held it high for the people to see. The men of the company repeated prayers, while the women wailed. Cand-hoen blessed the cup, put his strong bloodstained hands around Temrane's soft but learning ones, and together they poured the blood upon the altar.

Temrane could not watch. He felt his hands and his heart shaking. Inside he prayed, *Please, Hoen, let me be worthy. I have served you all of my days. I have given you the gifts you have demanded. I have forsaken my family. I have given up my role as the prince to serve you. Doesn't that count for something? Do I, the nephew and student of your great servant Cand, not deserve your blessing upon me?*

Then it was over. Temrane watched as Cand-hoen knelt and bound his loins with a cloth, covering his nakedness in the presence of women. Temrane knew then that it had happened. There was no need to cover the nakedness of a child. He had become a man.

• • •

Kreith quickly scanned the piece of land his father had chosen to defend. Jerome had always admired the strategic position of the Castle Andurin in Corigo, and he adapted his surroundings now to fit that model. It was hilly land, filled with valleys that could hide troops. A river ran to the south of Andurin and eventually flowed into the South Conmia. The castle edged on the little river. The boundaries of the river were marked by villagers who wanted to watch the battle, but did not desire to participate. It had been a good, strategic choice, one that Kreith told himself he would have chosen. But he had more men, and the men he had picked were good, quick-thinking warriors. Falcon was by his side, and the lords McIlree and Diones. With their help, he had picked the best warriors of their respective troops. There were not many village people who cared to fight in these mock battles, but Kreith chose from the eager faces.

The first stage of the battle was done. It was the duty of each commander and leader to reason first before fighting. This was done in deference of real battles and was a mere formality of the mock battle. The people did not want to watch the give-and-take of negotiation. They wanted the excitement of the battle without the danger.

Kreith divided his contingent into three troops according to various strengths and skills. He knew, of course, that in a real battle they might be separated by the use of and level of experience with weapons. But in the mock battle, mock weapons were used, made mostly from leather. Flats of swords were used, and it was left up to each person's honor whether or not he was mortally wounded.

His first mistake had been sending scouts. Even though he sent them into what he thought was an unoccupied area, only one of the five scouts had returned. Falcon had smiled a little at this first small defeat. He had known the mistake would happen, but preferred to let his pupil learn by this extremely good experience. Kreith could see right away the advantages the enemy had with the land. His father had chosen the highest hill, and the one farthest away from his enemy, as his command post. From here he could see whatever moves Kreith and his troops made. With smaller hills in front of his command post, he could station his men where he could see all of them, but Kreith could see none. It was an ideal location. But surely it had some weakness. Kreith began thinking as a defender.

"If I were on top of that hill, I would most expect an attack from the level plain that lies to the east. I would station half of my men there, and the other half I would place in the valleys." Kreith glanced at Falcon, but received no answer from the knight under his command.

"All right," he said to his three commanders, "Falcon, take your men to the east for a direct attack. Attack quickly and then retreat. We will kill as many as possible and hopefully lure the rest of them from the hills. Sound your trumpet as soon as you attack.

"Lord McIlree, as soon as attention is drawn from us and is placed on Falcon and his men, launch the catapults into the hills. Lord Diones, stand by with archers to kill any who escape the catapult. After each catapult volley, we will move forward to attack each successive defending line."

"Your highness," Diones said, "may I make a suggestion?"

"Of course."

"The river is of great asset to our enemies, but we can turn it to our use. I suggest that instead of the catapults we take those men, move them south behind the hills so they cannot be seen, and travel toward the river. We can then sail down the river and be at the door of the castle to launch a counterattack."

"But without the catapults our archers are hampered tremendously," Kreith argued.

"The catapults are too slow, your highness. It takes many men to drive them back and forth. We could be in position at the castle much more quickly by the river. The archers can set the catapults, launch them, and still have time to pursue any who escape."

Kreith knew this was a bold move, for it left the men on the river vulnerable. And yet, if attack was not expected from that quarter, they could take a distinct advantage there. He looked at Falcon and saw him smile. He knew in a real battle Falcon would not hesitate to give his opinion, but now he held his peace, wanting Kreith to think like a warrior.

"It is too risky," he said at last. "The men on the river would be entirely open to attack and could even be in danger from their own archers. We will stay with the original plan."

His orders were followed with speed, but Kreith could tell nothing from the expressions of the men under him. He did not know whether they agreed with him or not, whether his strategy was sound or weak.

Falcon's trumpet sounded quickly, signaling the attack had begun. The attack would be swift, and then they would retreat. He saw the majority of men in the valleys head toward the castle to repel the attack. Kreith listened for the retreat signal, heard it, and nodded to McIlree to launch the first catapult volley. As he hoped, the catapult scattered those it did not directly hit, and Diones and his archers picked them off as easily as target shooting.

The archers then moved forward toward the castle as Falcon's men struck again. This time many men in the valleys did not leave, but charged forward. The catapult could not be moved so quickly and the archers had to quickly shoot the attackers. Many of Kreith's men died in that assault, killing few, and he hurriedly regrouped.

The battle wore on through the morning and into early afternoon. Kreith's troops were badly depleted, and his only hope rested in the fact that his father's troops were suffering as badly. Kreith's few remaining archers did at last reach the castle and joined Falcon's men, effectively surrounding three of the four sides. Each side fought fiercely, but Jerome's men wore away at Kreith's until finally he was the only one left.

"Surrender," Jerome said, a smile in his voice.

"A king does not surrender, but dies with his men," Kreith countered.

"So be it," Jerome said and held up his sword. "We will do battle, the two of us."

Kreith smiled, this very much to his liking. He had trained many long hours with Falcon on his sword fighting and felt confident in it.

Jerome was pleased as Kreith repulsed many strikes that would have felled a less knowledgeable soldier. At last, moving quickly, Jerome maneuvered close to Kreith and was able to slip a dagger between an opening in his mail. Kreith was defeated to the cheers of the townspeople. King Jerome had again conquered.

"I have never come so close to being defeated," Jerome said to Kreith. "You have made me extremely proud and will someday be an heir worthy of the throne."

Kreith smiled, exultant. "I have had good examples, Father." He looked to Falcon and saw the beam on his face. His father's praise and his friend's smile were better than victory.

Kreith asked Falcon about Diones' suggestion and wondered if it would have been better.

"It is hard to say," he answered. "You, as king and being the most visible, would have most certainly been killed right away. Diones would have taken your place as ruler then, and you might have surprised enough men to make it worthwhile, but it would be very risky. I wouldn't have tried it."

"Then I did the right thing?"

"In that decision, yes. There were a few things I would have changed. We can discuss those tomorrow."

"But for the most part, I did well?"

Falcon put his arm around Kreith's shoulder. "Extremely."

• • •

Kreith raced across the green fields on his horse, never so full of life and the wonder of it as at this particular moment. He wondered if life would ever again be as sweet as now, or if it would be made up of moments like this for as many years as the Redeemer God gave him. The words of praise his father had spoken to him, his near-victory, the proud look of Falcon all swirled together in him, nearly intoxicating him with their deliciousness. There was only one thing that could make this day any better.

He saw her before she saw him. She sat under the golden trees, her dark hair like a shining beacon among the gold. His eyes swept the field, and though he saw her horse, he did not see her maid.

She turned at his footfall behind her, and smiles wreathed her face. "I knew you would be here."

His heart lurched at her words, for they spoke of a feeling that he also experienced, a feeling that made him want to jump in the air. He might well have done this but for the fact that he felt more of a man today, and he could not imagine a man such as Falcon jumping in the air because a girl said she liked him.

"What brings you back to The Fertile Valley, princess? I thought today was your brother's birthday."

"It is his birthday, but a woman is not considered a very important part of the Calli-kor."

He sat down beside her under the golden tree. "What is the Calli-kor?"

"It is when a boy becomes a man."

"How old is your brother?"

"Thirteen today. How old are you?"

He smiled at her forwardness. She seemed so different from the ladies of his father's court. "Seventeen. Why aren't women important?"

She became solemn, his words triggering again the questions she herself had often asked. "It is said that one day Velad, the goddess of the sea, seduced Hoen, the earth god, in order to gain some of his land for herself. Because of his attention to her, many lands were submerged in water. In order to punish Velad for her treachery, Hoen said that from thereafter Velad's daughters would carry water within them and would be forced to give it up at the birth of a child. Women are said to be born of the sea, men of the earth."

"Men and women are both born of the Redeemer God. There is no other."

"Then your women are important?"

"Some more than others, as are the men, and a man must be the final authority, but that isn't to say that women aren't important. It must be a very cruel thing to serve your gods."

"I don't think about it very often. Temrane does; it's all he thinks about. He is going to be a priest, even though my father forbids it. Is it a cruel thing to serve your god?"

Kreith didn't answer a moment. His mind roamed over the experiences in his short life, the words of his father, of Falcon, of the monks and teachers. They did not teach cruelty. He thought of the prayers he had offered, sometimes in weeping agony, as over his only friend's sick body before he had died. He thought of the tales of the Forgotten City and its inhabitants.

At last he replied, "It is never cruel, but it isn't always easy."

• • •

The priests' rooms in the temple consisted of little else than a pallet to sleep on and the god standing by the window to guard over the room.

There was a small table in the corner that held a basin on its top to wash with. Clothes could be stacked underneath. There was nothing else, for nothing else was needed. The priests' rooms were meant for praying and sleeping, little else.

Cand-hoen lay on his pallet in his room. He had closed the curtains to block out the sun, but it insisted on streaming in through the holes, reminding him of the celebration outside. His mind was numb with the thing he had done. He could not celebrate or pray or eat. The only thing he could do was lay on his pallet in his room.

"Why are you here?"

He turned and saw Fel-hoen standing in the doorway. He sighed and looked again to the ceiling. Surely it was more interesting than his brother.

"You have your celebration. You do not need me to be a part of it."

"You're right," Fel-hoen said, stepping swiftly into the room and closing the door behind him. "I do not need you to be a part of anything in my life. But unfortunately my son does not share my views."

"What do you want from me?"

"Let me make it clear, Cand. I want nothing from you . . . nothing. I want my son to have nothing to do with you. But there is a celebration going on that my son will not enjoy unless you are there."

"I am sure that his enjoyment means nothing to you. What do you really want?"

"He is the prince, and he will act like one. I'm sick of his speaking of you! His talk of the priesthood turns my stomach. After today, he will not see you again. Do you understand? He is a prince and he is my son. *My* son, not yours. If you wanted someone to follow in your footsteps, then you should have impregnated any of the foolish women who come to you for omens. They would gladly have given you a son. You've corrupted mine. Isn't that enough? Do you also have to corrupt my realm?"

Cand-hoen sat up abruptly. "Your realm! You have no right to this realm! You are the son of a priest. Instead of ruling people, you should be waiting on the gods. Instead of having servants, you should be Hoen's attendant."

"Still jealous, Candy?"

"Jealous of what? Of someone who wears a tin-plated crown and calls himself a king? Of someone who has brought the wrath of the gods on himself? Of someone whose own son has turned against him?"

"What have the gods ever done for you? They have given you

bloodstained hands and a temple that reeks of death! Don't try to taint me with your holiness that comes from slaughtered animals and sacrificed children."

"I have never sacrificed a child," Cand-hoen said quietly.

Fel-hoen also dropped his voice. "No, but your father did, and you stood by and condoned his act. Or have you forgotten that?"

"I shall never forget it. You seem to forget that she was my mother also, and her child my brother. I shall never forget, but I shall also never regret something done in obedience to the gods."

Fel-hoen's eyes darkened with a rage that wanted to consume. He spat at the god that stood by the window. "That is what I think of your gods." He strode from the room.

Cand-hoen sat in the deafening silence, his eyes still on the doorway where his brother had stood. He had said the words that needed to be said to Fel-hoen, but the words had been rote.

He let his eyes drift from the doorway to the window where the god stood. Against the beams of sunlight, the god was a dark, menacing outline.

Cand-hoen let his mind go back to the Calli-kor at the temple. The buck had been slain, and it was good. Temrane cut his chest in the manner prescribed and mingled his blood with that of the buck, and that was good. Cand-hoen had placed his hands over Temrane's, and they poured the blood on the altar.

But not all of it. Three drops of blood had landed on the floor at Cand-hoen's feet. Three drops of the precious blood that was not to be spilled or splashed.

But the worst of it had been that Cand-hoen concealed it. He had moved a little so that his feet were covering the blood on the floor. Temrane had his eyes closed and did not notice. The people did not notice. But Cand-hoen knew, and knowing would forever be to him like a fire that had gone cold. Temrane, his pupil, his nephew, the next priest in line, his beloved Temrane had failed the Calli-kor.

His eyes fell to the ground, unable to bear looking upon the face of the god any longer. Spittle dried on the feet of the god. Years of service to Hoen took over, and he automatically said a prayer of forgiveness for the sins of his brother. But inside he died a little, knowing that the sin he committed (he and not his brother!) would not be forgiven or forgotten.

He sighed deeply as though trying to expel the death inside, turned, and walked out to join the celebration.

• • •

"I love you."

Merry smiled. "How can you love me? You've only known me since yesterday."

"I don't care. I know I love you, and whether I know you for only a few hours or for years, my feelings won't change."

Merry's eyes sparkled with laughter. "I think I love you too."

"Let's get married."

"We can't get married!"

"Why not?"

"Kreith, be serious. My father is to pick my husband, not me. It wouldn't be right."

"And whose law is that? The gods?"

"I don't think so. If it were, my father wouldn't pay any attention to it. It is just the way things are done in Corigo. Besides, you are not rich, you are not a king's son, nor even the son of a knight. The only thing you are is handsome. How would you support me on your handsomeness?"

Kreith beamed at her. "But I am the king's son!"

"Don't play games with me, Kreith. You told me yesterday you were a farmer. I won't be believing any of this foolery now."

"But it's not foolery. I am King Jerome's only child. My mother is Queen Alexandria."

"Anyone who lived in Paduan would know those things, as well as the names of his knights and his knights' horses! You've made this up just so I'll marry you." She lay back in the tall grass surrounding the golden trees and watched the clouds decorating the sky. "I wish I could marry you."

"You will marry me. I'll find a way. I'll talk to my father, who is the king whether you believe me or not. Maybe he can talk to your father. That's what kings are supposed to do, isn't it? Marry off their sons and daughters to unite the land? I'll find a way, Merry."

"I hope so, Kreith, because I don't want to marry some old man who is fat and bald and will die leaving me a grieving widow in two months."

"You won't. I won't let you. If your father tries, I'll steal into Zopel and carry you away."

She sighed at the mention of Zopel, the very word reminding her of where she should be and how sick she was supposed to be. "I have to get back, Kreith. Elenu is keeping watch for me, but I don't know how long she can keep it up, and I don't want her to get into trouble."

"You can't ride all that way by yourself."

"I rode here by myself."

"But it was light then. It shall be darkening soon."

"You told me there were no robbers in these valleys, only in the cities. Did you lie to me again?"

"I never lie! There are robbers in the cities, and there might be on the road. But wouldn't you feel much safer if I were to ride back with you to Zopel?"

"Yes! Much, much safer!"

Kreith leapt to his feet and extended his hand, pulling Merry to her feet. In one fluid movement she rose on her toes and kissed his lips and then darted away toward her horse. Kreith, with tambourines, flutes, and lyres singing out a rhythm within his heart, ran after her.

• • •

Temrane watched the minstrels with a detached interest. Normally minstrels held as much fascination for him as for any other boy, but today he had become a man, and he wanted to share this new experience with Uncle Candy. When Candy had finally appeared, he seemed different, rather aloof himself. Temrane worried that there was something he had done amiss, but could not think what. He questioned Candy about it, and for a few minutes Candy would seem his old self. But then he would slide back down into a seemingly dark hole with no light and little air, a place where Temrane could not follow.

His father, in contrast, was in high spirits, bantering with the minstrels, dancing with Kenda as though they were much younger, pushing food on Temrane much as he had tried to push the festivities on him earlier. Temrane did not resist this time, however, and joined in the celebration as much as his serious, priestly nature would allow him. With each attempt at the merrymaking, Fel-hoen congratulated his son, and Temrane was not yet man enough to not try for the approval that had been so long in the coming. And when his father asked to speak with him privately, his heart had soared, thinking he had at last won his father's heart on this day of becoming a man.

The father and son walked away from the crowd, and if Temrane had expected his father to perhaps put his arm around him or at least a hand on his shoulder, he was nevertheless not disappointed when it did not happen. It would come in time.

"I want you to be prepared to ride tonight."

"Tonight?"

"When the castle has gone to sleep and the moon is at its height. I do not wish your mother to worry."

"Where will we ride?"

"There is a place in the Amil Mountains I wish to show you, and I have waited these long years until this very day."

He cares for me, Temrane thought. *There is something special that he has waited for so long to share with me, and now that I am a man we shall share it*. "What is it, Father?"

"I cannot tell you anything now. The time has been ripening for sixteen years; it can ripen a few more hours."

Temrane puzzled over this last statement. Sixteen years. Was this something for which his father had planned three years before his birth? "I will be ready when the moon is high."

"Good. I will wait for you in the stables. Go now and enjoy the celebration. You have earned it."

Fel-hoen watched Temrane rejoin the family and listened as he ordered a song from the minstrels. He tried to feel some kind of regret for what was going to happen. He was a father, Temrane was his son—surely there should be some remorse. But the child he had fathered was so unlike him as to make him almost an enemy, and he could feel no sorrow, but rather only a deep and pleasurable relief.

Eight

Batakis watched as the sun slipped below the horizon and the sky graduated from glorious pink to mellow orange and finally to relaxing black. Pinpricks of light had hinted of stars earlier and now ruled the heavens.

What a peaceful time, he thought. He loved the night. There was no better time than when the sun went down, leaving stars behind her like a bridal train and a coolness in the air that intimated Fall. His feast day had been full of children, laughter, and song, and now he rejoiced to have a few moments of quiet reflection.

He had an excellent view of the road from his perch here in the front window of his cottage, and earlier he had watched the people leaving the feast, each going home to his or her own quiet thoughts. Each feast ended the same; there was the sharing of the meal interspersed with singing and praying, and then talking and laughter would gradually die down as people left the fields to enter their homes and their own time of worship.

He abandoned his post at the window and lay down on the narrow bed against the wall. Loneliness welled up and rushed through him like a Spring stream swollen with the waters of Winter. Normally his loneliness was well hidden, and even he forgot it at times when the youngsters pressed close. The children were his entire life as he made toys, practiced magic, did tricks, sang songs, and played the clown. It was all done to cheer the children, and he supposed it was a good life. Everyone knew him; he had no enemies, and if he made the world a better place in which to live, then it was a good life. But it was also a lonely life, for he had no close friends. Everyone knew him, and everyone liked him, but he could never show himself to them. He had to keep his face happy even when he agonized inside. The laughter, songs, and jokes kept flowing from him, and there was no one to whom he could talk about his real feelings, real fears, real doubts, real loves.

The true darkness of night stole upon the room, masking things best not seen in the daylight. But Batakis could feel the wetness on his cheeks. The tears of a clown.

• • •

Niccola also appreciated the masking gloom of night. She had watched the celebration for Temrane until it had sickened her, but then she remembered and would smile a little. Lomeli had not understood; he couldn't remember a time when she had been as cheerful as she was tonight. She even had patience with Caldon when he insisted on playing with the rest of the village children, including his idiot cousin. "Go and play," she had said, knowing that soon all would be changed. The information she had searched for had finally, today, fallen into her hands. If she had believed in the gods, she might have made a sacrifice for this fortuity.

She lay quietly in the darkness beside Lomeli, grateful that his prying hands and questioning voice were at last stilled, for she had much to ponder.

It had been sixteen years since the overthrow of her people, sixteen years since a priest named Fel-hoen had ravaged her land, destroyed the beautiful cities of Corigo, and murdered every living thing from the lowliest sheep to the highest ruler. The highest ruler had been a wonderful king. Oh, perhaps he had been a little strict with the peasants, and perhaps he did take more of their crops than he needed to, but he was a true king. And his people didn't starve. Niccola remembered him strolling through the castle, his long, velvet, red robes trailing behind him on the magnificent marbled floor. Often she had sat in the doorway just to gain the privilege of this sight, a gangly young girl gazing on a king.

Sixteen years had passed since beholding that sight. Her last sight of the king had been a gruesome one. His body was nowhere to be found, possibly spirited away by the wizard with whom the priest sided, but his head, with sad and royal-looking eyes, was impaled on a post driven into the ground in front of the castle wall. Anyone who came to the castle looking for protection was met with this horrible sight of their king. Her father.

This had been only the beginning of the murders. Niccola had hidden in a now-horseless stable, listening, her eyes wide with fright, to the screams of death around her.

They never found her, and when this new king took up residence and began the city anew with the lords of Corigo who had betrayed her father, she became one of his first subjects, attaching herself to an old and senile couple, never daring to let Fel-hoen know that she was the princess of Corigo.

That would all change now. Of all the people in Corigo who attended the Calli-kor and the celebration for the prince, only two people knew that Temrane had not passed the Calli-kor, that he should have faced shame, humiliation, and expulsion today rather than a royal feast put on at the expense of the peasants. Only two people knew. She did, of course, the real princess of Corigo. The other was the priest, the king's own brother.

She smiled, even though there was no one in the darkness to see that smile. *At last.*

• • •

Captain Hirsch had been waiting in Crotalus' private rooms since sundown. He at last had the information that Crotalus desired, and with each fleeting moment he became more nervous. Crotalus had demanded this information by sundown. That had been two hours ago. Would Crotalus believe that he had been here that long, or would his anger be stirred by this apparent lack of obedience? If it wasn't for the fact that Hirsch was sure Crotalus would track him down and do some horrible thing to him, he would have left this army years ago.

He got up from the heavy wooden chair he had been sitting in for two hours and began to look around. This was the first time he had been alone in the private rooms, and his curiosity, although not usually very lively, pricked at him like a playful sword until he felt he could not stand it if he let this opportunity pass.

The desk in front of him was a good place to start. Large and ponderous, it filled the southeast corner of the room. Its dark and polished surface invited him to touch it, and he did, letting his fingers trail over its surface as though it were a woman to be caressed. He walked around its bulk and faced six large drawers, two columns of three on each side. He gently pulled on the wooden handle to each drawer, but they would not yield their secrets.

Upon the realization that he could not explore it, the desk lost all interest for him. He moved next to the bookcase against the far wall. Pleasure filled him as he looked at the volumes. He had not read a book in years. He had been taught how by his father, but though it was an occupation he greatly enjoyed, he did not have time for it now, nor much need.

Each book was covered with a dusty black animal hide, with no markings to indicate what each contained. He reached above his head and pulled one of them down. The handwriting that filled the pages was close and neat, clearly the handwriting of a wizard, but whether it was Crotalus or someone before him, Hirsch could not say. The title of this particular book was *On Night Dreams*, and it talked at length of the use of night dreams, interpreting them, inducing them, and so forth. He replaced it in its exact location and removed another: *On Extracting Blood*. As the first page contained a rather grim drawing, he hurriedly replaced it and went on to look at other titles: *On Basic Incantations*, *On Stealing Souls*, *On Herbs and Mosses*, *On Raising the Dead*. This last title intrigued him and he skimmed through it, wondering if this were really possible. Apparently it wasn't, as the book was not finished and looked to be a series of experiments in the field.

"They say that curiosity killed the cat. Do you suppose it also kills captains?"

Hirsch whirled around, dropping the book. He snatched it up and shoved it back among its brothers. He stood ramrod-straight. "I have the information you requested."

Crotalus walked over to the bookcase, a nasty smile on his nonexistent lips. "Are you interested in wizardry, Hirsch? Perhaps you would like to become my pupil? Or were you just trying to figure out what I could and could not do?" Crotalus grabbed the book Hirsch had just been perusing. "No, I cannot raise the dead . . . yet. I can move the body around, but the second I let go of it with my thoughts, the thing collapses. I can't raise the dead, but I *can* kill people, and in more hideous ways than you have perhaps imagined. Would you like a demonstration?"

Hirsch swallowed hard, trying to remove the spittle from his mouth, but the lump of fear in his throat prevented his spit from going anywhere. "No, sir."

"A pity. I was in the mood for some bone shredding. Perhaps another night."

"Yes, sir."

"Tell me what you have found."

Hirsch was only too happy to comply and babbled at length about the size of Paduan's various armies, finishing with the king's army at Beren.

"And who are the king's knights?"

"Cleve Palmer and Falcon Jaqeth."

"Only two?"

"There are lesser knights, but they are under these two."

"Cleve Palmer. I do not recognize the name. Tell me about him."

"There is not much to tell, sir. His father's name was Cleve, and he took it in the manner of the Paduans after his father's death. He has never been known by any name other than Palmer. His family was from Beren from the beginning. He joined the king's army two years after Falcon Jaqeth became a knight. He is considered the best friend of Falcon. There is nothing else. Would you care to hear the information on Falcon Jaqeth?"

Crotalus' eyes narrowed. "No. I know everything I need to know about him."

Crotalus sank further into his chair, his fingertips pressed together, his eyes closed. He remained like that so long that Hirsch wondered if he slept. He dared not move, though, and stood before the desk as straight as though his master still looked at him. At last his eyes opened, and Hirsch could see the smoldering hate there.

"Leave the information on the desk and get out. I will summon you if I need you."

Crotalus did not watch him leave, but instead concentrated on the material placed in front of him. He would find a way to deal with Falcon, the Dragon Slayer's son. He did not know as yet what he would do, but his outrage demanded something horrible, a long and torturous death.

He went to the bookcase and removed *On Raising the Dead*. His last experiment had been fruitless. He tapped his fingers thoughtfully on the book. "Soon, Rafaela, I will find a way. And when I do, I shall search the earth to find your bones. You shall again be mine."

• • •

Falcon stood silently before King Jerome, his guilt piercing him like a dagger. Jerome did not look at him, but stared out the window. Falcon wondered, but did not really want to know, what thoughts occupied his sovereign's mind.

Falcon had come to the king after the time of worship. Kreith had not yet returned, and Falcon felt the tendrils of worry creeping into his stomach.

Jerome, as could have been expected, noticed Kreith's absence and asked Falcon about it before Falcon could say anything.

"He rode into The Fertile Valley."

"When was this?"

"Right after the beginning of the hunt."

Jerome sighed. "I knew he was a headstrong boy, but he's also responsible. I might have thought it possible for him to rebel against me. After all, I'm his father. But to disobey you . . .! You're his hero, Falcon."

Falcon winced as the dagger of guilt was twisted by Jerome's words. "He didn't disobey me, Your Majesty. I gave my permission."

"You gave permission for him to ride to The Fertile Valley?"

"Yes, Your Majesty."

"Did you also give your permission for him to stay away this long?"

"No . . . but I did not specify a time when he should return."

"And why was it important for him to ride to The Fertile Valley?"

"I didn't want to say anything because I would have preferred Kreith to tell you in his own time, but I think I can tell you this much . . . There is a girl involved."

Jerome was long silent, looking out the window. Falcon wondered if perhaps the king was thinking of his own youth, which had been as stormy as a hurricane-tossed ocean and calmed only when he married Alexandria.

When Jerome turned, his face had softened, his worry lines were less pronounced. "You may leave, Falcon."

"Your Majesty, may I have your permission to ride after him?"

"No . . . You have a father and a sister who desire your presence. I shall ride out shortly. I am certain he is in no danger except perhaps the dangers of falling in love. And those dangers we know well, do we not?"

Falcon thought of black hair and enchanting eyes. "Yes, Your Majesty, we do."

• • •

Jerome stayed in his private study long after Falcon left. Thoughts of Kreith were not now as insistent as they had been. Another occupied his memories, the young man Falcon had been.

Falcon had officially joined the ranks when he was eighteen, but he had been trained and living the life of a king's knight from the time he was old enough to sit astride a horse. Jerome was glad to have him as a knight, for though he was a bit impetuous, he was also persistent. He never fought a battle he did not expect to win and he never gave up until he had.

Rafaela in those early days had been a match for him. Resolution marked everything she did, and she could be as unyielding as Falcon when she felt herself to be right. She was a lovely girl, with flashing eyes and a stubborn tilt to her nose and chin. The daughter of a tailor who lived in Amick, in northern Corigo, she had made her living working for other people, much as Ivy did now. Falcon had, in fact, learned the craft from Rafaela and taught it to Ivy. It was no wonder the clothes Ivy made seemed to sing with the craftsmanship that graced every thread.

When her father died, Rafaela became a businesswoman who needed no land and desired no husband, preferring the life of an itinerant to the settled life of raising chickens and scratching out an existence as the chickens scratched out grain from the ground.

Then she met Crotalus. With his high forehead, disdaining eyes, and powerful lips he held sway over women as a snake hypnotizes birds. He was only a fledgling sorcerer then, his own lust for women preventing him from developing great domination. But that changed when he met Rafaela. He detected in her a dark enchantress, a desire for control that needed only a little coaxing to become as great as his own. He saw her as his mistress in wizardry, his magic bride.

Falcon met Rafaela soon after the love affair with Crotalus began. With no intention of stealing her love from Crotalus, he struck a friendship with her, enjoying her argumentative spirit and her bantering tongue.

Jerome sighed deeply. Oh, the pain she had caused to two men . . . But even greater than this, the pain she had borne.

Of course, she had fallen in love with Falcon, and along with her love of him came a knowledge of the Redeemer God. Many things of which Crotalus spoke she now saw as wicked, an evil spawned by the enemy of the Redeemer God. This growing awareness, along with a growing love, forced her into leaving Crotalus, shattering his dreams of a bewitching and powerful union.

Unable to bear the thought of his dark love resting in someone else's heart, he bided his time until the love between the two was full. The poisoned arrow, meant for Falcon, found its home within Rafaela's breast.

Jerome closed his eyes in pain. The sorrow of that day had been great, not only for Falcon, but for those who loved him. Ivy had only been twelve, and it was doubtful that she remembered Rafaela very well, but she had wept with great tears for her brother, as did Farrel and Devona. Jerome, with the ache of love, sent Falcon away from the body. He did not willingly go, but at last Devona had led him away and ministered to him in his grief.

Jerome had taken charge of the body, carrying her himself into the castle, her long black hair flowing to the ground like blood. The poison had drained the color from her skin, leaving a porcelain translucence that even in death was beautiful to behold. He laid her upon a bed and was about to summon the priests to bury her when her eyelids fluttered. It had not been much of a motion, but enough to let him see the pain that filled those brown orbs. The pain did not come from the poison, he believed, but from the knowledge of the hurt she had caused Crotalus, even though he was following wicked paths, and to Falcon. She knew she had caused hate to spring into both hearts and that neither would ever forgive the other.

Jerome sat in the chair beside her bed and listened as the words of love and unworthiness poured from her. She believed she was dying and wanted someone to know of the love she carried, and would always carry, for the two men.

But she did not die. It was as though the words she spoke purged some of the poison from her body.

It was as she was speaking that Jerome decided. As painful as it might be, he would let the world believe that Rafaela had died. As the poison had removed forever the color from her skin, so the struggle within her heart had removed the spirit from her character.

She had been sent to the Forgotten City.

Jerome didn't know then, and still didn't know, if he had made the right decision. It had seemed right at the time. Now he wasn't sure. He had known it caused Falcon pain, but that agony was far removed from Jerome. Until now. He had glimpsed the depth of that pain on Falcon's face tonight, and he could no longer believe that he had done rightly. He had acted out of regard for Rafaela and his concern for her safety physically, emotionally, and spiritually. But what of Falcon? He still bore wounds that had never healed, and Jerome felt it was not right for the wounds to fester any longer. Falcon must be told.

The sudden movement at the door caused him to jump. "I'm sorry . . . I didn't mean to startle you."

He smiled at Alexandria. "I was deep in thought, but I am very glad to be roused from it."

"It has been a very full day. What news did Falcon have of Kreith?"

"Apparently he is in love."

"With whom? I have seen him pay no particular attention to anyone."

"Falcon would not say, but she does not reside in Beren. Kreith rode to The Fertile Valley to be with her. He is either there still or, being the gentleman he is, is seeing her safely home. I do not think we need to worry about him."

"I wondered how long it would be before we turned our thoughts to marriage."

"Will you be sorry?"

"I have heard that it is hard to lose a son, but I shall not be sorry. For what other reason do we raise our children than to release them into the world? And I feel we have done an adequate job."

"Even though his father is so old?"

She walked over to where he sat and placed her arms around his neck. Although in public a royal decorum had to be maintained, in private she was very affectionate, and after his thoughts of the night he was glad for her warmth.

"You are not so old. Kreith could not have had a better father, nor I a husband, nor Paduan a king."

He kissed her hand gratefully, for she always knew the right words to speak.

"I am going to bed. Are you coming?" the queen inquired.

"No . . . not yet. I have a few more things to think through, and then I shall ride toward The Fertile Valley and see if I can locate our wayward son."

"Will you be harsh on him?"

"I cannot be harsh on him when he has never before given me cause to worry. My own wild oats remind me to be gentle."

She kissed the top of his head and with a last, lingering caress left him to his night thoughts.

Nine

Fel-hoen's horse jogged silently beside Temrane. Memories crowded close in his mind, urging attention. Temrane's first question had been their destination. Fel-hoen had answered with a terse, "The Far Amils." The next question was a little harder to answer: "Why are we going there?"

How much should be revealed or concealed? Did it really matter? "It was a summer day, much like this one, sixteen years ago . . ."

He remembered riding into the Amils on horseback. The horse hooves striking the ground sent up an aroma of rich earth. Trees towered above him, blocking the sun's rays, creating dancing shadows on the forest floor. Sounds were muted here, as in a temple. He strained, but could only hear a few birds far away and the steady thump of hooves.

He had not always hated Hoen. There must have been a time, before the death of his mother, when he served Hoen along with Cand. But that time had been so long ago and his hate was so great that it obstructed the memory as completely as the trees did the sun. He did not want any longer to serve Hoen, but himself. He wanted wealth, fear, and power. He wanted to be king.

"Have you ever heard of King Lyca?"

Temrane's brows furrowed. "I don't think so."

"There is really no reason why you should have. He was the King of Corigo before I took the throne. He was a loathsome man. Luckily for me, I was born into a family of priests, and he had nothing to do with the priests. But for other villagers he was a cruel master. The people sweated for months to bring a good harvest, and then they were to turn it over to him for his larders. There is nothing wrong in that, of course. Any good king will fill his larders to put off famine, but he did not return much to the people. They were starving, and he liked it that way. None of his lords could do anything against him because they were weak from lack of food. There could never have been a revolt against him. Never. Do you understand that?"

Temrane didn't understand the urgency in his father's voice. "Yes, I understand."

"It's important that you do, because it explains what happened next. I wanted more than anything to be king. The gods meant nothing to me then, and they mean even less now, if that is possible. Don't look so shocked, Temrane . . . You have known my feelings for some time now. Your uncle stood by and watched my brother sacrificed to Hoen. I vowed then I would have nothing to do with the gods.

"Your uncle and my father were shocked at my talk of becoming king. It was not lawful for a priest to become king, and besides a king was already on the throne. And I was not a legal heir to it. It was at this time that I met Crotalus."

Fel-hoen paused at the name, his insides shuddering as he remembered that first meeting. His horse had only gone so far into the mountains before turning skittish. He had tied the horse to a tree and followed the ancient paths by foot, paths haunted by witches, or so the children of priests were told.

As he walked deeper into the maze of trees, the sun grew darker and colder. It was becoming less difficult to believe in the old tales.

He came to a clearing where mist rose from the ground. He stood on the edge of the mist, wondering if he dared to cross into it, when a soft voice, almost a whisper, surrounded and tugged at him: "So you want to be a king."

He could see no one, but he felt the presence just ahead of him. "Yes . . . I have heard that you can help me."

The mist dissipated, and in front of him stood the wizard whose name was only whispered in Zopel. He was taller than a normal man and powerfully built. His forehead was high and broad, unlined, his eyes yellow, like an animal; an evilly handsome man whose looks would flee from him within five years. Fel-hoen heard later that his commanding aspect was buried with a woman whom he had loved. But that was still in the future on this dark morning of his first meeting with Crotalus. The wizard had a reputation for raping any woman caught in these woods, and Fel-hoen thought he would do well to remember that and keep his young bride, Kenda, far away from these woods and this particular bargain.

"What kind of help do you want?"

"I need power. I need to sway men's minds so the lords of Corigo will fight with me against Lyca. I need strength to slaughter Lyca's men."

"And what will you give me in return?"

"Anything you wish."

Crotalus was silent for a time, weighing Fel-hoen's words carefully, as though they were made of gold. "You shall have what you desire. In return, you shall slaughter everyone that I have not given to fight with you. Every man, every woman, every child shall be cut down without exception. You shall cut the heart out of every male and bring it to me, but you shall not harm the female bodies except for what is necessary for death. These you are to bring to me. Male hearts and female bodies. Do you understand so far?"

Fel-hoen did not hesitate. "Yes."

"You shall also give me your firstborn son."

"On the day he is born?"

"No. I have no use for a puling, squalling brat. You will give him to me on the day he becomes a man. Agreed?"

"Yes . . . anything."

"Remember this vow, Fel-hoen, for I do not take betrayal lightly." He suddenly reached above his head and pulled a pigeon from the tree. He squeezed the bird in his hand until the bird was a mass of blood and feathers. He handed it to Fel-hoen, who took it gingerly. "Remember, the price may be very, very high."

Fel-hoen let his mind return to the present. He was unsure whether he had spoken his memory to Temrane, but the look on the boy's face told him he had remembered aloud.

"This was the only way revolt was possible, Temrane."

The look on Temrane's face did not go away, and Fel-hoen did not try to interpret it. He knew he should feel remorse, or at least a sense of sorrow for the loss of his son, but he felt none of these. He had known that eventually this day would come. He had in fact prepared for it, in that he did not allow himself to grow close to Temrane. And his revulsion at Temrane's attempts to enter the priesthood only made it easier for him to turn Temrane over to Crotalus.

"What will he do with me?"

"I don't know, but it will probably have to do with turning you into a wizard. From the things I have heard, he has always desired a student. He is not a true master until he has an apprentice, and I think you shall be that apprentice."

"Father . . ." Temrane whispered through dry lips. His father, riding in front of him, did not hear. He swallowed hard, hesitated, and spoke again. "Father, please don't turn me over to him."

"We made a bargain, and I do not go back on my word."

"But we could just return to Zopel. What could he do to us? Take the kingdom back? If that is all—"

Fel-hoen pulled up sharply on the reins, turning to face Temrane, who recoiled at the familiar face black with rage. "If that is all? If that is all indeed! My son, and I say that for perhaps the last time, the kingdom is everything! It would take much more than the words of a thirteen-year-old boy to make me give up the kingdom . . . much more!"

He wheeled his horse around and began cantering at a quicker pace. Temrane, in wretched and grim silence behind him, had no choice but to follow.

• • •

The Wastelands began to the north of Melram in the realm of Paduan, but they stretched west to the Amil Mountains and east to the Conmia Sea. People did not travel in the Wastelands—there was no need. But stories were told of witches that haunted the desolation, of winds that drove men mad, of wild animals that would tear humans to shreds. In reality, there were no witches and few animals. The winds were indeed hot and dry, but man's madness was due to other causes. The land was not good for farming, nor for raising much of anything except dirt.

The Forgotten City lay like a jewel in the Wastelands. In the northern tip, overlooking the waters, the city was once beautiful and wealthy. Tall buildings of stones, brick, glass, and clay told tales of architecture that no one had seen in hundreds, possibly thousands of years. Gardens still surrounded these structures—huge trees spreading leafy shadows over green grasses and multicolored flowers. Water was in abundance here, coming from the Conmia Sea and running through pipes that had been laid down at the time the buildings went up.

The fact that the Forgotten City retained its beauty amid so much ruin was due to Duncan. His mother and father had been the last inhabitants of the city and brought him up on stories of how the worshipers of the Redeemer God had been slaughtered here because they refused to renounce their belief. A few had remained in hiding, and through time the slaughterers died or moved on to other places throughout the world. Soon the city was forgotten. The few remaining worshipers raised their children and their children's children in peace. Through time the worshipers, called the Menontes (followers of Menon, the Redeemer God) died or moved on to other places throughout the world, and only Duncan's mother and father were left. They could not bring themselves to leave the city, believing as they did that it was holy, that the blood of their ancestors was steeped into the very ground of this land. *Menon* meant "The Abiding One," and if they were called by His name, they too would abide.

It was this heritage that Duncan received. He was thirteen when his mother died, standing on the edge of sixteen when his father died. He believed there was no higher calling for him than to stay in this city of the blood of his ancestors to carry on the work of his father and mother, studying the ancient books, maintaining the city in its wondrous splendor, worshiping Menon.

Of all people living now, only three knew that Duncan and the Forgotten City were not legend, and these resided in Beren: Devona, Farrel Jaqeth, and King Jerome. It was not known how Devona came by the knowledge of the Forgotten City, but she comprehended many things that were strange to others. Farrel and King Jerome had ridden together into the Forgotten City not long after King Jerome's victory in the first war of Paduan. Jerome was seeking a cure for his beloved friend Farrel Jaqeth, who had taken a poison arrow in the leg. The Menontes had been renowned for their knowledge of the healing arts, and Jerome wanted a cure that would restore the use of the leg to Farrel. None could be found, and the extreme effects of the poison were not known until much later.

Jerome and Farrel did not travel together again to the Forgotten City, and spoke of it to no one. As the ravages of the poison took effect in Farrel's mind, Jerome began to wonder whether Farrel even remembered the Forgotten City, and he also in time let it pass from his memory.

Rafaela brought the Forgotten City back into Jerome's thoughts, and he took her there, then spent a pleasant two days in Duncan's company before returning to Beren. Because of the nature of his mission, he never spoke of the Forgotten City to anyone and never again allowed it into his contemplations. The city and its proprietor must truly be forgotten in order to protect the woman who now reigned as the city's queen.

Rafaela understood but little of this. It had taken three months for Duncan to neutralize the poison that had been shot into her and long years to counteract the memories. Duncan was unsure how much she really remembered of the events, but he knew that the two men still stood out sharply in her memory – and in her heart. She loved both, and it was only her love of the Redeemer God that kept her from torment.

He watched her now as she bent over the flowers in an indoor garden, pulling weeds from around them, stroking the leaves clean, brushing away dead petals. She preferred the quietude of night for indoor gardening, and Duncan often wondered about her short hours of sleep. But her beauty was undiminished by the catnaps. Her long hair had been gone many years, as she favored the easy care of short hair. Duncan smiled a little. Who would have thought that such long, heavy, straight hair would become such soft curls around the face when cut. The dark brown of her hair accented the paleness of her face. Her natural color had been drained by the poison and although there were pink spots in the cheeks, she still remained pale. The eyes, chocolate in hue, sparkled more now and seemed to take in details that before would have escaped her notice. Her eyes caught him now, standing in the shadows, and her face flooded with smiles. "Hello, Duncan. I was wondering when I would see you. It has been near a week."

He came over and sat on the ground beside her, his knees cracking as he did so. "I'm not as young as I used to be. The ground is hard, and my body complains. I have been meditating much this past week."

"You have not taken the food I have left in the kitchens for you. Have your meditations made you forget food?"

"I suppose they have. I had not realized that I hadn't eaten." He patted his stomach. "You can't tell by looking."

"Come," she said, gliding to her feet, "I will make you something now."

"No . . ." He touched her hand, arresting her movement. "My meditations have been of a specific kind. We must talk."

She stared at him a moment, trying to read his thoughts, and Duncan could almost see the fear in her eyes. It had been a long time since it had been there, and he hated to put it back. She sat down beside him. "Which one is it?"

He paused a long time, then said, "I believe it is Crotalus." He watched her face carefully, trying to gauge the effect his words were having upon her. So far there was nothing. "Rafaela, we have often talked, and we have talked of many things. You cannot live with someone for thirteen years and not become a part of their life. You are a part of mine, and I love you as I have loved no other in this world. To say you have been like a daughter to me could not begin to touch my love for you. You have been more than a daughter. You have been a companion. I have taught you many things of the Redeemer God and the Forgotten City. You have taught me many things of the world beyond this city."

She smiled and placed her hand over his. "Dear Duncan, I could never have lived if it were not for you."

"Then you trust me?"

"Trust you! What a strange question. But I can see from your eyes that you do not jest. This must be a serious issue indeed for you to question my trust of you. I have entrusted you with my life."

"In all the talks we have had, and I know there have been many, you have never spoken of your great love for Crotalus and Falcon. Sometimes we have talked of one, at different times the other. I have never pressed because it was never important."

"But it is important now."

"It is to me. In the final balance it may make no difference at all, but it does to me."

Her eyes were lowered, so he could not see the expression in them. But he could hear her quickened breath and could see the color rising in her cheeks as she wrestled with the desire to suppress thoughts of the two men. "For your peace of mind I shall tell you anything."

"Then tell me of your love for them."

She pulled a few weeds from the ground and held the rich-smelling soil to her nose. Her eyes were closed as she lowered the dirt to her lap, her mind going back. "Crotalus was my first real love, and he awakened things in me that I never thought existed. It didn't matter to me that they were dark things. He talked often of the power we would share, and it seemed a good life to me. My love for him was sudden and overpowering and all-consuming. I loved him wildly, passionately.

"I did not love Falcon right away. In fact, I did not care for him at all. Oh, he was fun, and part of the fun was that we did not get along. We fought often. After a fight I would go into my rooms and fume at the way he was, and then I would almost as quickly forgive him because he was my friend. I would go to find him and tell him he was forgiven, and we would meet each other as he was coming to tell me that I was forgiven. Then the fight would start all over again. I realized my love for him slowly and after a long period of time. As I grew to love him more, I realized that some of the things we had fought about, such as the Redeemer God, were in fact things that were more important to him than life. That intrigued me, and instead of fighting we now conversed." She opened her eyes. "You know the rest."

"You did not, then, abandon your love of Crotalus."

"No . . . I never have. I have cried with bitter grief, sometimes wishing I could return to a time of simple love with Crotalus."

"Do you then love him more than Falcon?"

"At times, because it is an easier love. Falcon challenges me, urges me to higher things. I said that Crotalus awakened things in me. Falcon placed seeds within my heart and entreated them to grow. When I struggle with the growth, I love Crotalus more."

"Is it often?"

"Much less now than then. Are you asking me, if I had my choice which of the two would I choose?"

"I suppose I am."

"Set your mind at ease, dear Duncan. I would choose Falcon."

"Why, if you love Crotalus more?"

"It is only at times that I love Crotalus more, and at those times I feel that I am returning to something less than I am now, not more. I love Falcon with a love that is unshakable. It is a stable love. His love, and eventually mine, was based on something other than need. Crotalus, however, needed me horribly and would have eventually smothered me in that need, as he tried to do at the end."

"And yet you love him."

"My love for Falcon could not have existed without my first love of Crotalus. Besides," she said with a slight smile playing at her lips, "I was the only one to ever have loved him. Is there any creature that does not warrant our love?"

"No . . . you are right. He is a creature of the Redeemer God and deserves our love."

"Perhaps it is my continuous love that will eventually make him turn."

"Perhaps."

"Have I set your mind at ease?"

"You have."

"Tell me now . . . why does Crotalus concern you?"

"I don't exactly know. My heart is filled with dread, and it emanates from him. It is time for me to leave the Forgotten City."

"Leave! But you have long considered it sacred to stay here."

"Menon is asking me to leave. I must search for Crotalus. Some evil is abroad."

"Does this concern the sword you have spent so much time with over the years?"

"It may. I know the sword will be used again, but I don't know when or by whom." Duncan stood stiffly. "I am too old to be sitting on the ground."

This time it was Duncan who was detained by a touch of the hand. "Tell me why you wished to know which of my loves was greater."

"I wanted to be sure before I left that Crotalus no longer had any power over you."

She watched as he walked away, preparing for his journey. She turned back to the flowers, but did not see them, for the tears blurred the colors together. "Oh, Menon," she whispered softly, "the hurt is still so great. Crotalus does not have power over me. But Falcon does. Release me from a love that can never be."

• • •

Duncan gazed at the sword, its luminescence filling the dim room. He had considered taking it with him, but now decided against it. Apparently it was not for him to use.

He gathered a few belongings and food that Rafaela brought him into a small rucksack and threw it upon his shoulder. The time, he felt, was running short. He did not know what evil Crotalus was going to bring about, and he did not know how he was to abort it, but presumably Menon still had use for his old limbs and the love he carried inside him.

Ten

As darkness closed down on the Amil Mountains, the heights were not friendly, but were rather enemies to be feared or conquered. Fel-hoen felt he had subdued the mountains by his coming into them and his ride alone out of them. Temrane, left behind, feared the towering rocks, feeling that unfriendly eyes were upon him.

He had watched his father ride back down the mountains until he could no longer spot the slow jogging of the horse. He had wanted to shout to that quickly vanishing back, entreating him once again to forget the kingdom. But his begging had been unheard before – he knew it would be no different now. The king was as unyielding as the face of the mountain. If his father had any doubts about leaving his only son, he hid them well.

Temrane sat upon the ground, an oak tree at his back, and tried to justify this betrayal. He knew his father had never loved him, but he had always felt it was because of the priesthood. He had never dreamed that his father's hate would come to leaving his son to defend himself against a wizard. Pain rushed through him as he remembered his father's words: "The kingdom is everything." Greed had twisted his father's face into an ugly, alien thing. And Temrane especially agonized because throughout all, he still loved his father.

He peered around the tree, trying to penetrate the pervasive darkness. He heard sounds and in his fright imagined horrible monsters that would rend him to pieces. The wizard, whenever he came for him, would find only white bones, picked clean by ravaging teeth.

Temrane clenched his fists together, drawing blood into his palms in half-circles. He was no longer a child. He had faced the Calli-kor today and had been declared a man. A man would not fear the dark, nor a half-mad wizard. The thought calmed him, and he released his fists.

He stood and began walking in the direction he saw his father take. Just because his father—what pain that word caused—had left him here did not mean he had to stay here and await the wizard. He would return to Zopel, under cover of darkness if needed, and seek Cand-hoen. His father—Temrane shook his head; he no longer had a father—the king paid little attention to the goings-on of the temple and would not notice a new priest, albeit a young one, in the ranks.

A new thought grabbed him with such intensity that he stopped as suddenly as though hit with lightning. Perhaps Cand-hoen would not receive him.

No, he thought, starting again. Cand-hoen's love had always been strong, much stronger and surer than his father's. But Cand-hoen was also a priest, the high priest of Hoen, and as such would not hide Temrane from the king.

Wetness touched his cheek, and he hurriedly brushed it away. Had Hoen deserted him also? Why else would he allow his servant to be abandoned to a wizard? *But I am a faithful servant*, he argued. *My life has always been given to pleasing Hoen. I can feel the strength of the god within*. But as soon as the thought was formed, he began to feel that strength slip from him. It was being drawn away, taken back into Hoen to be given to a more deserving acolyte.

"Why?" he screamed to the stars that blinked back an answer if he could only read it. "Is it because I didn't love my father enough? Because I didn't please him? Or was it my greater love for Candy? Was I not quick enough in the Calli-kor? Please don't play games with me as you have with others! I am a faithful servant!" He began to run, knowing he could never run from the disgrace of Hoen's displeasure, yet trying to escape just the same.

"Where do you run?" The voice came out of the black sky as though the stars had gained voice. Temrane halted in his impetuous flight, his heart thudding painfully in his chest, his ears straining to hear.

"You cannot escape." Temrane whirled around, certain the voice had come from behind him, but no one was there. Laughter filled the forest, a low reverberation that caused Temrane to quake with fear. "I am a man," he whispered urgently and forced himself into stillness.

"Yes, you are a man." The wizard suddenly stood before him. "It is not a very nice birthday present to be betrayed by your own father, is it?"

Temrane said nothing. His father had said that Crotalus had lost his handsome looks years before, and it was true. Crotalus could not be called a handsome man, and yet there was something in his face that spoke of power, a commanding presence. Perhaps it was the strong nose, or the high forehead, the masterful height. His countenance was fierce, the eyes hypnotic.

"You hate your father for that, don't you?"

Temrane slowly shook his head. "I love my father," he whispered softly, and yet the thundering of his heart in his ears belied his words.

"You hate him. I know you do. It is all right to feel it inside of you. It is all right to say it. Go ahead and say it now. Say, 'I hate my father.'"

Temrane's mouth formed the words, but no sound came.

"Say it again."

He again mouthed the words, and at another urging from Crotalus the words came forth. "I hate my father."

"I understand your hate, for I understand betrayal, prince, perchance better than you can at your young age. Rule with me, and we shall in time make our betrayers very sorry for their choice."

Temrane felt the words rather than heard them, as though they came to him through a heavy mist. They rolled over him and penetrated deep within him. The wizard came closer, still speaking, although Temrane could not understand the words he spoke. He watched the sorcerer's eyes as the burning black pupils expanded, and he seemed to plummet downward within them until he closed his own eyes and was aware of nothing more.

• • •

Crotalus sat silently in his private rooms, watching the boy as he lay sleeping. Strange feelings stirred inside him. He wanted to protect him as well as teach him. If he didn't already hate Fel-hoen, he would hate him now for the pain he had caused to this tender one. Had he ever been this responsive? He couldn't remember. But he had loved sorcery and the dark arts. He had been an eager and willing pupil. Temrane would be the same in time.

Careful, his mind whispered. *You gave your love to someone once before, and she betrayed you.* He clenched his teeth in an agony of remembrance. That would not happen again. There would be no Falcon to steal the love away. This was a mere boy, not a bride. He did not love the child; he only wanted to control him. Still, it would pay to be cautious. There was much work to be done.

He walked to where his books were kept, treading quietly so as not to awaken Temrane. His hand first found *On Raising the Dead*. He carefully read over his last experiment. He had been so close. The eyelids of the corpse had fluttered. Of course, it could have been a mere muscle reaction, like the jerking of the arms, but Crotalus didn't believe that. He was close to an answer; he could feel it. Possibly the young and less desperate thoughts of Temrane would speed the breakthrough.

He replaced the tome and withdrew *On Stealing Souls*. He painstakingly went over the steps, each so intricate, so important. He remembered his words to Fel-hoen sixteen years ago: "The price may be very, very high."

"The time has come to pay up," he whispered as he watched the boy sleeping. "And you've only made the first installment."

• • •

Mists gathered around him, and somehow Temrane knew he was dreaming. He struggled to break through the mists and into the daylight, but something held him fast. He could hear someone talking, a low voice, kind and fatherly. Candy? It was similar in tone, but the inflections were different. He waited patiently, knowing that the owner of the voice was coming closer to him and would part the mists.

The man was short and round. The bald head gleamed through the mists like a light that matched his blue eyes. The teeth were straight and white in a smile that was the companion of the gentle voice. "Don't be afraid," he said to Temrane. "I am coming for you."

The man and the mist disappeared as Temrane was pulled up through the depths of sleep and awakened to Crotalus. "Come," he said. "I will show you your new home."

Temrane obeyed silently, but his thoughts as they went through the castle were on the man in his vision. He was not Uncle Candy, but this did not bother him. The appearance of the man had calmed Temrane as nothing else could have done, and although he was frightened of Crotalus, he would be willing to wait a short time for this man to come for him.

But supposing it was not a vision but merely a dream brought on by his own despair? He would wait a few days and see, but if the man did not come within three days—he could give him no more—Temrane would seek escape from the castle and Crotalus. He would return to Candy. He did not know if he would be welcome, or if the god would accept him, but it seemed a trivial point that could easily be dealt with when the time came. For now he would wait, please Crotalus as much as possible without arousing suspicion, and look for his salvation.

Eleven

Jerome rode steadily on the road between Beren and Zopel. His heart was light within him as he watched the sun edge over the horizon, purpling everything before washing it in gold.

His thoughts this early morning were more pleasant than those of the night. For a time he was able to put aside Rafaela and the strange love triangle he had disrupted and concentrate on Kreith. Although Kreith had thoughtlessly forsaken his responsibilities as prince, Jerome was willing to say only a little about this and hopefully talk about the girl who had made Kreith so forgetful.

It was at times such as these that he felt his fifty-eight years most keenly. Although his once-black hair had been streaked with silver for many years now and the lines were etched a little deeper around his eyes, he did not often feel the approaching of age. But as he thought about Kreith and his seventeen years, he grew a little older. Kreith considered him the king, but looked up to Falcon as a father. Jerome yearned to change that, and though he would fulfill his obligation as royal father and speak to Kreith about his precipitate leave-taking, he would also please himself regarding the new love of Kreith's young life.

It was as he was deciding these things that he spotted Kreith's horse in the distance. He did not speed up, but hung back patiently, hoping to glimpse his son's face before Kreith saw him. His patience was rewarded, and he saw a face flooded with goodwill, happiness, and youth. How much like his mother he looked with the golden hair and startling blue eyes! And how much he loved this young man who now whistled a melody taught him by Batakis.

The tune died on Kreith's lips as he neared and recognized his father. The duties he had neglected rushed into his mind upon the sight of his father— his king—riding in the very early morning, probably looking for him.

"Good morning, sir," he said with as much respect as he could muster.

"Good morning," Jerome returned with warmth and a trace of sternness. "You are out early."

Relief washed over Kreith's face as he thought that his father did not know of the evening's adventure. Perhaps he could keep the fact from him, even though he had never been good at lying. "Yes . . . It was a glorious morning for riding."

"So it would seem."

They rode silently for a time side by side on the wide road, occasionally passing a merchant traveling from one city to another, his wares clanking behind him long after he disappeared behind one of the many bends and hills of the road.

Kreith at last could bear it no longer. "I lied to you, Father."

Jerome raised his eyebrows.

"I am not out early—I am out late."

Jerome smiled at the look of worry on his face. "So it would seem," he said again.

"Will I be punished?"

"Do you think you should be?"

"No . . . Well, I guess I did leave without finishing my obligations at the feast, and I didn't tell you that I was going. But I did tell Falcon."

"Ah, yes, Falcon. That brings up another matter."

"What do you mean?"

"First, you caused Falcon a great deal of worry when you did not return. The second matter is more serious. Falcon is my knight, my highest knight. I expect him to obey me. His first loyalty is to me as king. His loyalty to you is subordinate to that until you take the throne. By giving you leave without my permission, he violated that trust."

Kreith's eyes were wide upon hearing this, his mouth open a little in protest. He closed it then, knowing his father was right. "I'm sorry, Father. I did not mean to cause either you or Falcon worry. Discipline me as you see fit."

Jerome wanted to chuckle a little at the manly submission of his son. He suppressed the urge, though, knowing that his words would remain a valuable lesson to Kreith. "Your punishment shall fit your crime. Because you shirked responsibility, I shall add one to it. Falcon shall be placed in your charge in this matter. Discipline him as you see fit."

"But it was my fault! I begged him to let me go! He should not be disciplined."

Jerome smiled at last, the lesson learned. "You must remember that as prince, and eventually as king, your responsibilities touch many more people than just yourself, and the consequences affect everyone. Perhaps for a discipline you could give him today off – he was up most of the night."

The words took a moment to sink in, and Kreith wasn't entirely sure what had taken place, but he returned his father's smile.

"What drew you from the feast and kept you gone so long?"

Kreith glanced sideways at his father, but did not see a bantering look. He was serious. Kreith still hesitated. The chasm between his father's age and his own seemed unbridgeable. How would his father understand what had happened to him? "I just wanted a ride and lost track of time."

Jerome sighed in disappointment, and then decided on another direction. "Your mother and I were talking last night about you. We feel that you are of an age to take a wife. There are several nobles who have daughters a little younger than you. I believe we could find a suitable woman to be your queen."

"But you can't!" Kreith cried, stopping his horse.

Jerome turned on his horse to look at him. "Why not?"

Kreith started, stopped, blushed. "Well, there's this girl . . ." he said at last.

Jerome let the smile that had been trying to escape diffuse over his face.

• • •

Alde watched as Bria finished putting the pastries into the window. Her hands had moved quickly and lovingly, almost lingering over the delicate and delicious creations. As she stood up to admire her work, he placed another rack of crossed cookies in the window.

"I don't want you spending so much time over that man."

She looked at him startled, unsure of his meaning. "Which man?"

"That Batakis."

"I didn't spend any more time with him than with any other customer."

"We don't need his business. Let him go elsewhere."

"For whatever reason?"

"For many reasons. The way he dresses is one. It's almost pagan. A man of God should not wear those colors, nor that style. It invites ridicule rather than respect."

"He dresses to please the children, Alde."

"But does he please the Redeemer God? A true follower should be more sedate, more serious. And the way he chases after that old woman is unbefitting a true servant."

"What old woman? You mean Devona?"

"Of course. He trails her from here to there and there to here as if she were the queen and he her footman."

"But they are friends."

"It is unseemly. They are not just friends. I would not be surprised to hear that he is her lover."

Bria gasped. "Alde, how can you say such a thing!"

Alde was prevented from replying by the smell of tarts that were almost too done, and Bria was glad to see him go. There was hardly a man in town more liked than Batakis and no woman more upright than Devona.

She smiled as she thought of Batakis' visit to pick up breakfast buns, declaring his intention to take some to Devona. His eyes had been soft, his mouth smiling gently. *Well, I'll be blessed*, she thought, *he does love her*. Not the sort of love, of course, of which Alde was speaking, but a true and devoted love.

"He loves her," she whispered, and then said it a little louder to Alde still in the back.

"It is not to be! She is at least thirty years his senior."

"And what of it? If they don't object, why should we?"

Alde appeared in the doorway, a dark, foreboding scowl on his face. "Because it is not right. And I will not have my wife condoning their sinful actions. Is that understood?"

He did not wait for her to answer, but stormed back to the ovens. Bria stared after him, a tear in her eye. How could he be so sure he was right?

• • •

"She is beautiful, Father, more beautiful than you can imagine. She has dark hair, like the night sky during a full moon, and it's long and wavy. She doesn't wear it pulled up, but it is pulled away from her face by combs. And her eyes! They're blue, but not like mine. They're dark blue like a storm. . ."

Jerome listened as his son counted off this wonderful girl's attributes. When Kreith paused to take a breath, Jerome interrupted. "But what is her name?"

"Oh . . . Didn't I tell you? Her name is Merry. Father, she is a princess. She is King Fel-hoen's daughter."

"Fel-hoen? From Corigo?"

"Yes. I saw him this morning after Merry went into the castle. He was returning from riding. He does not look much like Merry. He has blond hair, though not as gold as mine. Father, I love her. I haven't known her very long, but I know I love her."

"And does she love you?"

"I don't know. She thinks I am a peasant."

"Why not tell her you are a prince?"

"I tried, but she didn't believe me. Maybe she loves me because I am a peasant. Many women fall in love with men who are their inferiors," he said in a worldly voice that did not at all match his boyish face.

"That is true, and I suppose you could give up your crown for her, but why not try convincing her of the truth again? If she stops loving you, then you can throw away the crown. That will impress her."

Kreith looked at his father in amazement. He understood. Even though the last was said in jest, Kreith could hear the perception of his predicament behind the words. "Did you love my mother this way?"

Jerome laughed, and the laughter dropped years from his face. "I loved your mother with a passion that will never be surpassed. She, however, despised me."

"You? She loves you!"

"She loves me now, but then . . .! Ah, that was another matter. She was the most beautiful woman in the land and had many beaus. But I was the prince and could have her if I wanted her."

"Was she a peasant?"

"No. She was the daughter of a noble, and a number of years before I took her as my wife he and his men supported me in the battle against my father to gain Paduan. It was their support that swayed the battle and made me king."

"Did she love you once you became king?"

"No . . . She started to love me a little before that. She had despised me because I was considered a wicked man. I took my own pleasure where I found it and . . ." He paused, unsure how to phrase his past transgressions. "Well, let's just say I was never lacking for drink or female company."

Kreith listened to this confession in amazement. He had, of course, heard rumors of his father's past life, but he never dreamed that the stories were true and possibly even less wild than his father had truly been.

"I vowed when I saw her that she would be my bride and that I would change for the love of her. She, as a smart woman, did not believe that for an instant."

"But you changed," Kreith said wonderingly.

Jerome smiled. "I changed, and it has made all the difference in my life. Tell Merry the truth, Kreith. She can stand it. And then I shall bargain with her father. Perhaps we shall unite the lands of Paduan and Corigo."

• • •

Devona finished wiping the breakfast dishes, put them in a little cupboard that was next to the oven, and rejoined Batakis, who was sitting at the small table in the kitchen. "Tell me what you are really doing here. I know you didn't come all this way just to bring breakfast buns."

He leaned toward her, his eyes dancing merrily. "But they were great, weren't they?"

"That they were, but I have had nothing from Bria's ovens that hasn't been delicious. That still doesn't tell me why you came."

"I enjoy your face first thing in the morning almost better than anything else."

"Oh, Batakis, I hope you're not going to start on this again."

"On what again?"

"That we could make a good family together, that you love me wildly."

"Wildly and passionately, and we *could* make a good family

together. But if you don't want to hear it now, I shall save it for another time. I actually did come here for a very good reason. How's your wagon?"

"Still being mended. This is not only going to be time-consuming but money-consuming as well. For what they are going to charge me for putting on a new wheel, I could have almost bought a new wagon."

"I am going to ride into Zopel today and thought I would see if you would like to come."

"What are you going to Zopel for? You were just there the day before yesterday."

"It's a special visit for Temrane."

"Temrane? The prince?"

"Yesterday was his thirteenth birthday. I guess they have some kind of priestly ceremony with feasting afterward when a boy becomes a man. King Fel-hoen asked me to play for the feast since I am his son's favorite minstrel, but I could not because of our own feast. I thought I would go and see him today and give him a special birthday present from me."

Devona smiled softly. There was no one more kindhearted toward the children than Batakis, and for a moment she almost wished she were thirty years younger. "I would love to go. There are always things for me to do whether I am in Beren or Zopel. Could we make a stop at the Lidyl farm first? Jyn is rather anxious about his wife's first baby. I try to get by there often to ease his mind."

Batakis helped Devona pack the few things she would need, and then closed up the house for her. She chatted cheerily as they bumped down the road, and Batakis listened, half with his ears and half with his heart, feeling his melancholy of the night before slip away as it always did when he was with her.

Twelve

Fel-hoen waited until it was no longer possible to conceal Temrane's absence to tell Kenda about his deal with Crotalus. He knew she would be bereaved, so he placed much emphasis on the kingdom, on the fact that she would not be queen if it were not for the strength given him by Crotalus.

"How could you do such a thing to your own son!"

"Kenda, I did it long before he was my son."

"But the very thought of it! How could you do that to me?"

"You would have lost him in a year or two to the temple anyway. This way we can keep our kingdom and we don't have to listen to his talk of the gods day and night."

"You have gone too far, Fel-hoen. You have mocked the gods for as long as I have known you, but this time you have overstepped the bounds. The gods will punish you for this!" She began to weep uncontrollably as she sank to her knees, her fists beating her chest.

Fel-hoen stepped near her. He did not like causing her pain. Other than the kingdom, she was his one love. He touched her hair as though she were a child, stroking it, smoothing it. She jerked her head away and stared at him with red-rimmed, angry eyes. "Don't touch me! I don't want any part of you, for the gods will certainly punish you, and I don't want to be dragged along with you."

He slapped her across the face, the smack resounding through the room as the fingerprints stood starkly against the fair skin. "You are my wife and my queen. I shall touch you when I so desire. You have been married to me for a long time and knew what I was when we wed. You disgraced your family by marrying me against their wishes and against the wishes of the gods. You are a part of me. My damnation, if the gods choose so, is your damnation as well."

He strode from the room, slamming the door upon the now-silent sobs of Temrane's bereaved mother.

• • •

Niccola had narrowly missed the king's gaze as he stalked from her mistress's room. His face had been contorted and near purple in color, the words he mouthed unintelligible. His fists had clenched-and unclenched uncontrollably, and Niccola rejoiced that she had hidden herself in time.

She was at first distressed with the news about Temrane. Her victory of the night before seemed dashed to pieces as she listened to Fel-hoen's treachery. But her mind, although accustomed to despair, was not capable of admitting failure, and soon she was turning the situation over and over, finding how this could best suit her needs. There were several directions she could take. She could stir up greater animosity between Kenda and Fel-hoen and then insinuate herself into Kenda's good graces. This, she thought, would not be hard to accomplish. Approaching Cand-hoen and threatening him with her knowledge of the Calli-kor was another tack that might be profitable. Perhaps he could be bribed into helping her regain her kingdom. Along the same lines, but involving less dealing with the priest, she could expose Cand-hoen's lie about the Calli-kor and tell how Temrane's disappearance was just recompense for the high priest's corruption.

The latter idea appealed greatly to her, for she would love to bring down the entire family. Yet, other than satisfying her own desires, she could not see that it would bring her any lasting results. She toyed with the idea of becoming intimate with Fel-hoen in this time of his wife's withdrawal. She had attempted this before, but with little result. Fel-hoen was devoted to Kenda. Now, with Kenda's despisement of him, he might be more willing to be seduced. She could then reveal her knowledge of Cand-hoen to him. With his hatred of his brother, she could easily convince him to turn the people's wrath against the priest.

She would do all of this, of course, for a price: an equal share with him in his kingdom. If that came about, it would only be a matter of time before she could murder him, as he had murdered her father. Then she would rule the kingdom as she should have done all along.

She smiled a little. She could accomplish all of these things with one stroke. If she were careful, her duplicity would never be discovered. She glanced at the door to the queen's bedchamber. Quiet sobs still could be heard. Niccola could wait a few more minutes to go in and attend the queen.

She ran down the stairs quickly, careful to attract no attention, and went into her small apartment. As hoped, Caldon was still there finishing his breakfast before going to be with his father. "Caldon, I want you to take a message to your Aunt Freyda for me before going to your father."

He looked at her eagerly, always willing to do anything for her. She detested the look, along with the stupid eyes and dull mind of one who would never become anything more than a lowly leatherworker. "Tell Freyda that King Fel-hoen has consorted with a sorcerer and has given away the prince to be the sorcerer's pupil. Can you remember that?"

Caldon nodded and repeated the message back to her word for word.

"Go quickly then." She watched as he gulped down the remaining bread and ran out the door. Freyda, she knew, had a tongue like a dog's tail. The news of Fel-hoen's bargain with Crotalus would be common knowledge before the sun set tonight. And these superstitious people would be horrified at their king's denouncement of the gods. As the people's outcry against Fel-hoen grew, so would the intimacy between Fel-hoen and herself. She then would offer him a way out of disgrace by turning it toward his loathsome brother.

She almost laughed aloud with the ease of the plan. But there would be time for rejoicing later. Now she had a queen who needed comforting.

• • •

Lomeli watched Niccola from the shadowy corner of the bedroom. She had not seen him as she gave her message to Caldon, but he heard the words she spoke and saw the smile of self-satisfaction that graced her beautifully cruel face. He did not know what she had planned, but it surely had something to do with rising above her station. She would never be happy being the wife of a leatherworker, nor the queen's personal attendant. He saw it all with grief, but knew that nothing he had ever said or ever would say would change her heart.

As she left the room, he came out of the shadows to watch her ascend the steps to the queen's rooms. As soon as he could, he would go to the temple of Anok and make sacrifice there, not only for King Fel-hoen, but for Niccola.

• • •

Kenda drew the long, black, tattered cloth from the wardrobe and draped it over her hair. She did not look in the mirror that hung next to the wardrobe. It was considered mocking the gods to look at oneself in the death dress. She didn't know why this was so, but she obeyed nonetheless. One mustn't question the ways of the gods.

Kenda ignored the gentle knocking on her door, and in a few moments Niccola opened the door softly. "My lady, can I get you anything?" Her voice was filled with warmth and compassion.

"No . . . I am going to contemplate my disobedient life for a moment, and then I shall go to the priests."

"My lady, you have never been disobedient! You are a faithful wife and mother."

"I married against the wish of the gods. Being a faithful wife means nothing when you have married a man who scorns the gods. Better to be disloyal to him than to the gods. My son was taken away as punishment."

Niccola walked to where Kenda stood and for a moment felt a seed of real compassion for this woman shrouded in black. Although she had never touched her queen before except in helping her dress, she rested her hand on Kenda's shoulder. "Forgive me for witnessing your distress, madam, and for speaking to you in this way, but I cannot believe that the gods would be so cruel as to take away your son. The prince has gained favor with the gods, even if his father has not, and he will escape from this sorcerer and come to you again."

Kenda smiled a little, more for Niccola's sake than from any relief that she felt. "Thank you, Niccola. You have been more to me than a servant today. You have been a friend. I will go to the priests now. Perhaps they can help me find Temrane."

She swept out of the room, her chin held high, determination marking her step. She did not see the small smile that touched Niccola's lips.

• • •

Cand-hoen sat in stunned disbelief as Kenda related her story. Numbness had descended on him at her first words, and he struggled now to hear her remaining thoughts. As she finished, she looked at him expectantly, and he realized with a little shock that she had come to him not as the uncle of her son, but as the high priest. The knowledge angered him, for he loved the boy more than anyone in the world, and this news affected that love before any other.

"I know it has been many, many years since I have come to the gods, and perhaps this is my punishment. Tell me . . . what must I do to recover my son?"

He did not answer her immediately, for he was remembering his own sin before the god.

Kenda took his silence as the affirmation of the seriousness of her many sins. She lowered her head and gave voice to an idea she had conceived earlier. "I have heard that in the past young virgins were sacrificed to obtain favor with the gods, particularly Hoen. I am not young any longer, nor a virgin, but if it meant releasing Temrane from the hands of this sorcerer, I would do it."

Cand-hoen knew that her sacrifice would be useless, for it was not her sin that had sent Temrane away, but still he was tempted to give it credence. Sacrifices had purchased clemency before and might again. Perhaps it had been the sins of Kenda and Fel-hoen that had most offended Hoen.

"This is a very grave affair," he said at last. "I need to pray to the god for special guidance, for I do not know what is needed. Go home, observe all of the laws of mourning, and await my answer."

"What about Fel-hoen?"

Cand-hoen clenched his fists together to control the rage building inside him. "Your husband has forsaken the god, the priesthood, and now his son. You have not only this day lost a son, but a husband. Do not further anger Hoen by having association with Fel-hoen. He is dead to you. Do you understand?"

Kenda nodded. She would do whatever it took to get Temrane back – even if it meant angering her husband, sacrificing her daughter, or sacrificing herself. Temrane would be freed regardless of the cost.

• • •

Cand-hoen did not watch her leave, but hurried to his private room. He draped the window so none could see in, then covered the image of the god with a cloth so he did not have to look at that terrible face.

He reclined on the bed, staring at the ceiling, trying not to think of anything. Anguish lay on his heart like a stone that would not budge. He felt crushed under the weight, capable of doing nothing. Out of habit rather than desire he recited the daily prayers of Hoen, speaking softly, not concentrating on what he was saying, but letting his lips form the words anyway. These prayers calmed him somewhat, although sorrow still surrounded him.

The question uppermost in his mind was why Temrane had been taken. If it was his own disobedience, how could it have been planned sixteen years ago? It could not have been punishment to Fel-hoen, for Fel-hoen was not suffering at all. Indeed, it seemed at times as though the gods favored Fel-hoen. Kenda's disobedience was great, but not as great as his own; and besides, she was a woman.

The answer had to lie with Temrane. There had been some sin in the boy's past that he had not alluded to, for which he had not sacrificed. That was why he had not passed the Calli-kor and why he was now with a wizard.

The thought of Temrane being with a sorcerer, one practicing that which had been condemned by the priests, stabbed at Cand-hoen's heart. Perhaps this was also his own punishment, for he understood now that he loved Temrane more than he loved the gods, more than Hoen. It was an awful discovery.

He rose from the bed and stood before the god. He took the black cloth covering the god in both hands and yanked it away. Boldly he looked into the face of the god. "I despise you," he spat. "And I defy you to stop me from searching for Temrane. Do your worst to me, but I shall never cower before you again."

• • •

Two thoughts struggled through Farni's mind as he watched his newborn daughter suck rapaciously at Freyda's breast. The first concerned the child. She did not seem to be gaining weight. It was true she was only a few days old, but she had the sickly look about her that Lis had had when she was born. Farni and Freyda were perhaps being further punished for their disobedience.

His second thought did not seem connected to the first, but the indignation in his heart told him it was so. His nephew Caldon had just given them the news of King Fel-hoen's treacherous disobedience. It was true that this should shock any god-fearing person. To have the king throw off the respect and honor of the gods was to incur wrath on the realm. This was indeed an appalling and frightful thing. But the resentment that had grown in him since Anne's birth blossomed full-flower into bitter hate that left acid in his mouth as he heard of the king giving up his son.

His son! How Farni had prayed and sacrificed and worked and bought costly incense all to purchase the goddess's blessing of a son, and all in vain. And then this king, who had been disobedient from the very start, hands over his son to a worker of magic!

Angry and harsh words rose to his mouth. He bit his lip to keep from saying them, but the pain was too deep, and the words spilled out despite the clenched teeth. "Why do you punish me? You have given me two sickly daughters, and then to further laugh at me you bring me this pain. What have I not done for you? Tell me and I shall do it!" Hot tears coursed down the anguished face. "If you had given me a son, I would never have given him away."

The torrent of words ended, and in time his tears dried. The calmness of exhaustion came over him, and he sat down in the dirt to contemplate what was to become of his family and his country. His anger at the goddess would not bode well; it never did. *Ah well,* he thought as he rose from the ground, *what's one more thing to sacrifice for when there is so much sacrificing to do anyway?*

• • •

Devona and Batakis had chatted happily together, enjoying each other's company on the drive from Beren to Zopel. Batakis was in the middle of a story concerning one of Zopel's children when he suddenly stopped mid-sentence.

Devona leaned over him to see what had arrested his attention. The stretch of road they were on now was the outskirts of Winni and Drucker's farm. It was beautiful land, still containing much of the grass that was lost further north of Zopel. Foothills rolled gently here to become rocky and mountainous as they turned into the Amil Mountains.

Winni and Drucker raised a few crops here—enough to eat well, but not enough to sell. Their sheep wandered these hills, munching on the sweet blades of grass. The pigs, their main livestock, were quartered on higher, less grassy, and more muddy land, close to the house. The sight of a pig here in this grassy area was indeed unusual. But what had caught Batakis' eye was Winni slaughtering a pig.

Batakis stopped the wagon, and the two watched as the small woman wrestled with the large pig, finally slashing its throat. They could see the blood spurt from the wound, sparkling darkly in the sunshine before Winni caught it in a cup.

"Does Winni always slaughter her own hogs?" Devona asked.

"No, they always take them to the butcher. He pays more for a live hog because it makes fresher meat. It's not even harvesttime. That hog shouldn't be ready for the market for at least another two months."

"But look how big he is!"

"Do you know their son Jasper? The last time I talked with him, he was telling me that was his personal hog and that it was the best. He said it was sure to bring more money than any of the others."

"Why would she slaughter her best hog two months before it was ready?"

Batakis hopped down from the wagon. "I don't know, but I think I'll go ask her. Want to come along?"

Devona let Batakis help her from the wagon, and the two strode across the field to where Winni knelt by the dead animal, its blood flowing sluggishly now from the neck and into a sacrificial cup. She looked up as they approached and nodded to them grimly.

"Do you want help hauling him to the town?" Batakis asked.

"No, but thank you. It is to be part of my penance to drag him to town without the benefit of a wagon or a man."

"Is that why you slaughtered your best hog before its time? For penance?"

"You haven't heard then?"

"Heard what?"

"The king has disgraced the gods. He has given his son over to a sorcerer, one named Crotalus. He would have done much better for everyone, including Prince Temrane, if he would have sacrificed him on the altar to Hoen."

"I'm not sure I understand, though, why you sacrifice your best hog."

"Drucker says that the king's disgrace is our disgrace because we have pledged our allegiance to him. If I took the pig to market, the butcher would be allowed to keep the blood and make his own sacrifice with it. If I slaughter it, we can give the blood at the temple, and our family will be blessed for it. We all need Hoen's blessing if we are to pull through this terrible time. Two weeks ago I saw a raven fly across the moon. I knew evil was in store, but I didn't realize it would be this bad. I must make penance for not warning the priests of the omen. The king's downfall is my downfall."

She turned back to the now-bloodless pig, dismissing them. After all, they worshiped a strange god.

Devona and Batakis were silent on the final stretch of road to Zopel, each contemplating the news Winni had given them of the prince. Devona thought of his golden head as it emerged into the world thirteen years ago, the mother's eager delight as she took him in her arms. Batakis remembered the dark eyes glistening with laughter, a smile creasing the cheeks and eyes as he listened to the funny songs of Batakis. Batakis' heart wrenched within as he thought of Winni's words. Temrane was gone.

Thirteen

Temrane spent the day in the care of Crotalus. Together they wandered the battlements to overlook what Crotalus called "his realm." They went into the armory, so Temrane would know what to expect from Crotalus' army. Crotalus spoke to many of the men Temrane saw in the castle, but none spoke to Temrane. Crotalus did not tell him who any of them were, and although a few of them glanced at the prince, none were brave enough to dare a few words with the boy. They knew well how Crotalus treated those who disobeyed him: escape was impossible, death certain.

The vision of the fatherly bald man was never far from Temrane's thoughts. He had ceased to consider this a dream. It had the quality of a vision, and though he had somehow displeased Hoen and was now out of his sight, the vision reassured him that a strange god still watched over him.

As Temrane observed the fear and respect Crotalus generated in his army, he could not help but be impressed. He wondered what had caused this respect. It was not long before he found out.

He and Crotalus had finished touring the castle and were approaching Crotalus' private rooms. As Crotalus was telling him about the books of magic he would teach Temrane to read, sounds came to them from within. Temrane wondered who would be in the private rooms of a wizard while the wizard was gone and glanced at Crotalus. The face he saw shocked and frightened him. The eyes narrowed until they were slits in a face darkened by fury. Nostrils flared as the chest heaved air in and out. Crotalus seemed to grow in height as he grabbed the door handle and flung the door open with a force that knocked several books from the shelves.

Captain Hirsch stood behind the desk, a dagger in one hand that he had used to pry open the desk, and a gold orb in the other. His eyes grew wide as he watched Crotalus' slow approach. He looked quickly around, realizing the distance from the desk to the window was too far for an escape attempt.

"You cannot escape me, you little fool," Crotalus spat. "I was tolerant when I found you looking through the books that contain magic spells. I will not be lenient this time." He stepped closer to Hirsch and tapped his chest with one long, bony finger. "Experience the beating of your heart, Hirsch. Slow, rhythmic, almost soothing. Now it begins to get faster, but not yet unpleasant. You feel as though you have just run up the stairs. Faster now. Ah yes, I can feel it flying. You can hardly keep up with it. Faster now. You can feel your life furiously beating away. Your heart is throbbing, almost bursting."

Sweat beads popped out on Hirsch's upper lip and brow. His mouth dropped open, and he began panting as though he had indeed run a very far distance. Eyes popped as he tried to breathe, as he sought without success to still his straining heart. He was slowly shaking his head, but he could not speak. His own heartbeat kept him from begging for mercy.

Temrane watched with growing horror as water poured down the man's face. He could almost hear the sound of the man's heart as it raced to its inevitable end. Temrane could bear it no longer, and out of compassion for the man rather than good sense or bravery he screamed at Crotalus, "Stop it! Stop it!"

Hirsch dropped suddenly to the floor as Crotalus released him, the gold orb falling from his hand and rolling to Temrane's feet. Crotalus turned to Temrane. "I forget that you are still tender." He looked down at Hirsch's heaving body. "There is no sense in killing him today. It will wait."

He walked to the door, flung it open, and hollered for Shallis, Hirsch's second-in-command. Shallis appeared in record time, and though his eyes wanted to stray to the body of his captain lying on the floor, he did not dare and kept his eyes straight ahead.

"Shallis, as of this minute you are the captain of the army, and your first duty is to take this maggot to the dungeons where I shall attend to him later, according to my own pleasure."

Crotalus spoke to Temrane without looking at him. "Pick up the orb and hold it in front of you." Temrane did so. Crotalus passed his hand over it. A green mist instantly rose from the orb, swirling, mesmerizing.

A shape rose from the mist—a lock of hair here, a rounded shoulder there, and although the mist sunk back down into the orb, the image of the woman remained—a miniature reality, solid in her makeup, bewitching in her beauty.

"Her name is Rafaela. Remember her well. She is the reason for everything we do—the spells, the experiments, the ruling of worlds."

"She's beautiful," Temrane whispered, not able to take his eyes from her. "Is she a goddess?"

"If there were such beings, she would be one. Rafaela is dead, prince, and you will help me find her and bring her back to life."

Temrane wanted to weep at the words, though he hardly knew why. Surely she was too good and too beautiful for the gods to let die. As he watched her image, it wavered as though before a melting blast and was replaced by another image, one that Temrane instinctively knew Crotalus could not see.

The man was short and round, his bald head gleaming. The light that shone from his blue eyes warmed Temrane, even in the chill of the castle. "Don't be afraid," he said to Temrane. "I am coming for you."

The image descended, and Temrane gave the gold orb to Crotalus. The vision had again comforted him when he most needed it. He was captive to a wizard whose brain was eaten by power and hate and a desire Temrane could not name. That he was dangerous was a fact almost beyond mention. But Temrane had nothing to fear. One was coming for him.

• • •

Crotalus had seen the vision descend upon Temrane as a cloud shrouds a mountaintop. He probed the vision with his mind, but could not gain access. Fury awakened again in his breast, but his disciplined will squelched it like a bug on the table. There was no sense in frightening the boy. Soon he would have what he wanted, and the boy would willingly serve alongside him.

He motioned the boy away and watched him make his way to his own room. Temrane acted as though the room were a sanctuary. The sooner Crotalus could break him, the better.

Crotalus had wanted to move slowly in taking over the realm of Corigo, but circumstances demanded that he move forward *now*. It would be better to capitalize on Temrane's fear of him and the boy's anger at his father before he forgot. Temrane might enjoy seeing the father who betrayed him squirm before the powerful wizard.

The book on stealing souls lay facedown on the desk where he had left it. He stroked it lovingly, regarding it as sustenance for his ever-ravenous will. The question of where to start had been resolved for him almost from the beginning. It was tempting to start with the king himself, but that would be of little value. Better to start with the small children and let the fear build to a pitch that would feed his power. Where to store the souls until he decided to dispose of them was a question that needed a bit more pondering. It had to be a place far from Zopel. Indeed, it would be best to have it removed altogether from the realm of Corigo. Amick, near the border of the Wastelands, might be far enough away if he could not find anything better. He pulled a map of Paduan in front of him and scrutinized it. Eschay was possible; so was Melram.

Rising quickly, he summoned Shallis. "Send a scouting party to Eschay and Melram in the realm of Paduan." He handed Shallis the map. "Note the number of people in each, the size of any armies, any buildings that are large and have been abandoned. Do it efficiently, for you have witnessed my wrath."

Shallis scuttled from the room, no doubt wondering if he should entrust this mission to anyone less than himself.

Eschay and Melram. Crotalus wished it could be Beren, and that the first victim might be a certain knight in the king's army.

Oh, how he wished he could use the soul-stealing on Falcon Jaqeth! But he knew from bitter experience that a cloud of protection surrounded Falcon, and his magic, strong as it was, could not penetrate it. He would have to use cunning and intelligence in trapping Falcon. But he didn't want to just kill him. He wanted Falcon on his knees before him. He wanted to witness on Falcon's face the pain that he himself had felt as Rafaela was stolen from him. He wanted Rafaela to be at his side as Falcon's life slipped away, so Falcon could see that Rafaela had always loved *him* and would never leave him.

But Rafaela was dead, and his experiments were bringing him no closer to her. He would use an illusion if nothing else. He wanted Falcon to feel the torment of betrayal before he died.

He leaned back in his chair. Feeding his hate always exhausted him. Somehow he would gain both the realm and the soul of Falcon Jaqeth.

• • •

She ran through a field of green grasses and flowers still tender in age. Yellows, reds, and pinks flooded his vision, and the smell of the flowers as she ran through them rose up and filled his nostrils with enticing sweetness. Clover was woven in the long, dark hair that floated on the air behind her.

He awaited her approach. He held out his arms and in an instant she was in them, pressing close, warming him though he had not realized he was cold. She tilted her head back, and he looked into eyes the color of the fertile earth. She caressed his cheek with one long finger, tracing the jawline. He drew her closer and kissed her with longing and regret, and a deep wound inside began to heal. His soul was comforted . . .

When Falcon awoke, the sun was high overhead, already past noon, and the smell of flowers came from a vase on the table by his bed.

He did not sit up, but closed his eyes tightly, almost willing himself back to sleep, back to Rafaela. She had been so close, so vivid. It had been thirteen years, and yet she was as clear in his mind as though he had just seen her. He rolled over on his side as the waves of grief washed over him, urging him to remember every detail of her. For years he had pushed away memories of her by thinking instead of Crotalus. Hate had served him well. But today there was something insistent about the memories; so he let them come.

He did not cry aloud, for the pain was too deep. No sigh escaped his lips, for the regret was immeasurable. Only a single tear crept from the eye to the bed as he remembered the dream and the look of ineffable joy on their faces.

• • •

Cleve Palmer finished inventorying the weapons and put aside the list with a pleasurable sigh. It was a small job, one he could easily have passed on to a lesser knight or the armory guard, but he enjoyed being in this room with its glint of steel and smell of battle. There was something deeply satisfying to him in checking the swords for nicks, rubbing down the leather, handling the weapons that had brought down the evil king of Paduan and had exalted King Jerome. History was thick here, and Palmer breathed in the mystery of it.

He handed the list of needed repairs to the armory guard and walked to Falcon's house. He knew that Falcon had been up all night and therefore slept this morning, but surely he would be up by now.

He knocked on the door and entered, calling Falcon's name. Falcon hollered from the rear bedroom that he would be out in a minute. Palmer heard the sound of water splashing and knew that Falcon was bathing Farrel. Ivy took on most of Farrel's care, but Falcon did not think it proper for a young woman to bathe her father. So he did it himself every morning. He came out of the bedroom, drying his hands.

"Have you been at the armory?"

"Yes. I gave the list to the guard."

"Were there many items on it?"

"No . . . just a few nicks on a couple of the broadswords, and a saddle was ripped. We may have mice. I left a note to the guard to check for them. Is Ivy doing her rounds?"

Falcon nodded, and Palmer thought he looked weary. The lines etched around his eyes were a little deeper than before, the mouth haggard this morning. Concern washed over him for his friend. "Falcon, have you ever thought of getting a boy from town to help care for Farrel?"

Falcon's eyes snapped with lightning. "Are you saying I can't take care of my father? He gave me life . . . How can I give him less? His care is no concern of yours."

Palmer, stung by the harsh words, involuntarily took a step backwards and instantly the fire died in Falcon's eyes. He rubbed a hand over his face. "I am sorry, Palmer. You have been more than a brother to me, and I have no right to speak to you in such a manner. Forgive me. I have thought of getting someone to help, but Ivy will not stand for it. She loves him fiercely and couldn't bear someone else attending him."

"You had spoken once before of a husband for her. If you found one, would she leave your father to marry?"

"She says no, but my father could live for years yet. She could still marry when she is older, but finding a husband for her then will be much harder, and if she desires children she had better have them soon."

"And what about you, my friend? Why will you not marry? There are many pleasant women in Beren who would be honored to be the wife of the king's highest knight."

Falcon laughed briefly, but Palmer could see the hints of death in his eyes. "Rafaela?"

Falcon nodded. "I dreamed of her."

"It's been thirteen years, Falcon. It's time to let her die."

"I can't. I feel her around me sometimes, as though she weren't dead, but alive and searching for me."

"Falcon," Palmer said in his gentlest tones, "she resides now with the Redeemer God. Let Him heal that part of you that she possesses, so you can continue to serve Him."

"Sometimes I despise Menon, Palmer, and I know I can't say that to anyone but you. Sometimes I want to turn my back on Him, but I know He will not let me. I wish I were ignorant of Him, but He has not granted me that. He let her die because of an evil wizard, and I can't bear that and don't know if I can forgive Him."

Palmer, having no words with which to respond, sat silently. Falcon was comforted in his presence and knew that had he wished, Palmer would listen to the angry and hurtful ravings of his troubled soul.

Their talk was interrupted by Ivy as she came through the door. She stopped upon seeing Palmer. Falcon, though immersed in his own grievings, could see the blush that colored her cheeks and the light that filled her brown eyes, even as she quickly turned away. *She's in love with Palmer*, he mused. One look at Palmer and he knew the feelings were returned. Palmer's gaze, as she apologized for interrupting them and then disappeared to tend to Farrel, yearned after her.

It is time, Falcon thought, *it is time to let Rafaela die and concentrate on the wondrous things that are happening right now. It is time for a husband to be found for Ivy*. He chuckled a little, but Palmer, still lost in his reverie, did not hear.

Fourteen

In his vision Cand-hoen again stood on the grassy knoll overlooking Zopel. The lion stood beside him – large, proud in his bearing, glorious in his presence. Gold and silky hair glinted in the sunlight as he tossed his magnificent head. Hoen stood at the place of the temple, as in the first vision, facing the lion. But this time the god did not look powerful or grand. He looked like stone and gold and earth. Cand-hoen turned questioning eyes to the lion next to him, but the lion was gone, and in his place stood the lamb. Cand-hoen's questions were forgotten as he saw that the lamb was wounded in the side; blood soaked the white fleece. Cand-hoen placed his hand over the wound, trying to stop the flow, but warm blood seeped through his fingers and dripped onto the ground.

Cand-hoen awoke from the vision slowly. He did not understand, and his mind recoiled at the lack. He was the high priest; if he could not discern the meaning in his visions, who could? In all his visions the lion and the lamb were central, but he did not know what they signified. They were one, he was sure of that, but it was the only thing of which he was sure. And always Hoen was beaten down, somehow overpowered by the other. It was baffling.

He arose now and stood before the god. He gazed upon him with sorrowful eyes, and suddenly he was doubled over with pain. It originated in his abdomen and sent flares of torment into his chest and set his lungs on fire. Agonizing tendrils crept through his intestines and bowels, turning them to water. His legs ached, and he could not stand.

The pain subsided for a moment, and Cand-hoen leaned weakly against the feet of the god, knowing that another wave would soon follow. This had been the pattern of the days following Temrane's disappearance, his only relief coming during the all-too-brief vision.

It was easy for him to think that perhaps Hoen was punishing him. And well he deserved it! He had openly defied the god and spurned his presence. How natural it would be for Candy to rely upon the god to bring respite from his pain. But Candy knew it was not Hoen but his own guilt that smote his insides like a swordmaker beats the metal until it assumes the shape it was destined to have. He wanted to cry to Hoen for forgiveness, and yet something held him back. His anger at Hoen had gone, but it left behind a desolation so vast that he was destitute. He did not feel that Hoen would not forgive him, but rather felt that Hoen *could* not.

"Uncle Candy, are you all right?"

He started at the voice that penetrated his black despair. Merry knelt beside him, her blue eyes filled with apprehension. He took her hand and let her help him up and onto the bed.

"Yes, I'm all right. Just some stomach pain, but it is gone now."

She stayed kneeling in front of him, her hands holding his, and for the first time in a long while he thought about how beautiful she was becoming and how glad he was that she was his niece. He had grown so attached to Temrane that he did not have much time for Merry, and he now felt the lack of that.

She looked up at him, and he was troubled as he looked into her eyes, for they were not the usual cheerful orbs, and her face carried a solemn look. "What is it, child? What troubles you?"

A tear formed and trembled on the black lashes. But she did not blink those wide eyes, as though she knew that letting one tear escape would bring a flood of others. "I can't bear Temrane being gone, Uncle Candy. Mother grieves as though there were no future, and Father simply doesn't care."

He stroked her hair. He had no words of comfort to give her. As if she read his mind, she shook her head. "I don't need you to say anything about them. I'm worried about you too, because you loved Temrane more than any of us did. And I'm worried about Temrane most of all, Uncle Candy. Mother told me that he is with a wizard right now. Uncle Candy, we have always been taught that the wizards are evil and that we are to have nothing to do with them. I know I've never paid much attention to the teachings of the priests or the gods, but Temrane has, and it must be torturing him to be with one whom the gods have forbidden."

He let the words pour out of her, not trying to comfort or rebuke, only listening. He was amazed at her love of Temrane and her concern for his well-being, that even though she had little use for the priesthood and the gods she knew Temrane did and therefore it was something of value.

At last she was silent, but even the silence carried pain and grief. She bit her lip, as though making a weighty decision, and looked at him with eyes that contained no more tears but a steady resolve.

"Cand-hoen, I have come to offer myself to the gods for Temrane." He started to speak, but she shook her head, cutting off his speech. "Don't try to discourage me, and don't think Mother sent me. I know she talked with you about sacrifice, but she wasn't really serious and came only because she's hurting so much right now. She just wants the pain to stop."

"And you don't?"

"I want Temrane's pain to stop. That's the only thing that matters."

Candy swept her to his chest in a fierce embrace, burying his face, wet with tears, into her hair. How good she was! He felt as though he had never truly seen her until today.

"I am still young, and I have never known a man. Would I not make a pleasing sacrifice to Hoen, even though I am a woman?"

The thought, although neither more nor less than what he had previously taught, was suddenly repugnant to him. "Merry, you would make a very pleasing sacrifice, but I cannot accept. The god has not told me to take a sacrifice, and I should be very sorry at losing you as well as Temrane. Yes, you are a woman, and the gods do not think highly of women. That is a pity because I shall always value you."

She looked at him strangely for a moment. "I met a man the other day who talked about the value of women and men. He said that his god created both and loved both equally."

"What god is this?"

"Kreith said he is called by many names, but he is most known as the Redeemer God or Menon."

The sudden pain was like a punch in the stomach. His sight went black. He doubled over and inadvertently cried out.

"Uncle Candy!" Her hand was on his forehead, and he remembered instantly his mother, the mother who had been sacrificed for her sins. Pain again ripped through his insides, leaving ashes in the wake of the blazing fire.

"Shall I call for someone?" He recognized the edge of panic in her voice and struggled to resume a sitting position. The pain lessened when he did so and in a moment had passed.

"No, it is gone."

"Candy, what's wrong? What is happening?"

He smiled weakly, patting her hand reassuringly. "I'm afraid I have angered the god. It shall be put right in a few moments. It is nothing to worry about."

The look of concern did not diminish.

"I am all right. Tell me of this man. Your eyes are lit by small suns when you speak of him."

"His name is Kreith, and he lives in Paduan. He is a farmer."

"And he worships a strange god."

"Yes. Am I angering the gods terribly by falling in love with him?"

The priest inside him answered yes. He looked over at the god. Ah well, what did it matter? He was already so deep within the mire of deserved punishment, what did one more thing signify? "No, the gods are not angry. Your father probably will be for falling in love with a simple man. A princess should be the bride of a prince, not a farmer."

"Perhaps. But if one became a prince because of handsomeness or kindness, he would be one. Sometimes there is no justice in the world."

Candy looked again at the god, dark and vengeful, biding his time over unrepentant servants until he could deliver the final blow. "You are right, Merry . . . Sometimes there is no justice. Come, I shall walk you back to the castle, and you can tell me more of this wonderful young man."

• • •

The rock that flew through the castle dining room window, shattering the glass, was accompanied by loud, raucous shouts from the street. "Death to the king!" Fel-hoen surreptitiously looked out the window. He could see no one individual but indeed throngs that seemed intent on deposing him. He did not know how word of Temrane's departure could have spread so quickly, but it had, and with amazing accuracy. Perhaps it was because these simple, superstitious people could think of nothing worse than consorting with a wizard.

He swung around with alarm when the door opened behind him, fully expecting to see angry peasants, but instead saw Niccola. He watched her carefully as she walked to the sideboard, still loaded with food from the midday meal, and began making a tray to take up to her mistress. Kenda had not been out of her rooms and had not spoken with him since her talk with Cand-hoen. In order to placate the gods, she was observing rigidly all the laws of grieving, and Fel-hoen could expect no attention from her.

Niccola, on the other hand, had been particularly solicitous of him, and he could not help but respond to her advances. She was a beautiful woman, graceful in carriage and fair of feature. "Niccola," he said softly, "when you have finished with her ladyship, come back here to me. I need companionship."

He noticed that her dark eyes warmed to him, but her voice and manner were as proper as they had ever been. "As you wish, Your Majesty."

She returned in only a few moments, and Fel-hoen gestured to her to take the seat beside him. "You intrigue me, Niccola."

"I, Your Majesty?"

"The realm is turning against me, I am dead to my own wife, all are in rebellion but for you. Tell me why you remain loyal."

Niccola smiled, and Fel-hoen was captivated by her dusky eyes and smooth skin. He reached out a hand and cupped her chin. He saw in her eyes the bewitching spells, the enclosing net; yet he was helpless in her grasp. "Tell me what you want," he murmured.

"Make me your mistress," she said so softly that it was but a whisper. "Make me your mistress and I shall restore the kingdom to you."

"Restore my kingdom? Are you a witch as well as a beautiful woman?"

Niccola laughed, and the net drew tighter. "No . . . I simply know secrets."

"Tell me."

"I will not tell you all until I possess an equal share of your kingdom, but I will tell you this much to whet your appetite. The secret I shall tell you will turn the people's wrath from you onto your brother, Cand-hoen."

Cand-hoen! His breath came a little faster; his eyes narrowed. How good it would be to have revenge on Cand-hoen! His mind's eye saw the mob storming the temple, dragging Candy from the altar into the street, tearing his clothes from his body and exiling him.

"I will not interfere in your rule. I only ask that upon your death, I will reign over the entire realm. You can bring Cand-hoen down and have the peoples' loyalty returned to you. Isn't this worth half your kingdom, Fel-hoen?"

Fel-hoen's head was swimming with the nearness of her, the captivating fragrance of her hair, the cool hand pressing against his chest. "Yes," he whispered urgently, "it is worth it. Come to me tonight after dark, and we shall discuss this secret." And then his lust would wait no longer. He grabbed her to him and crushed her lips against his own, the net entangling him inextricably.

A strangled cry from the doorway broke them apart, and Fel-hoen saw an angry Cand-hoen watching them. Fel-hoen let Niccola slip from his grasp. She walked to the doorway, and Cand-hoen did not look at her as she passed by. But she gazed at him insolently before turning to Fel-hoen. "Tonight, my king."

Fel-hoen smirked at Cand-hoen's horrified countenance. Once he might have felt guilty at being caught in such a situation by the high priest who was also his older brother. But now he felt only contempt for the office and scorn for the one who held it.

"So associating with wizards is not enough defiance for you! Must you grieve the gods and your wife further by dallying with a servant girl?"

"The gods mean nothing to me, and my wife is very quickly coming to mean the same. It is none of your business, Cand."

"None of my business? The wrath of the gods is going to be poured out on the realm because of your disobedience and you say it is none of my business! What of Merry? What if she would have walked in here with me? How would you explain this to her?"

"She is a girl . . . I am the king. I need to explain nothing. Why are you so concerned with Merry?"

"She came to see me. She is very upset at Temrane's absence. She offered herself as a sacrifice to bring him back."

Fel-hoen's face darkened. "Don't touch her, Cand."

"I have no intention of using her as a sacrifice for your sins. I just wanted you to know that your sin is not affecting you alone."

"I don't want you near her. You corrupted Temrane and turned him from me. I won't have you doing the same with Merry."

"I turned Temrane? I? You hated him from the very beginning, and your conduct with this sorcerer only proves it. Temrane turned to me because he knew I loved him. Maybe Merry is doing the same thing. You have never loved anyone except yourself. Don't come to me when your downfall comes."

Fel-hoen watched him storm out the door. Heated words burned his tongue, words he longed to say to the brother he despised, but he held them in. "Tonight," he whispered softly, "tonight I shall know everything I need to know to bring you down, and then my rage shall be satisfied."

• • •

Niccola came to him in his rooms later that night while the entire castle slept in virginal innocence. Their coupling was marked by a hunger on both sides, more a passion for power than for pleasure. After the need was satiated and both felt a measure of control over the other, Fel-hoen demanded to know Niccola's secret.

He could only discern her form in the moonlit room as she sat by the open window, not caring if any of the villagers could see her. But he could sense the small, greedy smile that touched her lips.

"You must first keep your end of the bargain, Fel-hoen. Give me something so I can know I hold half the kingdom."

He rose and walked silently to the tall wardrobe in the corner of the room. Niccola could not see his machinations, but she listened as he opened several drawers, some very small, heard keys turning in locks, and finally heard a whoosh as a drawer slid out on rollers as if by magic.

Fel-hoen removed the drawer and brought it to the window. Moonlight glistened on jewels, rings, crowns, and orbs. The first thing she spotted was a large crystal ball, the size of a man's fist. It glowed and pulsed in the light, almost a living being.

"What is that?"

"It belongs to a wizard. If I desire, I can call him with that. Don't touch it! The last thing I want is to summon the wizard."

Niccola's breath caught in her throat as she spotted a large single ruby cut in the shape of a pear. It was a ring her father had given her mother after a successful campaign over the sea. And now this barbarian held it.

She picked it up to look at it better and saw Fel-hoen smile. "It is a beautiful piece."

"Yes," she said, still holding it, "but it is worthless to me. It does not prove kingship of the realm. Give it to me as a sign of loyalty, and give me your signet ring to be the sign of the kingdom. I know that to rule you must have the signet ring and the orb. I will have one, you the other. If you die, I shall have the signet and therefore the right to the orb."

"And if you die first, then I shall retain the kingdom."

Niccola hesitated a moment, wondering for the first time if there was a threat implied in this. "Of course."

"Tell me the secret."

Niccola picked up the signet ring and held it and the ruby tightly in her hand. She waited as Fel-hoen replaced the drawer. He sat down on the window seat beside her, and just as she was readying herself to speak he interrupted her. "One thing before you begin: If I don't think the secret is worth half the kingdom, I shall kill you."

A chill ran through Niccola, but she disguised it by smiling fondly at him. He picked a good moment to alarm her, but she was his match. "As I said earlier, the secret is about your brother, Cand-hoen, the high priest to Hoen. The high priest is to be faultless before the god. He, above all people, should not lie with another's wife, or murder, or tell falsehoods. Now we both know that has not always been the case with the priests. Some priests are more wicked than the people they serve and almost approach the wicked ways of the gods themselves.

"Cand-hoen, though, has always been upright. You may not have liked some of the things he did, such as killing your mother and younger brother, but it was done with the blessing of the gods and therefore the approbation of the people. But I have found something, Fel-hoen, that your brother did against the god himself."

"How long ago was this?"

"I am no fool, Fel-hoen. I realize that something done even ten years ago would be of no value to either of us. This was done just days ago, immediately before you gave Temrane away, so his wickedness could not be attributed to grief."

Fel-hoen felt the stirrings of excitement. "Tell me."

"Temrane did not pass the Calli-kor. Three drops of blood fell to the floor, and I watched as Cand-hoen covered them up. I heard as he lied to the people and pronounced Temrane a man."

Fel-hoen let these words sink in, measuring their weight. The ritual meant nothing to him, and whether Temrane passed it or not could not interest him. But it was everything to the people. Cand-hoen had protected one who should have been expelled from the community.

"Leave me now," he whispered to his lover. "I want to be alone to consider the implications of this and how best to exploit it."

Niccola slipped from the room as quietly as a cloud passes over the moon, leaving darkness in its wake.

• • •

Fel-hoen stood at the window where only an hour before Niccola had sat. Sleep would not come to him. His mind was too full of the scandal. Oh, he wished he could shout to the sleeping village of the treachery of their beloved priest! He would make Cand-hoen crawl to him. Perhaps if he crawled far enough, Fel-hoen would grant him pardon and let him remain as a beggar inside the city.

A small chuckle escaped, and soon another and then another. Laughter resonated through the village, causing animals to stir and dogs to howl. His laughter was cut off, however, when he heard a small, almost insidious snicker behind him. Crotalus stood by the bed, a nightmare come to life.

"Share your mirth with me, King Fel-hoen. What has caused you to make such a loud noise in the middle of the night?"

"What do you want?" he demanded. He had always been fearful of Crotalus, but now Crotalus had what he wanted. There was nothing more to fear.

"Just some quiet conversation with an old friend. How are you liking your end of the bargain? Do you enjoy being without your son?"

Fel-hoen relaxed somewhat, but he still did not trust the wizard. Something in the smooth voice and easy stance said that he was not done dealing with him yet. "It was done for the good of the kingdom."

"Hah! Spare me your guilt-ridden justifications. I am enjoying your son, Fel-hoen. He is making a very good pupil. Beware of him, however. He is carrying a powerful hate inside him against you. When he becomes a mighty wizard, he may turn on you."

"Are you threatening me?"

"I have no need to threaten, for you are not in a position to bargain. I have decided that I want to rule this kingdom."

"That is impossible!"

"Not for me. Nothing is impossible for me, Fel-hoen. That is something you would do well to remember. Give me the kingdom."

"And if I refuse?"

"It would not be wise."

"What would you do? Kill me?"

"Hardly. The kingdom would go to someone else if you died. No . . . I shan't kill you yet, pleasing as that might be." He reached a hand inside his robe and pulled out a round bottle with a glass stopper. Mists swirled within like early morning fog. "Do you know what this bottle contains, Fel-hoen? This is your daughter trapped in here."

A cold hand clamped around his heart as Fel-hoen ran from the room and down the hallways to Merry's room. He expelled a lungful of breath as he saw her still form on the bed.

Crotalus stood smiling in the doorway. "She is such a beautiful child, Fel-hoen. She almost makes me regret taking your son." He came into the room and, standing beside the bed, reached out and stroked the dark hair that lay like the night on the white pillow. "So lovely."

"Don't touch her!"

"But why not? She is not truly here, Fel-hoen." He held up the bottle. "I have her soul. Only her body remains. If I remove the stopper, her soul will escape and will never be found again. Look deeply at your daughter's soul. It is light and airy, hardly any darkness to it at all. It almost sings. She is rightly named Merry. Would you like to hear your daughter? Her soul is crying out to you. Shall I remove the stopper and let you listen to her cries?"

"No! You lie to me. She is here . . . She sleeps."

Crotalus slapped Merry's face, and though her head snapped to the side from the force of the blow, her eyes did not open. "She sleeps? She may as well be dead, Fel-hoen. I am being generous to you. Her soul remains with me, but I shall give her to you in exchange for the kingdom."

"I shall not deal with you again."

"Then I shall begin stealing all the souls in your kingdom. I shall first close the wombs. No children shall be born to Corigo again. Then I shall steal the souls of the young. I want your kingdom to feel the fear of me as I steal their children and then their wives and lovers and eventually their king. If you do not relinquish the kingdom to me, you shall soon be king over nothing. You shall have bodies filling your streets, but they shall be lifeless. Your crown will be a mere mockery. Give it your most serious consideration, Fel-hoen. I will keep Merry to remind you of the cost. The wombs I shall close tomorrow. The first children shall be taken in two days."

Fel-hoen sank to his knees beside his daughter's still form. The imprint of a hand stood out starkly against her fair skin. He gathered her in his arms. Holding her close, he wept.

"Two days, Fel-hoen." And the wizard was gone, leaving the king to bitterly weep alone.

Fifteen

As Devona neared Zopel in her newly repaired wagon, she could hear the wails of the townspeople. She had been urgently summoned to Zopel early that morning. No message had been given her other than the summons, and she wondered what evil had befallen the people to cause the moanings of grief. It was a sound that began low in pitch and rose until it was almost a shriek. Other voices took up the wails, creating a sound that was inharmonic, grating on the nerves.

There were no people in the streets, no children playing, no business being conducted. Except for the laments, the town might have been dead. A shiver trickled down her spine.

Suddenly there was a flurry of skirts in the street as a young woman flung herself in the road in front of Devona's wagon. "Please, Madam Devona," she moaned, "please make supplication from your god for us. We have been calling on all of our gods for days now, but they do not hear. Perhaps one more god would help."

Devona climbed down from the wagon and took the young woman by the shoulders, hoping to calm the shakes that racked her body. This was one of the newly-married women who had lately become pregnant, Devona was sure of it; yet, this girl was not with child. She saw then, on closer inspection, the bloodstained dress the woman wore.

"When did you lose your child?"

"Four days ago."

"Why wasn't I summoned sooner?"

"I was the first, Madam Devona, and I knew the gods were angry with me because of my many sins. I thought that was why they took the baby. But, Devona, that isn't it! They took *every* child. There is not one pregnant woman left in Zopel—some say the world." Tears coursed down her face as she collapsed into Devona's arms.

"Come . . . You are not well and should be resting." Devona led her into the house, steadily pressing down every thought of what the woman had said. Until she could give it her full consideration, she would give it no consideration at all.

Bustling around the small kitchen, offering whatever words of consolation she could find to the new husband, Devona made a bowl of steaming herbal broth that she hand-fed to the grieving mother. She then stroked her forehead and smoothed her hair until exhaustion took over, the moaning was silenced, and she slept.

"I will be back soon to check on her. I want to see the other mothers."

The story was the same in every house she entered. The abdominal pain had been the greatest during the night, and sometime before morning each had released the tiny form beginning to grow. Some believed it was their own sin that caused the gods' anger. Some said it was the sin of the king that had brought on this evil from the gods. Others said the wizard with whom the king had trafficked caused the deaths. Devona heard enough to be fearful for the people.

After seeing the eleven pregnant women in the town, praying with each and offering comfort, Devona sought out the priests. Only one was willing to speak with her: Cand-hoen. The others felt only more evil could come from letting a worshiper of a strange god in among them.

"The people are on the edge of panic. They come to me offering sacrifices, and I accept them. They ask for omens . . . I cannot give them. I myself have angered Hoen, and for me there is no forgiveness."

Devona puzzled over his words. Of all the priests in Corigo, Cand-hoen was her favorite. He was devout, and yet streaks of humor ran through him that made him delightful company. He was also one of the few who never turned his back on her, despite her strange god. "Why is there no forgiveness for a priest?"

"Because I will not offer sacrifice for myself." He peered at her intently for a moment. He liked this odd, old woman. He had never admitted it before his defiance, but her god attracted him. Now, in the pain of his loneliness, he decided to talk with her. "I am in rebellion, dear lady."

"Rebellion against your god?"

"Yes. Does that sound strange? I would imagine that it does. It feels strange to even say it. I am rebelling against Hoen for taking Temrane away. Hatred burns in my soul against those who did this. You see now why I cannot give omens to the people—I have none. The visions remain, but they are not for the people, and they are not from Hoen."

"The people feel that Hoen is punishing them for something. What do you believe, Cand-hoen?"

"If I were a true priest, I would say that Hoen was punishing the people for their sins and punishing me for mine. I would say that Temrane was taken away because he was a sinful boy—not a man, mind you, but a boy."

"But you do not say these things?"

"No. I believe it is the result of a bargain my brother made sixteen years ago with a wizard. I smell the wizard's hand in this. I don't know what he wants, perhaps the kingdom itself—it seems a common bargaining tool these days. And my god, who once seemed so powerful, stands helpless beside the wizard's lust for power. Perhaps that was, after all, the meaning of my visions, because Hoen was impotent in those also."

"Perhaps your displeasure will soon lead you to begin a search for truth."

Cand smiled. "I know of what you speak. You speak of your god, called Redeemer, who recognizes no other gods. He is a strange god, this Menon. He does not desire sacrifice, but offers deliverance freely. What would a poor priest like me do in his temple?"

Now it was Devona's turn to smile. "There is always service to be done." She waved toward the numerous books and scrolls that filled Cand-hoen's room. "And always much to learn. More than enough for infinite lifetimes. Search for truth, Cand-hoen, and it will find you."

"I will bargain with you, dear lady from Beren. I will search for truth if you will do me a favor."

"I shall do it as long as it does not compromise the Law of Menon. What is it?"

"Talk to Fel-hoen for me. I am sure that his dealings with the wizard have brought about this present pain. I would love dearly to recover my nephew from this magician before he is harmed, but there is an additional reason. Each day the people's grief grows less and the anger grows more. Although there is no love lost between Fel-hoen and myself, I do not wish to see him harmed. He is perhaps the only one who knows how to contact this wizard. He is my only hope to reach Temrane. But I fear that the people will try to take his life. The sins he has committed cry for his blood, and the villagers would like nothing better than to kill him and receive again the blessings of the gods. Will you talk to him for me?"

"I don't know if I can change anything, but I will certainly speak with him."

As Devona rose to go, the uproar Cand-hoen had predicted began. Devona could hear loud voices bawling in the streets, calling for the death of the king. "He is responsible!" "Let him die!" The words were angry, the voices vengeful.

They ran into the street and were swept along by a tide of people hurrying toward the castle. Cand-hoen tried to reason with a few of them, but his voice could not be heard above the mass.

The mob came to a halt before the castle, underneath the public window where King Fel-hoen and Queen Kenda had addressed the multitudes for sixteen years. A chant was taken up: "Death to the king! Death to the king!"

The window opened and Fel-hoen stepped out, accompanied by Kenda and Niccola. Immediately people grabbed rocks from the ground, ready to hurl them at the king who had caused the gods' wrath to fall upon them. Niccola flew to the rail of the balcony and held up her hands. Silence descended like a heavy cloud.

"Please . . . hear what your king has to say before you proceed with this evil act."

Fel-hoen stepped to the balcony, his stern countenance defying the rabble. His kingly form and royal bearing made more than one pair of eyes turn away. "My people, I understand your anger and fear. You have believed lies that said I had dealings with a wizard. You believed I gave up my son to be his pupil. I come before you now to speak the truth! I did not give my son to the wizard. Crotalus came into my castle as a thief and stole my beloved son. Why, I asked the gods over and over, why, why, why?"

A quiet murmur ran through the crowd at the king's words. They could see his fists jammed into his stomach in pain, the tears rolling down his face in grief.

After a moment Fel-hoen straightened, his face calm and noble. "My loyal followers, it was revealed to me by the gods why Prince Temrane was stolen from me." He pointed to Niccola. "This woman, who eats and breathes and moves among you, saw a heinous evil done against Hoen. This woman, who is one of your own, saw why this punishment has befallen us."

He let his eyes sweep the crowd, faces expectant, eyes bright. He had swayed them. Niccola had been right—they were ready to destroy the one he named.

He turned his eyes suddenly to Cand-hoen, pointing to him. "You, Cand-hoen, high priest of the god Hoen, you lied to the gods and to the people. Temrane did not pass the Calli-kor. Three drops of sacred blood fell from the cup to the floor, and you covered them up. You lied to the gods by declaring Temrane a man. You are no longer a priest and must now forfeit the priestly name. The blood of the children is on your head, Cand! Receive your punishment!"

Fel-hoen raised his arm and let fly a stone he had concealed. The fury of the people now boiled over, and rocks pummeled Cand-hoen's body and Devona's as well as she tried in vain to shield him. She tugged at his arms, leading him away through the throng that wanted his death. As rocks hit his head, he stumbled and fell. People fell on him, striking blow after blow, until Cand lay still. One by one they rose to leave.

Devona fell by his side, wiping the blood from his forehead with her hand. She put her head on his chest and discerned a very faint heartbeat.

A man knelt next to her. "We must take him into the castle before they come back! I know a room that is not in use. No one will find him there."

Together they carried Cand through a castle that had grown somber and laid him on the bed in a small room that looked as though it had once been used by servants.

"He's not dead, is he?"

"No, by the Redeemer's mercy." She looked at the man in front of her, the wrinkled and brown face, the strong hands and even stronger character. "Who are you?"

"My name is Lomeli, ma'am. I am the leatherworker for the king. It was my wife standing beside him today. She shouldn't have done it."

"Thank you for your help. I hope it won't get you in trouble."

"Trouble has fallen on the whole land. If it visits me personally, then it does. I won't change what's wrong and what's right to avoid it."

"You are a rare man, Lomeli. I will thank the Redeemer God many times for you. I would like to stay here with him and care for him. He is still in much danger."

"I'll arrange to get you some food and anything you may need to take care of Cand-hoen. Do you wish me to send a message to your family?"

Devona considered this. "Yes . . . Find Batakis, the minstrel in Beren. Simply tell him where I am. I don't want him to worry."

Lomeli nodded and slipped out of the room, leaving Devona to her ministrations. As she wiped blood from Cand's bruised face and examined his body, she spoke to the Redeemer God. "You spared him today for some special reason. He agreed to search for truth. You are the truth. Let him find You, Menon. Let him find You."

Sixteen

The lights of the inn shone brightly in the gloom, causing the cheer to again rise in Duncan's heart. How strange his heart was, he thought. He had lived without human companionship for many long years, and it had not troubled him. Then Rafaela came. He loved her dearly and missed her achingly, but at first did not require another to take her place. He had traveled through the Wastelands quickly, wanting to be out of the barrenness that enveloped his body and threatened to darken his soul.

Then he had come to Amick. Ah, what a wonder that town had been! There were so many people that he had wandered around for several hours just looking at them. The sounds of dancing, singing, worshiping, eating, fighting all fell on his ears like the sound of bells. He felt as though he had been deaf but could now hear.

But Amick was a long time ago, and the joys he had felt at being among people had vanished, leaving a void that yearned to be filled. He wanted fellowship, and the lights of the distant inn promised it.

He hurried to get to it, passing a sign that read *Andurin*. He knew Andurin was a small mining town in the foothills of the Amil Mountains. He wasn't sure exactly where Crotalus resided, but knew it was somewhere in this great stretch of mountain ranges. He hoped to at least find someone who knew of Crotalus.

The sounds of music and laughter greeted him even before he walked in the door, making his heart light. The inn was well-lit, if a bit stuffy, and men crowded into every table, spilling over into all corners of the room. He was immediately pulled into the revelry of one table, slapped on the back innumerable times, and had a mug of ale slammed in front of him.

The men had been talking of their day's dig, but stopped and eagerly asked Duncan questions. He felt at once welcomed and at home among these friendly miners. He gladly told them who he was, but when he mentioned his destination the room grew silent. All eyes seemed to bore through him. Faces became guarded.

The man across from Duncan, a young, handsome miner with friendly brown eyes, spoke as though for the entire room. "If ye be a tradin' with the wizard, ye'll find no kind word here, friend."

Other voices mumbled in acclaim.

Duncan smiled and spoke loud enough for all to hear. "He stole something that didn't belong to him. I am going to recover it."

"He seems good at that lately," said an old man two tables down. "He stole the king's son less than two weeks ago."

Duncan's heart beat faster. *The king's son. Menon, is that what I am to recover? Protect him until I arrive.* "Has the king done nothing to rescue the prince?"

"Ach! What can be done 'gainst a wizard? I hear tell that he plans to ride with an army to slaughter the wizard and steal back his son." The young miner shrugged. "But only the gods know whether his army can beat a wizard, and they not be tellin'. If ye be lookin' to recover somethin', ye had best be about your business."

"Yes, thank you . . . I will." Duncan finished his ale, threw a coin on the table, and rose to go. Silence escorted him out.

Duncan had planned on spending the night at the inn and was disappointed that his dealings with these people had to be cut short. Perhaps it was best. If it was a king's son he was after, it was best to get him as soon as possible. On the other hand, if he and his horse did not rest, neither would be able to go very far.

He was still grappling with what to do when he heard a step behind him. He whirled around, unsure as to who would have followed him out. The young miner leaned against the building, appraising him with his eyes.

"Where ye be stayin' tonight?"

"I was just going over the possibilities myself."

"Come," he said, walking over to Duncan, "ye can stay with me and stable your horse in the barn."

• • •

Devona sat in Fel-hoen's anteroom, waiting for an audience with the king, as she had done most of the day, going over and over what she would say to him. Lomeli had been strictly against her speaking with the ruler, arguing that it was too dangerous to let him know that she still resided in Zopel. Fel-hoen was sure to remember that she had been with Cand. Against his sound reasoning she could only offer her belief in the will of the Redeemer God.

His will had been revealed to her two nights before. She had been dozing in the chair next to Cand's bed when she suddenly awakened. Immediately she felt a strong pull to speak with Fel-hoen, and although she resisted it she soon came to believe that it was the pleasure of Menon that she do so.

The next night revealed to her the same appeal, and this time she could not resist. She had at once sought a hearing and waited with a growing sense of urgency and anticipation at what Fel-hoen's reaction to her presence would be.

At last she was escorted into the throne room where Fel-hoen listened to complaints, advice, threats, and bribes daily. It was not lost on Devona that he looked haggard and drawn. Blackness encircled his eyes, and his golden hair seemed to have lost much of its shine. His hands fidgeted with his staff.

"For what reason does the midwife of Paduan seek an audience with me?"

"It is the will of the Redeemer God, called Menon, whom I worship. He has shown me your struggles, King Fel-hoen, and I have come with a suggestion."

"What do you know of my struggles?"

"I know that your son resides with the wizard Crotalus. I know that the people you had hoped to turn against Cand-hoen are not yet satisfied. Their children are being taken daily, and they are anxious to do anything that might return the children to them. I know that you are quickly repenting of your bargain with Crotalus."

The look he turned upon her was faraway, pondering, his staff gently tapping on the floor. "Repenting? Yes, it is a good enough word. I suppose it is what I am doing."

"I have also heard, King Fel-hoen, that you intend to ride into the Amil Mountains and bring back your son."

"I am resolved to do battle with Crotalus. However, I do not have the manpower. My army is quickly deserting me. The lords, no doubt, speak of dethronement. And you come to tell me that you have a suggestion? You are only a midwife and are not even of my kingdom."

"Yes, Your Highness, it is true I am a midwife. But I am first the servant of the Redeemer God, as are we all meant to be. It is His bidding that I do."

Fel-hoen slammed the staff down in one swift motion, sending defiant echoes through the throne room. "I desire to hear nothing of the gods. I am sick of the gods. Tell me your counsel and then go before I lose patience."

"I know of Crotalus, Your Highness. There are a few people in King Jerome's realm who have had dealings with him and know him for what he is. If you plan on rescuing your son from this wizard, seek King Jerome's counsel. He is a wise king and no friend of any wizard. The combined armies could well overcome Crotalus."

The staff tattooed a thoughtful rhythm on the stone, and for a time Fel-hoen did not speak. When he did, it was merely to dismiss Devona.

She walked from the throne room perplexed. She did not know what her counsel had accomplished, or what the king's action would be. She only knew one thing for certain: she had done the will of Menon.

• • •

Temrane slept fitfully, waking for long ages of time only to doze and awaken again from the nightmares. During his periods of consciousness, he could hear screams coming from the dungeons. He imagined this was Hirsch, the one-time captain of Crotalus' army. Temrane had asked Crotalus to spare him once, and now Temrane realized it had been a mistake. Hirsch was spared from death to be tortured.

Temrane shuddered at each drawn-out scream, praying that it would stop, sure it would not. But here he was wrong, for it did cease, but the sounds that came instead made him long for a silence as complete as death itself. Thuds fell regularly on the body. Then came a snapping sound as bones were broken. Hirsch occasionally moaned, and thus Temrane knew he still lived.

The next time Temrane awoke, the castle was silent. His ears strained to receive impulses, but there were none to receive. Death, it seemed, had indeed descended upon the castle.

He lay quiet for a long time, wondering if there would ever again be a morning. He had not had a vision of the kindly man for two days, and he had begun to doubt the reality of it. Perhaps he wished so desperately for rescue that his frightened mind had willingly produced one. Or maybe it was only Hoen taunting him. He was no longer sure of anything.

When he heard sounds from Crotalus' room next door, he held his hands over his ears, not wanting to hear more torturing. But the sound that came through was, in its way, worse. Crotalus was laughing.

It was not the good-hearted laugh of merriment, but a cruel cackle, a delight in another's suffering. What power Crotalus received from tormenting weaker souls escaped Temrane, but he knew that Crotalus fed on fear like a snake dines on a rat. Even for the short time Temrane had been with Crotalus, he recognized that Crotalus would do anything or harm anyone to nourish his lusts.

Temrane had angered him earlier in the day, and he had seen Crotalus struggle with controlling his great displeasure. Temrane had been genuinely fearful that Crotalus would destroy him, but apparently his rapacious need for a pupil forestalled his wrath.

It had been in the morning, just after Crotalus had gone over maps of Paduan. He seemed in an expansive mood, talking of great things the two of them would do, the wondrous magic he would teach Temrane.

He produced, as if out of the air, the image of the woman. His voice softened, almost murmuring, caressing. "First I will teach you of the things I have already done. Then we shall study how to raise the dead. I am counting on you to have new ideas."

"But you can't raise the dead," Temrane replied incautiously.

Crotalus' eyes darkened. "I am the greatest wizard alive or dead. Don't risk my wrath."

"But when someone dies, their soul is gathered into the all-soul of Hoen. They are no longer."

Crotalus spat on the ground. "That is a myth you would do well to forget, boy. There is no Hoen, no gods. In your world as of now there is only one you worship and adore, and it is I. Learn this lesson now, or I will be forced to impress it upon your mind with lessons you will not soon forget."

Temrane was silent a moment, watching the old man's hands stroke the image of Rafaela. When Crotalus spoke, his voice was again calm. "Soon she shall be with us. She is the most beautiful woman in the world, and the power within her is great. When she is recovered, you shall worship her also."

"I will not worship a woman!" he lashed out, the years with Hoen still a habit with him, even though his faith was shaken.

Crotalus threw back his head, opened his mouth, and let loose a howl that echoed through the entire castle, ringing from the walls, beating the ears. It was a howl of death, a rage at the one who dared to speak against Rafaela. He looked at Temrane, who fell back from the fury in the black and yellow eyes. It was as if a fire that had been smoldering had suddenly burst forth in full flame, scorching and devouring.

"Leave my presence! Do not seek my face again today lest I grind you into the dust!"

Temrane had left the room, stumbling in his hurry to escape. He sought the sanctuary of his own quarters, remaining there the rest of the day and night, trying to shut out the sounds of torture and cruel laughter that came from the madman.

He turned over in his bed and pulled the pillow around his ears in an unsuccessful attempt at silence. He thought of Candy and wondered if his uncle hated him for somehow disobeying Hoen. He let his mind wander over his last few days, then weeks, then years in Zopel, searching for his sin. He instinctively felt that it had been during the Calli-kor, but he could think of nothing, no sin that had merited Hoen's wrath. Perhaps it was all just the whimsy of the gods. But in that case it made no difference how he lived his life, whether good or bad. Good was obviously not rewarded any more than bad was punished. His days here with Crotalus proved that.

As he slipped from melancholy to despair, he heard a slight sound at the window. Hope sprang in his heart, and he leapt from the bed. Glancing at the door to make sure it remained closed, he hurried to the window.

The man of his vision stood on a rickety ladder, smiling at him. "Come, boy, we haven't much time."

• • •

Duncan had awakened early in the morning, the sun not yet lighting the small cabin of McNyre. McNyre had been of invaluable help the night before, and Duncan was most sorry to be leaving the company of the miner who had befriended him. McNyre had once traded with Crotalus ("when I was younger and not near so wary") and therefore knew the way. He drew maps for Duncan and made a floor plan of the main doors and windows of the castle.

"Where would the prince be held?"

McNyre's warm, brown eyes held their gaze steady on this strange little man before him. "I knew from the minute I laid eyes on ye that ye were searchin' for the prince. Why do ye risk your life for such as him?"

"My God tells me where to go and I do His bidding. What is the prince like?"

"He be a young man now, though just barely, by about two weeks. 'Twas on the night of his manhood that he be spirited away by the wizard. He be of not much use to his father. He wanted to be a priest."

"The king didn't like that?"

McNyre snorted. "The king doesn't like much of anything, but he especially has no use for the priests and the gods. Imagine a god sending you to get the prince."

Duncan smiled. "Well, my God is a bit unusual."

McNyre had shown him where the prince might be held and then talked of roads to get there and back, hopefully escaping the notice of the wizard, which he did not think likely.

Duncan had been glad for his help and thought of him with fondness and regret as he dressed and headed for the barn to ready his horse for the long and possibly dangerous ride. He was surprised, therefore, when he found not only his own horse saddled, but McNyre's mount as well. McNyre was coming around the corner of the barn, hauling a pack and wearing long boots and heavy furs on his back. He carried a much-worn crossbow with him.

"I couldn't let ye go on alone. These be strange and sometimes dangerous woods, and ye may need a friend."

Duncan let the delight he felt show on his face as he helped McNyre load the horses and the packs they would carry. They started out from McNyre's cabin as the sun was pushing its way over the horizon.

The morning was spent in silent riding, McNyre struggling with his fear of a certain evil wizard and Duncan contemplating on the prince and what he was to do with him once he got hold of him. His immediate thought was to return Prince Temrane to his own land and his father. This seemed a logical course of action, and yet he hesitated. He balked at sending the prince back to a father who did not care for him. He sensed danger, but was unsure whether the feeling came from his own heart or from the Redeemer God. He left the matter undecided in the Redeemer's hands. Possibly a way would become clear when he was with the prince.

They ate the bread and dried meat McNyre had packed near a clear brook that offered them drink. The sun was high over head, bearing down with midsummer tyranny, and Duncan felt he would be glad to return to the Forgotten City with its cool breezes and fragrant air.

"Ye look like a man who is thinking of home."

Duncan smiled. "You are very perceptive. I *was* just thinking of my home."

"Tell me about it."

"What do you wish to hear?"

"Ye be a wary one. Ye do not tell anyone your true mission – ye do not talk of yourself nor your homeland. But I can tell this much. Ye rode in on the road from the north. Ye did not come from Zopel, as ye did not even know the king's son was gone. So I start to think that maybe ye hail from Beren. Ye talk as some of them talk. But ye be different. So, do ye come from Eschay? Nay, ye are not a farmer. Melram? Melram is deserted. Perhaps somewhere further north? Do ye ride in from the Wastelands, Duncan?"

Duncan considered what to tell McNyre. The people of Corigo were a suspicious lot, and the Wastelands were considered the dwelling-place of the gods. But McNyre had been a friend to him when none other would offer aid. McNyre was risking his own life in traveling with Duncan; Duncan could do no less than trust him with his secrets.

"Yes . . . I live in a city in the Wastelands that is known to only a small handful of people. I live there with one other."

"Are ye a god?"

"No. There is only one God, and it is He whom I worship and serve."

The questions then spilled out of McNyre as fast as water pouring from a jug. Where was the city? What was it like? Who built it? Duncan laughingly answered all questions, feeling again the warmth of companionship and wondering at the same time if he would ever be able to go back to a solitary existence.

At last the miner's questions seemed to dry up. Duncan became serious again as he pondered his wisdom in disclosing so much about the Forgotten City. "McNyre," he said at last, "there are only three people in Beren who know of the Forgotten City, and now you know of it. Do not disclose any of this until it is settled with the wizard one way or the other. If he were to discover the whereabouts of the city, it could mean death for many, many people."

"I appreciate your warning, and your trust in me is not without good foundation. I shall speak of it to no one. Tell me of the other person there. Is it your wife?"

"No. I have never had the pleasure of a wife. Rafaela is a woman of thirty-five years. She came to me when she was twenty-two, her soul much scarred. And although I have never enjoyed a wife, I feel I have had a child. I could not love a daughter more than I love Rafaela."

"Is she beautiful?"

"She has an outward beauty that is only surpassed by the beauty of her spirit, which is generous and loving."

McNyre looked wistful. "Perhaps someday I could come to your city and meet this beautiful lady."

"She is not the woman for you, my friend. She is already loved by two strong-willed men, and one of them is the wizard we seek."

"The purpose of your warning, then, is clear. Among others, ye wish to protect this Rafaela."

"Crotalus would destroy everyone and everything in his quest to find Rafaela. Right now he believes her dead. It is best to leave it so."

"May your God keep watch over my lips. I will guard your secret and hers as surely as I would guard my queen. But come . . . The sun does not wait for us and our talk of worlds of which I have only dreamed."

Repacking their belongings, they headed further into the Amil Mountains, searching for the trails that would lead them to Crotalus.

• • •

When they finally stopped for the night, darkness had been their companion for many hours, only a sliver of moon slicing through the night. The silence had grown with the darkness, each too tired for conversation. Bedrolls were brought out and horses relieved of their burdens, all in a hush that secured the men together in accord.

Duncan drew the blankets tightly around his neck, hoping to shut out not coldness, for it was a balmy night, but snakes. He breathed a sigh of a prayer to the Redeemer God and fell asleep almost instantly.

He awoke what seemed only minutes later, but he knew from the position of the moon that it was much later. He struggled to remember what had wrenched him out of a deep slumber. Someone had called his name. He started to sit up, but was held back forcefully by his shoulder.

McNyre leaned over and whispered in his ear, "Be still. There be marauders in our company."

Duncan lay absolutely still, hardly daring to breathe. He heard McNyre rise slowly, almost imperceptibly. Duncan strained his eyes to watch his movements and saw him grasp the crossbow and load it with an arrow in one fluid movement. This was a man used to hunting.

Duncan saw two men searching the packs, both well-muscled, trained men as though from an army. One man was tall, wearing leather boots and a chain-mail vest, obviously the leader. The other was shorter and dressed all in leather. These men were apparently after more than money.

McNyre crept closer. "Move away from the packs slowly," he said in a voice that chilled Duncan with its strong authority.

The men began backing away, hands lifted halfway. Suddenly the leader of the two bent down and grabbed something from the ground. In one swift motion he threw it at McNyre. Duncan hollered something, he was unsure what, but it was enough of a warning for McNyre. He dropped to the ground, and the weapon sizzled past his ear to land by Duncan's feet.

McNyre fired the arrow before either man could move, and it dropped the bleeding leader to the ground. The other man bolted for the cover of the woods before McNyre could reload the bow.

McNyre turned to Duncan. "Gather your things quickly. They were not thieves, but were searching for us. The one who escaped will surely bring reinforcements."

McNyre picked up the enemy weapon and handed it to Duncan, who received the deadly-looking boomerang with trepidation. "Ye may need it before this trek is finished."

Duncan was hurriedly throwing his things in the pack and rolling his blankets when he spotted the dead body with the arrow still protruding from it. He stood above it, feeling a dozen things he had never felt before and experiencing some that brought back painful memories of the Redeemer's people in long-ago ages.

He lay down the pack and knelt beside the man.

"What are ye doing?"

"We can't just leave him here like this."

"Duncan, we can't take him with us."

"We can at least give him a proper burial." Suiting action to words, he struck the boomerang into the soft dirt and began to dig a hole.

"Duncan, those men could be a-comin' for us any time. If they find us here with a dead man, they will kill us as certainly as the sun comes up in the morning."

"Then help me dig and we will get done faster."

McNyre sighed and dropped down next to Duncan, digging furiously with his hands. "Ye be a strange one, Duncan."

"My people long ago were slaughtered – almost every one of them. They were killed without dignity, but did not die without dignity. I am the only one left, and when I die, the secrets and knowledge of my people will vanish forever. I am the caregiver. This one here, although not of my people and not of my God, was still created by the Redeemer God. Because of that, I will treat his death with dignity."

They finished the task and laid the man in the rough grave. As they covered it over again with dirt, Duncan bowed his head and placed his hands across his chest as though he too were dead. "Menon, it is given to us to live but briefly on this earth. A flicker and we are gone, while You have no beginning and no end. Have mercy on this man's soul."

McNyre had no reply, but he greatly pondered the words spoken by Duncan in a voice filled with a million sorrows.

• • •

The next night the castle was spotted, and Duncan rejoiced in his heart that at last the prince was to be rescued.

Seventeen

Zopel was dying. A traveler passing through Zopel to the Amil Mountains and the land that lay beyond would hear not the sounds of commerce and daily trade, but a weeping that no king, priest, or god could assuage. The cries came from the depths of the souls that still remained, but within months they would be gone also. Zopel would then be a silent land, a barren desert where once children had played and life had flourished.

Many lost faith in the gods and believed that the world was simply winding down to a close. Some tried to placate the gods with further sacrifices, and the city stank with the odor of burned flesh and poured-out blood. Most of the people believed that Cand still lived and therefore the gods' anger continued to burn against them, making protection impossible. They organized large parties of men to comb the woods, even searching so far as the Amil Mountains where it was forbidden to go. But he was not found, and more children's souls were stolen by the wizard or by the gods — it no longer mattered which, as both seemed the same.

If only Cand could be found . . .

• • •

Devona took care that Cand should not be discovered, but she could not be insensible to the danger that surrounded him. And Cand was not the only one in jeopardy. Twice daily Lomeli came to the hidden room in the castle bringing food for Cand and Devona, medical supplies he had stolen, and valuable reports of the town's condition.

The disposition of the people continued to grow worse. Less easily were they appeased by the king's words, and their outrage was aroused to a murderous intent that sought a victim. One day even Batakis, normally loved by the people, was greeted with angry words and hurled rocks as he hurried to the castle to meet with Devona.

The four sat around the only table in the room, Cand looking rested but grim after skimming the surface of death. "It is too dangerous to remain here," Batakis said.

"I don't want to move Cand yet. He is still weak. The long trip to Beren could very well kill him. I worked too hard to save him to have that happen."

"But if the townspeople find him here, they will kill all of us, and it is only a matter of time before they search the castle."

"Batakis, I appreciate your concern," Cand said, smiling at the passionate young man, "but I can't leave. If Temrane were to escape from the coils of that snake, where would he find me?"

"Where will he find you now?"

"Please, my friends, I have endangered your lives enough. Go back to Beren."

Lomeli broke the silence that followed these words. "Devona, Batakis is right. We could all be killed. If I constructed a leather sling to attach to the wagon, Cand could lie in it and would not be jolted by the rocks in the road. I have made many for young babies—I could make one for a man. Cand, I will still be here should the prince return. I can lead him to you in Beren."

Batakis looked first to Devona and then to Cand. Both faces were concerned, but neither argued with the plan that Batakis obviously thought excellent. "All right then," he said, "Lomeli, how long will it take you to build this sling?"

"Give me two nights. I will work on it privately, so I won't bring questions upon myself."

"Good. I will see if I can find a large piece of canvas to cover the wagon. Cand, get as much rest as you can. It may be a long trip. Devona, gather enough supplies in case we need to go into hiding on the road. We leave in three days' time."

• • •

Farni lay stretched out on the ground, face in the dust, arms outstretched painfully to the side in the manner prescribed by the goddess Velad. Inside the small cottage he could hear Freyda weeping softly.

His arms screamed for relief, but he remained in supplication facing the sea until the sun touched the horizon of the water. He stood then, walking slowly into the cottage, feeling a heaviness on his heart that no amount of prayer could ease. There was nothing further he could do. The goddess was silent.

Freyda lay on the single bed in the cottage. She had been crying for many hours, and Farni could see the ravages this left upon her face. He put his hand on her shoulder to still her sobs. "Freyda, it is not so bad. We knew when they were born that they were a punishment to us. At least we do not need to feed them."

He stroked her head and rubbed her back until the sobbing stopped and the deep breaths of heavy slumber took over. He left her side and went into the other room to watch his daughters.

Anne, being the youngest, had gone first, about three days ago. Lis, with her frail legs and dull eyes, was taken this morning. He stared at their inert forms, wondering where their souls had gone. Were they lonely? Frightened? Or perhaps happy to be free from the feeble shells that housed them? He didn't know. The only thing of which he was sure was that despite his words to Freyda, he wanted them back desperately. There was nothing he wouldn't give to have them returned.

Some people had given everything, and yet that didn't stop the horrible loss of children. Some spoke of starting the human sacrifices again. Perhaps the gods had been particularly offended by something and desired human flesh to atone.

At least I do not have that pain, he thought. *I would rather have my daughters' souls roaming the world free than to sacrifice them upon a god's altar.*

Instantly he fell upon his knees, weeping at his sinfulness. To offer a child in tribute was considered the loftiest calling, the greatest show of loyalty, the highest price to be paid to a god or goddess. If one was sacrificed, the gods had to bless.

But Farni was unwilling to give that oblation.

For a brief moment he struggled with his hatred of the gods and a sudden recognition of a way of life that enslaved. For a brief moment a door blew open with wisps of cool, Spring air, uplifting and purifying. But the years of habit were strong, and the door that had let in a ray of light was forcibly shut by the darkness.

He went outside where the sky still showed a bit of red in the west. Facing the sea where Velad ruled, he lay in the dirt, facedown, arms outstretched, vowing to remain in the position of supplication until the goddess's heart was softened toward him.

• • •

Fel-hoen yanked the curtains closed so he could not see the faces of his people. But though he could shut out the sights, nothing would stop the sounds. He had not believed Crotalus would really do this. But child after child was taken, leaving behind a fragile housing that was gradually crumbling. He had watched Merry's body growing weaker and wondered how long she could survive without food. He had been pouring liquids down her throat, as he had advised other families to do. But without food, what hope was there?

What hope was there for any of them? Unless he did something to stop Crotalus, the adults would be stolen also, and his kingdom would be one of corpses. He indeed saw this as clearly as Crotalus had intended.

"Come, my love, do not brood," Niccola whispered from the bed.

"Our kingdom is falling. The only solution I see is to give Crotalus what he wants. Perhaps after that, we could kill him and regain the kingdom."

"Don't be a fool. He will not allow you to live that long. I know his kind, Fel-hoen. He survives and grows stronger from others' fears. The terror that grips the kingdom now is nothing compared to what he will do when he has free rein. I have a better plan. Will you listen to it?"

Fel-hoen shrugged. "Why not? My lords have not advised anything worth listening to. Why shouldn't I begin listening to the counsel of a woman?"

"The midwife suggested you seek an audience with King Jerome of Beren. I concur."

"You're mad!"

Niccola smiled faintly. "Perhaps . . . But maybe I am more versed in politics than you, my lord. Offer to unite the two realms under one king. You need his help or your kingdom will be lost to a wizard. With his help, Crotalus would be defeated; he cannot withstand two armies. Jerome surely could see the expediency of such a move. He will rule the kingdom with you as advisor. Once Crotalus is taken care of, you can kill King Jerome, and you will have gained both dominions."

"It would be a good plan if Jerome did not have a son."

"But Beren practices different laws. They will not set up a king before his eighteenth birthday. The son will not be of age for another year. The kingdoms would naturally be turned over to you as the chief advisor, providing, of course, that you killed Jerome before the prince turned eighteen."

Silence billowed around Fel-hoen like a living thing, breathing, anticipating, urging his answer. "I will leave tomorrow."

• • •

The wagon jogged over the less-traveled roads between Zopel and Beren. Because of Cand's injuries, the pace they set was slow and gave Cand much time to think.

At first he thought the god had truly deserted him because of his lies and later his rebellion. He had lashed out in anger at Hoen for letting Temrane fail the Calli-kor even though Cand knew he was worthy. Temrane had an eagerness for the gods that could not be found in many men, and he had been groomed for the priesthood since his earliest days. There had been no unworthiness . . . Cand was sure of it.

Then came the betrayal and Temrane's disappearance. Again Cand's fury was turned toward Hoen. If indeed the god was hostile to Cand because of the corruption of the Calli-kor, then why punish Temrane?

Cand's anger gave way to disillusionment and finally doubt. He spoke of this to Devona one day while she sat beside him in the wagon trying to ease his boredom.

"I begin to wonder about the whole of my life. I have taught the people to sacrifice to Hoen because that is the way to procure blessing, and yet looking over my past I see that sometimes the blessings do not come. I think of someone like Farni who sacrifices over and over to Velad and she does not bless. Before, I would have said there was a secret sin, something he had not sacrificed for, but now I am not sure. The sacrifices seem to be a waste."

Devona spoke softly in contrast to Cand's agitated tones. "Sacrifices seem to be a waste only because they must be given over and over again."

"Ah, how wonderful it would be if there could be only one sacrifice." He looked at Devona. Her composed countenance spoke of inner harmony. Her blue eyes were like tranquil pools that beckoned one to exchange the anxieties of life for serenity and assurance. "You don't sacrifice to your god, do you?"

"No . . . The sacrifice, the one sacrifice, has been made. To offer any more would indeed be a waste and an insult to the One who made the sacrifice."

"But who could make a sacrifice that would be final?"

"Only a God."

"I had a vision once, a very long time ago . . . But no, that is impossible."

"What was your vision?"

"I have never told anyone, and I'm not sure I can tell you."

Devona smiled at him and patted his hand. "When the time is right, you shall tell me. Rest now and remember that doubting is only evil when the evidence is in front of you and you refuse to believe. But doubting such as yours is a quest for truth. Believe this, Cand: your quest shall be satisfied."

• • •

Temrane held on lightly to the man called Duncan as they rode through the hills with McNyre behind them. Duncan and McNyre chatted easily about the mountains, the towns of Amick and Andurin, the condition of the roads, and whether it would be a hard winter or not. Occasionally one would break out in song, the other joining in, and the hills would ring with the sound. They seemed to be old friends, and Temrane might have felt left out if he didn't have so much on his mind.

He didn't recognize any of the landmarks they passed, and though he had heard of the mining towns of which McNyre and Duncan spoke, he knew where neither of them lay in relation to Zopel.

Whether he should trust these men was something else that occupied him. The thought of trust hadn't occurred to him as he climbed out the castle window and let Duncan help him down to the horses waiting below. He was too full of fear and the nightmares he had witnessed with Crotalus to think of whether to have faith in these men or not. Neither looked particularly dangerous, though McNyre did carry a crossbow. Common men did not carry weapons such as that.

And what would Crotalus do when he discovered Temrane's disappearance? The powerful wizard would not just let him go; he would search for his pupil long and far. And when he was found, what then? Perhaps he should have avoided Crotalus' tortures by remaining with him. Then he remembered Hirsch's last screams and the horrible laughter from the evil sorcerer. No, flight was better. Perhaps even now the wizard was planning something just as atrocious for his pupil to punish the disobedience.

Temrane shuddered at the thought, and Duncan, feeling the movement, broke off his song and turned. "Are you cold, young prince, or do your thoughts make you tremble?"

"I am not a prince anymore. I'm not anything."

Pain twisted through Duncan. "Ah, that is where you are wrong, Temrane. Perhaps you have yet to discover who you are. McNyre, are we going to ride all night?"

"Ye are in the lead, old man. I think that we be a sufficient distance away to stop and rest a bit if it pleases ye."

"It does. My backside was not shaped to be forever on a horse."

They rode a mile more while searching for a suitable area that was secluded and not easily surrounded. At last it was found, and the bedrolls were brought out again. Temrane immediately crawled into one, pulling it close around him as though to shut everyone and everything out.

Duncan helped McNyre with the horses. "He does not trust us," he said.

McNyre grunted softly. "Would ye? He doesn't know us or where we come from. Duncan, the only reason he came away so easily was because he be mortally afraid of the wizard. And with good reason, I might add."

"I had hoped . . . Ah, well . . . The Redeemer has His purposes."

"Ye will have to earn his trust, Duncan. And so will your god. That one has an anger toward the gods right now that may be difficult to overcome. Go to sleep, Duncan, and quit worrying about him."

"Are you coming?"

"No. I don't trust the wizard, and I don't doubt but that those men are still looking for us. I want to keep watch."

Duncan nodded. "Wake me in a couple of hours so you can sleep." Then he too slipped into a bedroll. He was just beginning to doze when Temrane spoke.

"Where are you taking me?"

Duncan gathered his thoughts a moment. "I can't tell you right now."

"Why can't you take me home?"

"It was what I first wanted to do. But the Redeemer has shown me the danger of that. Apparently your city is under siege by the very wizard from whom you escaped. Your death is certain if you return."

Temrane sat up quickly, his voice agitated in the dark. "But my uncle is there . . . He must be in danger too! I have to help him!"

"Help is being prepared. We must wait."

"You don't understand! He is the only one who loves me. I must return to him."

"There are many who love you, young one, including the God who watches over us all. Rest now. We will know when it is the best time to return."

Temrane lay back again, and Duncan could hear him tossing for many minutes. Then he heard the sobs. He wanted so much to reach over and comfort the boy, to take him in his arms, cradle his head as that of a baby, stroke the hair, and tell him how much he was loved. But the time had not come yet for that. McNyre was right. Duncan would have to earn Temrane's trust.

• • •

Duncan came awake at the sound of Temrane's screams and grabbed the first thing that came to his hands. The saddle he had been resting his head on was then hurled toward the attackers who held Temrane, but one of them knocked it out of the air, and it fell to the ground harmlessly. Duncan was then seized from behind, his arms jerked back and up. The pain turned Duncan's world black for a moment. When his vision cleared, he saw three men holding Temrane as a fourth bound his arms and feet together as though he were an animal bound for slaughter. Three or four men were also behind Duncan, tying his wrists together. The fire began in Duncan's shoulders, spreading through his chest. He tried to relieve the pain by moving, but was only rewarded with another upward jerk by the men behind him.

"Let the boy go."

"Quiet, old man."

"Let me speak with the leader."

One of the men stepped away from Temrane. He was tall and broad of shoulder. Brown hair matted over his ears and onto his face. "I am the leader. You can say one thing, and then I want silence or my men will beat you into silence."

"The boy is of no concern to you. Let him go and I will give you what you want."

The man laughed. "You are not in a position to bargain. I happen to know that this boy is wanted by both a wizard and a king. That makes him a concern of mine. He shall make his future home with whoever pays the most."

"Let him go!"

"Silence! You have no money, nothing to bargain with but your miserable life. The king or the wizard may purchase you also. They may want the privilege of ending your life, but be assured that it does not mean much to me, and I would just as soon end your life here as listen to you all the way back to the camp."

Duncan struggled against the men holding him, kicking two of them, one in the knee, one in the crotch. Despite the pain in his shoulders, he wrenched himself free from the other two as they swung their fists at him. "I will die a thousand deaths before I let you harm the boy!"

A kick from behind sent Duncan sprawling at the feet of the leader. The man then raised his boot and brought it down on Duncan's back. Other men joined the fight, and Duncan could only fight back with his feet. He was kicked in the groin and abdomen. His ribs cracked as they met with heavily booted feet, and his vision swam as fists landed on his face and ears.

He knew he could not long remain conscious and struggled to hold on. But the repeated blows were too much to fend off. As his sight turned red, then mottled, and finally black, he heard Temrane screaming his name. Then all was silent.

Eighteen

"Palmer's in love with you."

Falcon did not miss the light blush that spread over Ivy's cheeks like sunrise. "Palmer has imagined himself in love with me for years," she replied airily.

"Has he? I never noticed. Doesn't it seem strange to you that a man who is thirty-eight years old would only imagine himself in love? That usually happens to boys around fifteen."

"I don't know what you're talking about." She swept the breakfast dishes up from the table and headed for the washtub.

Falcon grabbed her wrist. "Come, Ivy . . . Sit down and talk."

"You're not talking, you're teasing."

"I know, but I'm done with teasing. I want to talk seriously."

Ivy looked in his eyes and decided that he was sincere, so she sat down.

"Do you love him?"

"Does it make a difference?"

"Of course it does! It's my responsibility to make sure the husband you choose is upright and trustworthy."

"Husband? My, you certainly do move quickly for someone who has not noticed his best friend's feelings in two years."

"I am heartily ashamed of that and intend to make recompense. Do you love him?" When Ivy remained silent, he said, "I could choose someone else for your husband. It's within my power, though not within my will."

"I do not wish to marry."

This was said so softly that it quieted Falcon's bantering tongue a moment. At last he put his hand over Ivy's. "It's not right to remain in this place out of obligation when you love someone else. Your place should be at his side."

"I do not stay out of obligation but love. My place is here."

"No . . . Your place is out in the world. Ivy, I have always thought of you as my baby sister, and then as an annoying little girl. It seems like I woke up one day and found someone very different living here. You have become a very beautiful and very talented woman. You can't spend your life as a slave to someone who hardly knows you anymore. Palmer loves you. It's a real love, not imaginary. Do you doubt that?"

"Yes, I do. How can you know? Have you spoken with him? Do you know his feelings?"

"No. But I have eyes, and I see how he feels. Are you telling me that the two of you have never spoken of this?" Ivy shook her head. "He does not know how you feel?"

"No. I try and mask my feelings when he is around because I don't want him to know. It would only hurt him in the end."

"Then it is my duty as your brother to speak with him on your behalf. There is no one in the entire realm of Paduan who would make you a better husband."

"It can never be, Falcon. I will not leave Father."

"We will find a way, Ivy."

A large tear slipped from the corner of Ivy's eye and crept down her cheek. "I do love him, Falcon," she whispered.

Falcon drew her to him and stroked her hair. "I know."

• • •

Falcon found Palmer in the armory, polishing a sword that had known much fighting from the early wars. "Tell me, Palmer, if you marry will you spend less time in this place?"

Palmer laughed. "Only if my wife is very pretty. Have you noticed that every time we are together we talk of marriage? What do you suppose that means?"

"That it is very often on our minds."

"Maybe it means we are getting old. We are regretting the youth we have lost and are pining for things we have left behind."

"Not all of us have left behind the thought of marriage."

Palmer straightened up with a surprised look. "You? Who is she?"

"Not me, Palmer . . . You."

Palmer chuckled. "You must be mistaken."

"I saw the look on your face when Ivy came into the room the other day."

"The sun must have been in your eyes."

Falcon sighed. "You are as difficult as she. I ask her if she loves you, she says no, and I know she is lying. I ask you if you love her, you say no, and I know you are lying. I finally got her to tell the truth. You could save me much argument if you would do the same."

"She said she loved me?"

"She did."

Palmer smiled a little, fingering the sword absently. "You know, there was a time when I thought she might love me. I had only loved her a little while and was trying to get the nerve to ask you for her hand. But I waited, and as I waited I began to doubt if she had ever loved me at all. Every time I came around, she left. She would hardly say a word to me when we met in town. So I said nothing to you because I didn't want her to marry me if she did not love me."

"She told me that she was trying to discourage you because she didn't want you to be hurt."

"How could she hurt me?"

"She doesn't want to marry."

"Farrel?"

"Yes."

"Then we shall wait."

"At least your courtship doesn't have to be in secret."

"Does she know you were coming to talk with me?"

"She didn't want me to, and I think she would be embarrassed by it. She will be in town tonight taking fittings. Maybe you could meet her then."

Palmer smiled again, his mind reeling from the suddenness of his good fortune. "You were not angry?"

"Why should I have been?"

"You are a very jealous, protective older brother who might have thought that no one was good enough for his sister, and I did not wish to lose a friend."

"You have my blessing. I could not be more pleased with her choice or yours."

"Ah, my friend, now if we could only find someone for you."

"Perhaps I should begin looking. It is time to silence the past. Maybe now that you are attached, the cook will take a liking to me."

Palmer laughed, and the two talked over their prospective futures until the sun was high in the sky.

• • •

Falcon's steps as he headed home were light and his thoughts of a happier aspect than they had been in some time. His heart felt calm, at peace. On sudden impulse he entered the chapel that fronted the main road.

The chapel was of red stone and wood that had weathered gray. Green plants climbed up the hallowed walls, threatening to overrun the small building with burgeoning life if not for the priests who faithfully trimmed the foliage. Windows were high and on the side that received the morning sun.

The place seemed smaller than Falcon remembered. He had not been in the chapel for years, since Rafaela's death. The chapel that day had been cold, huge, and remote, far removed from the world and workings of humans.

Falcon had raged silently against Menon, using his duties as knight as an excuse to stay away from the chapel. But of course Menon was not locked away in a building, nor could He be silenced by Falcon's refusal to enter the chapel.

Falcon knew what Menon required. He was to trust. Rafaela was not to become a goddess to him as though he were a pagan. She resided in his heart only because she first was loved by Menon. She was a child of the Redeemer God, as was Falcon.

Falcon stood for a moment at the front of the chapel, unsure what to say and knowing at the same time that it didn't matter. Menon knew all things and indeed had drawn him to this place and time.

Shunning the benches that filled the chapel, he sat with his back against the wall, facing the windows. He closed his eyes and breathed deeply of the mystery that was the Redeemer God. He let his mind play over the events of the last thirteen years, dwelling especially on any shortcoming that Menon brought to his attention.

As the sun went from midday light to the first faint tinges of sundown, Falcon wept and prayed, confessing his bitter ire at Menon for the last thirteen years, surrendering to His will, relinquishing his hold on Rafaela without in the least ceasing to love her. He recognized now, as calm and a feeling of purity washed over him, that to truly love Rafaela was to give her to the Redeemer God. He could not love her as a husband, but he could love her as did Menon, with a love that nothing could remove.

Menon had withdrawn the ache from his heart and had shown him a higher way. With joy Falcon embraced the knowledge and left the chapel humbled and full of wonder.

"Ho, there! Sir knight!"

Falcon turned at this beckoning and saw a man riding toward him on a black steed. His practiced eye saw that the horse was of a royal house, disciplined and well-trained for battle. The man, although dressed in simple travel clothes, sat erect in the saddle and bore himself with obvious nobility. Falcon noticed immediately the odd gold of his hair and his dark skin. The knight was sure he had never seen the man, and yet he smiled at Falcon as though sure of his reception. But the smile did not light his eyes.

"I am Fel-hoen, king of the realm of Corigo, from the castle at Zopel."

Falcon bowed his head with respect. "I am Falcon Jaqeth, of the king's army. How may I serve thee, Your Majesty?" he asked courteously, although the king's name had caused an odd ripple of pain to start in his midsection. He longed to return to his own sanctuary, and yet knew this was not Menon's way.

"I seek an audience with the King of Paduan. I have arrived later than I expected and shall await the morning to speak with him. Is there lodging somewhere?"

"Your Majesty, I would be remiss in my duty if I allowed you to stay anywhere but in the castle. If it pleases you, I shall escort you to the castle and find a manservant to look to your needs and those of your retinue."

"I am traveling alone; there are no others coming. I do not wish my presence to be greatly known until I have spoken with your king. I am sure that the inn of this city is most comfortable."

"As you wish. Continue down this road for yet another mile. It will take you into the town proper. The inn fronts this road on the left side. Ask for Zeire and you will be well taken care of."

"Thank you. I shall mention your kindness to the king."

Falcon watched as the King of Corigo rode past, and again he felt the tremor in his stomach. He hurried home, anxious to be rid of the feeling by losing himself in other occupations.

By the time he reached his door, the pain had worsened. Tension bunched up in his shoulders like knotted ropes; his legs ached with strain.

"Are you feeling well?" Ivy asked as soon as he entered.

"Not very."

"Do you want me to stay?"

"No . . . I will be fine."

"Devona should be here any minute to see Father. Perhaps she can give you something."

"I'll speak with her. When did she return to the city?"

"This afternoon. She and Batakis brought a man with them from Zopel. He looked badly hurt. He is staying with Batakis until he is well enough to return to Zopel. What's wrong? You have an odd look on your face."

"There are strange things going on, Ivy, and I wish I understood them."

"What things?"

"I'm not sure I'm at liberty to say. Don't worry about it. Go on . . . Take your fittings. I'll be all right."

After Ivy left, Falcon went in to see his father and found him sleeping. He was disappointed, for he felt the need to speak with someone. He fixed his dinner and ate in a silence which was most welcomely disturbed when Devona knocked on the door. She too perceived that he was not well.

"I don't know what it is, Devona. I'm not sick. My muscles are tight all over, and I don't know why."

"When did it start?"

"Just a little while ago. I was speaking with a man and it almost seemed like his presence caused it, although I know that is ridiculous."

"What man?"

"A man from Zopel," he said cautiously, unsure whether he had a right to name the King of Corigo to anyone.

The effect of these words on Devona, though, was clear. Her breathing grew rapid, her eyes narrowed. "Who was it, Falcon? I must know immediately."

Years of trust in the midwife loosened his constraint. "He told me he was the King of Corigo . . . Fel-hoen."

"And did he tell you what brought him to Beren?"

"He did not say except that he wished to speak with King Jerome."

Devona slowly tapped her fingers on the table, taking deep breaths to calm herself. At last her breathing slowed and her finger-tapping became less insistent.

"You did right to tell me, Falcon. A man's life hangs in the balance even now, someone King Fel-hoen would very much like to see destroyed. And by naming the man, you also have found the source for your own malady. You have not heard the news from Zopel of the prince's disappearance?"

"No."

"I thought not. Ah, Falcon," she said, placing her hand over his as tenderly as a mother, "how I wish I could spare you more pain. But apparently that is not to be. Your sensitive nature feels the pain even before the knowledge is given. King Fel-hoen gave his son away around the time of the Feast of the Redeemed."

A deep line creased Falcon's brow in puzzlement. "That grieves me, as it should any servant of Menon. But I sense that you speak of a personal pain."

"Yes, and it must be told. A wizard received the boy in a bargain struck many years ago. Temrane is to be the apprentice of Crotalus."

Blackness washed over Falcon as if in a wave. His muscles twisted in anguish. Anger, hot and thick, rose up and nearly choked him with its strength. He struggled against it, closing his eyes in fierce concentration, his hands shaking with the effort. He was dimly aware of Devona massaging his shoulders with her powerful fingers. He opened his eyes and forced himself to speak around the fury that filled him. "Why does Fel-hoen seek Jerome?"

"Fel-hoen, for whatever reason, and I don't trust him, wants his son back. The people of Zopel are ready to kill because of this and indeed have tried to take the life of the priest who now resides with Batakis. I counseled Fel-hoen to seek Jerome's help. Perhaps with both armies, Crotalus can be overcome."

Falcon leapt to his feet and headed for the door. "I must see Jerome immediately."

"No!" Devona's voice was filled with authority, and Falcon stopped. "You are in no condition to advise the king. You are thinking with your heart and not your head. I know if you had your way you would ride right now into battle against Crotalus. But you are a warrior, Falcon. Think like one. There will be time tomorrow, after Fel-hoen has counseled with Jerome, to speak with him."

Although he wanted to argue, he recognized the wisdom in her words and remained silent.

Devona, seeing that her words had been effective, went into the other room to see Farrel.

Falcon listened to her chatting with him about the various happenings in the town. She talked lightly, offering no hint to Farrel that anything out of the ordinary was going on. His father's responses were lucid for a change, and Falcon was glad to hear it.

Devona came out shortly and laid her hand on Falcon's arm before leaving. "Go in and speak with your father. He is a great man with much insight." She turned again at the door. "Do you know how to kill a dragon, Falcon?"

"Of course . . . Father has told me many times. You seek its weakness first, and the rest is easy."

Devona smiled. "Yes. You are a fine man, Falcon, but with a weakness that is evident to your enemies. Don't let it be that which destroys you."

He puzzled over her words as she put on her shawl and left.

She was a wise old woman, so he took her advice and went in to his father.

• • •

Palmer waited until he saw Ivy coming out of Bria's house. He saw her turn the corner and go back up the main road. He caught up with her, falling into step beside her.

"Do you mind if I walk with you?"

Ivy's heart wanted to crawl up her throat, but she steadied herself and said calmly, "Not at all."

For a time it seemed as if these would be the last words spoken between them. Palmer, although joyous inside, was unsure how to begin. Ivy was gratified by his attentions and yet too shy with him to know what to say.

At last they reached the house of Jeffen and Constance. Ivy was to fit the children for new clothes, a rare treat for them and for her. She did not often get the chance to make new children's clothes, as old ones were usually handed down from generation to generation.

Ivy put her hand on the gate and turned to Palmer. "Thank you for walking with me."

Palmer grabbed her hand. "Don't go in yet. Stay and talk with me for just a minute."

"All right, but only for a moment."

Palmer didn't let go of her hand, even though he felt that she wanted to flee from him. "Ivy, you know how I feel about you. I sometimes think the whole of Paduan knows how I feel."

"Palmer, please don't do this," she said, removing her hand.

"I know you love me too."

"Did Falcon talk with you?"

Palmer did not wish to implicate Falcon in this, as Ivy could very well be angry at him, but he would not lie. "Yes . . . this afternoon."

"He had no right . . ."

"He had every right. He's your brother, and he only wants to see you happy. Would I make you happy, Ivy?"

She turned away quickly so he would not see the tears in her eyes, but he sensed them. He touched her shoulder and gently turned her toward him. She came into his arms as though she belonged there. "Ivy, there is nothing in this world I wouldn't do for you. I understand your love for your father and the duty you feel. I respect that and would not ask you to change. But it doesn't change my love for you."

"I cannot leave him, Palmer. It would break my heart to have someone else attend him in his final days."

"I would not ask you to leave him. Our marriage will wait until the time is right. But as Falcon said, at least our betrothal does not need to be secret."

Ivy smiled up at him, the joy in her heart spilling onto her face until Palmer was sure he had never seen anyone so beautiful in his life.

"I don't wish to keep it secret. I want the whole world to know."

"We could start with Constance and Jeffen as long as we are here."

"We could at that."

Palmer pushed open the gate, and they entered the house together.

• • •

"I am sure that he is the one causing all the evil in Corigo," Falcon said to his father.

"I do not doubt it."

"But I can stop it."

"How?"

"He wants to see me dead. I am perhaps the only one who could flush him out and kill him."

Farrel sighed at the impetuosity of his son. "That would not be wise."

Falcon forced himself into calm again. "You said that before, but you did not give a reason."

"You did not ask for one."

"I am asking now."

"But are you ready to hear? Your anger and bitterness block out all else."

"He killed her, Father!"

"He killed her thirteen years ago. Falcon, you said you had spoken with Menon, that you had released her. What does Menon tell you now?"

Falcon thought over the question a moment. "I don't know," he said humbly. "Perhaps I have never known."

"Son, your anger at Crotalus is warranted, and your love for Rafaela is strong. But just as you felt that your love was holding you back from the Redeemer, so does your bitterness. It is not justice that you want, but vengeance. Give the revenge and hate to the Redeemer, as you gave your love of Rafaela to Him. Your bond with Menon will not grow unless you leave your wrath behind."

Falcon had no answer and so sat in silence with his father as he slipped into forgetfulness and then into sleep. He watched the flames in the grate burn down to embers and pondered the things Menon had told him through his father.

Much later he heard Ivy come in the door. She stopped upon seeing him. "Is he all right?"

"He's sleeping. He was very lucid tonight."

"Devona said he would be more rational the closer it got to the end. Do you suppose he has much time left?"

"I don't think so. Ah, Ivy, I shall miss him when he's gone, and yet he does not deserve our pity, for he shall reside with the Redeemer. I wish he could see you married before he dies."

Ivy smiled. "Perhaps he shall."

Falcon smiled back at her. "Are you angry with me?"

Ivy walked over to him and put her arms around his neck. "Yes, very . . . But I forgive you. I'm going to bed." She walked to the door and smiled at him one last time. "I am the happiest woman alive."

Nineteen

"I must say I am a bit surprised at your presence here, though you are most welcome."

Fel-hoen smiled. "I know our kingdoms have had little chance to cross paths, but I come seeking your counsel."

"If you choose, I can summon my knights and lords. They advise me in most matters."

"I choose to present this to no one but yourself at this time, King Jerome. After you have heard me and have given me an answer one way or the other, perhaps you shall choose to inform your knights and lords. My own knights and lords are even now ignorant of my visit. I wish to know your counsel before I enlighten them."

"As you wish."

"You have no doubt heard many rumors from Zopel about my son."

Jerome waved his hand in the air. "There is a saying among my people: 'The evil of one who pays heed to rumors is only surpassed by one who spreads them.'"

"A most worthy sentiment. However, I wish to tell you the truth regarding my son. An evil wizard, Crotalus by name, came to me on the night of my son's thirteenth birthday. He demanded that I turn the kingdom over to him or the consequences would be dire. I, of course, refused. The next morning I learned he had stolen my son, Temrane, the Prince of Corigo. Crotalus demanded my kingdom in exchange for my son. If I did not comply immediately, he would steal the souls of the children."

Fel-hoen leapt up and began pacing in front of Jerome. "What was I to do? Whom was I to abandon? My son, my flesh and blood, the heir to my throne – or my people who entrusted their lives to me? Ah, bitter decision! I decided the only course of honor was to ride against Crotalus' army in battle. Perhaps my kingdom would be conquered and Crotalus would reign, but at least we would die valiantly."

Jerome sat in stunned silence. He felt he had just witnessed a superb performance that almost demanded applause, and yet what if he were wrong? He did not know Fel-hoen, did not understand his inner workings. Perhaps he was telling the truth, in which case Jerome could only join his forces to Fel-hoen's army.

Against this logic, he could only put a very slight feeling he had that Fel-hoen was lying. But did that change anything? Crotalus needed to be stopped, no matter what the cause. The pain he had inflicted on Rafaela and Falcon was still fresh in Jerome's mind. Prince Temrane needed to be rescued from Crotalus whether he had been willfully handed over or kidnapped.

"Is your army expecting battle?"

"Yes. They are ready to ride at my command. But what is an army against the wiles of a wizard?"

"You speak truly, but in that case what are two armies against the wiles of a wizard?"

Fel-hoen sat down and leaned forward, his eyes bright. "But Crotalus will not expect two armies. And I also, King Jerome, have heard rumors. You have a knight in your camp whom Crotalus wants desperately to see dead."

"Who told you this?" Jerome asked quietly.

Fel-hoen sensed the shift in the conversation, the uneasiness in Jerome, the sudden coolness, and so backed down. "It is talk and, as you said, nothing to which we should pay heed. However, if Crotalus suspected that this knight resided in Beren, he might turn his dark magic here. His great hate for this knight could very well be his undoing."

"I find it hard to believe that Crotalus would not already know these things. But it is no matter. Crotalus' reign of terror must end. I shall join my army to yours against a common enemy, and I ask only one thing in return. Your daughter has caught the eye of my son. I propose that she be given in marriage to him and that the two kingdoms be united under a single rule."

It was now Fel-hoen's turn to be surprised. He had fully expected to unite the kingdoms under the rule of Jerome, as Niccola had suggested. Now, killing Jerome after such a bargain would mean nothing until the prince was also killed. It would have to be done with haste and perhaps look like an accident, but it could be done.

"It is an unusual request, but one I am not reluctant to meet. However, I must tell you something in total disregard for what it may do to our bargain. Princess Merry was the first soul to be taken by Crotalus. Her body lies in the castle, but her soul is captured and held only Crotalus knows where."

"Then it shall also be the first released when we defeat Crotalus."

Fel-hoen stood up and made a slight bow. "King Jerome, I thank you most heartily. I shall return to Zopel and confer with my knights and lords. I shall send word when we are in agreement."

Jerome watched Fel-hoen leave and then summoned a scribe. "Tell Falcon Jaqeth and Cleve Palmer I wish to see them immediately."

"Is there anything else, sire?"

"Yes. Take this message to the Lords McIlree of Eschay, Diones of Chantey, Sipple of Yartenn, Thomas of Vierne, and Ulster of Keffram: 'Council of war in three days.'"

•••

Duncan became conscious slowly, the world coming into focus and receding again for three full hours before he could attend to his condition. His shoulders ached as though they had been pulled loose from their sockets, and for all he knew they had been. A thick rope pulled his wrists and ankles together behind him, arching his back painfully. He twisted his head slowly from side to side to take in the camp.

Temrane was beside him, watching him with bright, mistrustful eyes. He too was tied ankle to hand. The men who had captured them sat around a fire, and Duncan could smell the delicious odor of meat, causing a small ripple of hunger to flit through him. There were eight men, and none paid attention to him and Temrane, preferring for the moment their stomachs rather than their prisoners. The men were settled between Duncan and the horses. Duncan could not feel anything behind him, but he sensed wilderness. Apparently the men were confident that Duncan would be unconscious for quite some time because he had been cast aside, out of the way.

"How long have I been out?" he whispered to Temrane.

"From sunrise this morning. It has been dark about two hours."

"Did they hurt you?"

"No. Are they Crotalus' men?"

"No. They are mercenaries. If they were Crotalus' men, I would not still be alive, and you would no doubt be in the castle by now receiving whatever punishment Crotalus metes out to people who desert him. Tell me of our captors."

"They have not even come to see how we are. Every now and then one of them turns around to make sure we are still here, but that is all. I was only waiting for you to awaken before trying to escape. I think I can work my hands loose."

"Do not try anything yet. Let us wait until full darkness overtakes them and they sleep. They will certainly place a guard on us, but we could better fight one man than eight. And perhaps by that time McNyre will have come."

"McNyre? You are daft, old man. It was he who betrayed you. He is far away from here, counting his money."

Duncan sensed the boy's hostility and probed the wound gently. "You said he betrayed me. Did he not also betray you?"

"No. I did not trust him. I didn't even like him. Therefore he could not betray me."

"But you are here, in captivity."

"Yes, but McNyre's deception did not touch my heart. He was not my friend, as he was yours."

"So you can only be betrayed by a friend."

"Yes," Temrane said softly. "Only by someone you love very much."

"Then you shall never love again?"

"No."

"Ah, my young friend, then you shall never know life's joys."

Temrane looked long at Duncan, and Duncan was astonished at the ancient and battered expression in the eyes. "Maybe not, but I shall never know life's sorrows either."

Duncan could only reply with an anguished prayer to the Redeemer for the inner life of the boy. He could do no more at this time. He did not consider for a moment that maybe the boy was right and McNyre had deluded them. McNyre's heart was true and his loyalty secure, he was sure of it. Duncan was, however, exceedingly afraid that McNyre had been killed by these very men, and it was a fear not easily dispelled. He could not help but feel responsible for whatever fate befell McNyre, and so he offered a prayer for him also.

So, with prayers on Duncan's part and stony silence on Temrane's, the night passed, and one by one the men around the crackling fire fell asleep. Duncan waited another hour to be sure, but he saw no movement. He could not believe they would not even put a guard on them.

He was just beginning to make a tentative move toward freeing himself when he saw some kind of activity around the fire. He could not make it out, but he held himself still and whispered to Temrane to do the same. One of the eight men rose from the fire and stole toward them.

Duncan's heart sank; there would be no escape attempt. The man was heavily hooded, and as he came nearer he threw back the cover. Duncan smothered a cry as he saw it was McNyre. He knelt by Duncan and ran his hands over the knots.

"I'll have to cut the bonds. Are ye seriously hurt or can ye ride?"

"I think I can ride. Anything to get out of this. Temrane, can you ride?"

Temrane eyed McNyre distrustfully. "Yes. I am unhurt."

"Have you been a part of their group the entire time?" Duncan asked.

"Not quite." McNyre removed a knife from his robe and began

sawing carefully at the ropes. "They surprised me at my post and had knocked me out before I could utter a cry. I think they meant to leave me for dead. When I came to, ye were gone. I've had occasion to track animals before, and tracking them was much easier, for they left clues everywhere they went. I just joined in as though I belonged. I have only been waiting for all of them to sleep. I could not fight them alone."

Temrane had begun to wiggle a bit, impatient to be released. "Why cut the ropes? Can't you untie us?"

"No . . . The ropes are tied through your crotch and would put pressure there if ye tried to escape. I could not untie them without putting you through excruciating pain that could possibly wake the entire camp. Be patient. I will be there in a moment."

Duncan relaxed his muscles a little more at this bit of information and then asked, "Did you happen to hear any news while you were with them?"

"No. But we cannot be certain that word was not sent to Crotalus. They are looking for ransom money. If they sent word, it will take at least two days for the message to reach Crotalus and hopefully that long for Crotalus to find that we've escaped. But it is not long enough. When we are free, we must ride hard and continually. We cannot afford a rest now."

"We should also avoid Amick and Andurin."

"At all costs. It looks as if I am destined to travel to the Forgotten City with ye, Duncan."

Duncan's ropes fell away, and he began to slowly move his legs and torso around, feeling the throb of the beating he had taken resound through every bone and muscle. He watched as McNyre freed Temrane and then came over to help him toward the horses. Walking took intense concentration for Duncan as each step sent agonizing flames through his body; he bit his lip to keep from crying out.

They approached the horses slowly, giving the animals a chance to get used to them. Duncan knew if they made any sudden moves the horses would bolt, proclaiming the escape of the captives to the entire camp.

Temrane glided onto a horse and watched impatiently as McNyre helped the ailing Duncan onto a horse that had been quickly saddled. "Do you have strength enough to guide the horse?"

"I think so."

McNyre mounted a horse and grabbed the reins of the remaining horses. "We will take these with us. We may need them."

They were moving slowly when one of McNyre's horses shied as a shadow passed over the moon. The horse jolted into Duncan's horse, causing it to stumble. Although the movement was slight, it was enough to cause Duncan to cry out in extreme pain as he struggled to right himself on the horse.

Instantly the mercenaries were jumping up from slumber, yelling to each other, grabbing for weapons. McNyre eased his hold on the extra horses and hollered loudly. The horses scattered into a moon-drenched field and then away. McNyre slapped the rump of Duncan's horse to get it started. "Ride hard!" he shouted to Temrane, who immediately kicked his horse's sides and followed Duncan.

McNyre raised his crossbow and let fly two arrows in rapid succession. Each found a home. McNyre released one more arrow before spurring his horse to follow Duncan and Temrane.

The remaining men ran after him a short time before realizing they could not catch a man on a horse, nor could they recapture their other horses. Luck had left them to sit and wait until Crotalus came to fetch them. Crotalus would no doubt be extremely wrathful at the loss of the boy. None of them liked the prospect.

McNyre caught up with Duncan and Temrane. Both had wide, round eyes. They slowed the horses to an easy jog. "Sorry, Duncan," he said, "I didn't have time to bury them."

Duncan smiled weakly. "No matter. We will leave it to the One God to bury them in His own time."

"Ye look very pale. Can ye make it to the Forgotten City?"

"I hope so."

"We cannot stop to rest. Crotalus' men will be after us very soon."

"I hope we can gain a fair amount of ground on them. I hate the thought of leading Crotalus to the city," Duncan said quietly.

"Perhaps the boy and I should go on to the city and ye should turn to Andurin or Eschay to have your wounds looked after."

"No . . . We have a chance of losing Crotalus' men once we reach the Wastelands. The winds blow strong there and will cover our trail. I have healing medicines of my own and can best protect the boy on my own soil."

"But I do not wish to go," Temrane said. It was the first time he had spoken since fleeing the camp, and both men turned in their saddles to look at him.

"Would ye rather be captured by the wizard?"

"No . . . I want to go home."

Duncan dropped back a little and rode even with Temrane. "You have no home right now, Temrane. Your father gave you away, and I shudder to think what he would do if you were to turn up in his city again. The only safe choice right now is to press on to the Forgotten City. We shall know which way to go when we get there."

"How do I know that going with you won't be worse than staying with Crotalus?"

"You don't . . . that is true. You don't know me, you don't know McNyre. But you do know Crotalus. Could we be much worse?"

"No, but . . ."

"There aren't any buts after that, Temrane. We are who we are. I follow a God called the Redeemer who told me to get you. I did that. And now I will await His leading again, and you will wait with me."

"My uncle is a priest to the god Hoen. Does your god recognize Hoen?"

"No. There is no god but the One True God."

"There cannot be one god, old man. There are many, and Hoen is the greatest of them all. My uncle serves him, as I was to do before I was found unworthy. I was cast from his presence. I need to make sacrifice and restitution for my sins, but I cannot do that here. I must be in his presence to do that. Please let me return to my uncle."

"I cannot at this time. Perhaps things will change when we reach the Forgotten City, but for now we must travel on."

"Could someone at least send word to my uncle when we reach the city?"

"That at least can be done."

Duncan spurred his horse as much as his aching body would let him, and the three rode swiftly throughout the day.

Twenty

Drucker sat in the dank, fetid temple awaiting the decision. Kalei played at his feet, her blonde hair a light in the shadowy holiness of the temple. She tugged at his leg, wanting him to stoop on the floor and play with her as he sometimes did at home. He reached down and stroked her hair, feeling it wind around his fingers as though it too wanted to frolic with him. Kalei turned a bright and trusting smile on him, and he swept her up from the floor to cradle her in his arms.

"Who's my girl?" he whispered against her ear.

"Kalei," she whispered back and put her arms around his neck.

He brushed her hair away from the ear and kissed it softly. She giggled as the touch raised goosebumps on her arms. "I love you, Kalei."

"I love you, Daddy."

Galion, the high priest of Hoen now that Cand was gone, stepped through the curtains and faced Drucker.

"I have sought the god's face long on this issue. My decision is to receive the child in Hoen's name. You shall be blessed greatly because of the sacrifice."

Drucker nodded curtly, his heart wanting to turn back. But he could not – serving the god must come first. He cuddled Kalei close and whispered again in her ear. "Do you remember who this man is?"

"He is Galion."

"That's right. He is the priest to Hoen. You must go with him now and do what he tells you to do. Can you do that for me?"

Her arms squeezed his neck. "Yes."

Drucker handed her to Galion. "Will there be any pain?" he murmured through the tears that sprung to his eyes.

"No. It shall be very swift. Go in peace, Drucker, and go in the god's blessing."

Drucker watched as Galion put Kalei on her feet and led her behind the curtain to the holy altar of the temple. Drucker thought of her silky, blonde hair and the smile that had always tugged at his heart.

"Who's my girl?" he said softly.

There was no answer.

• • •

Falcon strode into the council chamber, but hesitated when he saw Jerome in an attitude of prayer. Jerome looked up, and the thought crossed Falcon's mind that the king had suddenly grown old. "I came as soon as I received your summons, Your Majesty."

"And Palmer?"

"Palmer rode to the North Woods this sunrise. I sent the messenger after him. Do you wish me to take leave until he can be here?"

"No . . . It is better this way. I can talk with you privately now about a matter that has been weighing on my mind since the night of the feast."

"What is it, my king?"

Jerome rose to his feet. "Let's walk in the gardens. This is such a cold place, a place of death. Wars are decided here, strategies made that lay waste to good land and better men."

Falcon looked at Jerome wonderingly. He had never heard the king speak in such tones. Jerome had fought bravely during the wars; there had been no hint of this disposition. A knight couldn't very well find war distasteful. Of course, peace was always to be hoped for, but Falcon felt there was very little promise for it in this world, and if there was to be war, then he would fight with every virtue he possessed.

"Is there to be war?"

"Yes. Regretfully, I see no other course."

Falcon was pleased. He knew the war had to be against Crotalus, and it would give him great pleasure to ride into battle against his most hated enemy and destroy him. He smiled a little, though Jerome did not notice and went on speaking.

"Crotalus is planning on taking over Corigo, and he must be stopped. I have summoned the lords for a council in three days. But I want you and Palmer to know of my initial plans."

He paused a moment and took a deep breath of the fragrant air, air that smelled not of blossoms and perfumes as in the Spring, but the musty, rich aroma of the earth. It was a good smell, the essence of virility and life. It gave no suggestion of the coming Fall and Winter. Springtime was serene like a newborn baby; Winter spoke of dissolution, and even its colors were ashen; Fall was an old man vaguely recalling days of youth and glory. But Summer! Ah, Summer was robust and flavorful, life bursting through the seams of the earth. It seemed almost a sacrilege to speak of war in the Summer.

"I want Palmer to lead our army against Crotalus."

"What!" Falcon stopped on the path and stared at Jerome as though the monarch had lost his faculties.

"There is something else I need you to do."

"Send Palmer!"

"I cannot. It is for you and you alone to accomplish."

Heated words leapt to Falcon's mouth, but Jerome held up a restraining hand. "I have always delighted to call you and Palmer friends, but I am still your king."

Falcon stilled his tongue a moment. "I understand that, Your Majesty, better than anyone . . . but . . ." His voice became very quiet with pleading. ". . . you know how I feel about Crotalus, Jerome. I implore you, don't take this from me."

"I said I have thought long about this. War is no place for personal vengeance. Clear heads and hearts are needed to lead an army. Do you deny this?"

"No."

"Then will you respect my wishes as your king?"

Falcon closed his eyes. *No!* he wanted to cry out. He wanted to grind Crotalus beneath his heel; his heart would not be satisfied until he had wrung the life out of Crotalus himself. But he could not say that now, nor go against his king.

He opened his eyes. "Yes, I will respect your wishes." As he said the words, his heart opened a little, releasing tension. Although he was still disappointed, he was no longer angry.

Jerome was well-pleased. "This thing that needs to be done is for you alone, as I said before. I must confess, Falcon, that I have hidden something from you for many, many years and have now discovered I was wrong. When I first made the decision, I thought it a good one. But I have grown older, and now I see that the choice was not mine to make."

Jerome turned and looked at Falcon. The knight's dark brow was creased, the green eyes stretching for understanding of Jerome's riddled words. Jerome smiled a bit sadly. He did not know if his words would bring happiness or anger . . . possibly both. "Falcon," he at last said softly, "Rafaela lives."

• • •

Cand had watched the sun go down the night before, then waited to watch it come up in the morning. His vigilance had been unbroken, although Batakis urged him to take rest.

"I don't understand what you are watching for," Batakis complained just before dawn.

Cand did not turn his eyes from the window. "I am waiting for a change."

"What change?"

"Any change. Something should be different, and yet life goes on much the same as it always has."

"I still don't understand."

"Nor do I, my young friend. Please go to bed. When there is a change, I will let you know."

Batakis had finally relented. He wanted to keep watch with Cand, but his bed and the busy day ahead called to him, and he at last slept as orange flames shot through the morning mists.

Batakis awakened mid-morning and found Cand still stationed at the window, his back straight and eyes clear. But there was a despondency in his face that was not easy for Batakis to read. "Does this mean there has been no change?"

"None."

"What change were you looking for?"

"Anything." He sighed deeply. "Anything at all."

Batakis moved a chair close to Cand and sat down beside him. "I can see that your heart is deeply troubled. Perhaps if you shared it with me, it would ease your burden."

Cand dragged his eyes from the scene he had been viewing for the last twenty-four hours. "I will try, but I cannot hope for you to understand—I don't understand it myself."

"But at least you shall not be alone."

"That is true . . . Batakis, since my earliest days I have served faithfully in the temple. I have made sacrifices, I have interpreted omens, I have procured monies for the temple. Was it all done for nothing, Batakis?"

All of his life Batakis had wanted to tell the Corigans of the True God, but now he found it wasn't as simple as he thought it would be. He had not reckoned on the pain of loss in Cand's eyes. "What change were you looking for, Cand?"

"My god has left the world. I wanted to see what difference his departure would make. It made none. Everything is still the same. The sun still came up this morning . . . The birds still fly. There should be purple grass and a green sky. Or at least a rip in the heavens that the stars fell through. All these years I have been mistaken. My god never left the world because my god was never a part of the world. Am I right?"

"Yes," Batakis said kindly.

"Devona once said that I was on a quest for truth. I believe I have found it."

"No . . . You can't stop there. Yes, you were mistaken, and by turning your back on your old ways you have found truth, but it is only a partial truth. There is a God, one God."

"You say there is one god, I have said there were many. What makes me wrong and you right?" Cand asked without animosity, but rather with a strong desire to understand.

Batakis sat quietly, but his mind raced and skipped over possible answers, discarding them all. The truth was, he just didn't know.

• • •

"I didn't know what to say to him," Batakis said as Devona patiently worked in her kitchen. He loved the smells in her house. When he was young, he would try to distinguish the many different fragrances, but it was impossible to determine more than two or three. There was the sweet aroma of benry leaves that, when boiled, made a drink to relieve morning sickness. Savory smelled most strongly in the room. Pungent, almost bitter, its leaves could be added to vegetables or chicken to enhance the taste. He watched now as she squeezed the musky scented oil from the minga fern into a jar. Minga was used for scrapes and cuts; every household contained a jar.

"You are too hard on yourself," she said with the trace of a smile.

"I should be hard on myself, Devona. I have walked with the Redeemer God since childhood. I should know the answers to these questions. Perhaps I haven't walked as closely as I have thought."

"It is always good to question because that is when we grow, and you should always stretch yourself in your walk. But you are trying to tell Cand things he will not understand until he has grown a little. It is like trying to explain the mysteries to a little child. You don't give the children who come to you nothing but facts. What do you tell them?"

"I tell them of the things they can see."

"Exactly. Show Cand first what he can see. Tell him how you feel, what is in your heart. There is nothing wrong, Batakis, with not knowing all the answers. None of us, this side of the Redeemer's Country, will ever know everything. Tell him what you do know and what has happened to you."

"And then what?"

"Then listen. Cand has a great pain, perhaps the greatest a person can experience, but in that hurt are seeds of great joy. Listen to his pain. He does not need dispassionate facts, but a loving heart. And that," she said watching him fondly, "is exactly what you have."

He reveled under her gaze that was almost a caress, and vowed that someday he would tell her *all* that was in his heart.

• • •

Falcon lay on his back in a field of wheat, its golden-green color like a blanket covering him from prying eyes. He stared at the sky, his mind trying to make sense of all he had heard. He had no doubt that it was true. *Rafaela was alive!* He would ride immediately after the council for the Forgotten City. Palmer would lead Paduan into war against Crotalus. His enemy as good as dead and his lover alive—this was something he had dreamed of for thirteen years.

He heard a sound like horse hooves in front of him, so he sat up. It was Palmer.

"Aggh! You frightened me! Do you always lie in wait in wheat fields to startle unsuspecting knights, or is this a special occasion?"

Falcon laughed aloud. "This is a glorious occasion, Palmer. Nothing shall ever surpass this."

"I was summoned from the North Woods by a messenger from Jerome. What is happening?"

"Much, my friend. Come . . . I'll walk to the castle with you."

Palmer dismounted and, taking the reins, began to walk.

"I don't quite know where to begin," Falcon said.

"Begin with the news that has your eyes dancing and the laughter in your voice."

"Very well. It is a good place to begin. Rafaela did not die thirteen years ago. She lives in the Forgotten City."

Falcon expected this news to bring surprise and delight to his friend's face, and he was not disappointed. "How do you know this?"

"Jerome confessed it to me. He was trying to protect her from Crotalus and perhaps, even though he didn't say it, from my trying to possess her. I was wrong in that, Palmer. That was how Crotalus' love turned into a bitter and vicious thing. He wanted to own her . . . as did I. But no longer. I am prepared to love her as the Redeemer loves her and for however long He chooses to let me."

"And there really is a Forgotten City?"

"There is no longer the city of which we heard when we were children. That was destroyed many years before our time by enemies of the Redeemer. But there is a city, and one man is the caretaker. He is the only remaining Menontes, and he has cared for Rafaela these many years." After a pause he continued, "There is also to be war against Crotalus. But I won't say more of that until we are in Jerome's presence."

"I can see that much has happened in my absence. Does it seem to you that things of which we only dreamed yesterday are now happening with remarkable speed? Perhaps it is the end of all things."

"It seems a good way to end. Life has never been so sweet," Falcon said and then wished he hadn't. The thought brought a cloud over his soul. His country and king were about to enter a war in which many people would die. Innocent children even now lay in a deathlike slumber from which they might never awaken. It was true that his joy over Rafaela should not be marred by this, but it was wrong to rejoice over the war that would put an end to his enemy. *Forgive me, Redeemer,* he whispered in the sanctuary of his soul. *If there be any way to stop Crotalus other than war, please show us the way. If there be any way to turn his heart, turn it.*

The rest of the walk to the castle was spent in companionable silence, and Falcon felt a calm in his heart at the prayer he had uttered. He was unconscious of the fact that he had prayed the most pure and highest prayer of his life. He was soon to need all its power.

• • •

Lord Soaje paced up and down Fel-hoen's Great Hall. He was a big, impatient man, used to his own way. He had been summoned along with the other lords for a council with Fel-hoen, and so far had been left waiting. The king's advisor had not even been in to welcome them or to tell them of the king's delay. "King or no, if he does not come within the hour, I ride back to Andurin."

"Surely he does not plan war, does he?" Pelaro, the Lord of Amick, asked.

"Who knows?" said Lord Kies of Mandor. "I hear so many rumors, I do not know which to believe and which to ignore."

"I have heard he rode into Beren," Lord Tegmen said. "The people of Derrich think perhaps he means war against the Paduans."

"So what is he doing?" Soaje said derisively. "Warning King Jerome?"

"If we are to have war, it will be against Crotalus," Pelaro said.

"I would much prefer war against Paduan. Crotalus' castle is much too close to Derrich. He could easily overtake it."

"Crotalus could easily overtake any of us," said Kies softly. He was a quiet man, fond of his lordship and fearful of war. Mandor was given to him because of his father's loyalty to Fel-hoen during the siege. Kies was a child when Fel-hoen took over Zopel and the realm of Corigo, so he had never been in a battle, much less a war.

"Fel-hoen is a fool if he is thinking of going to war against Crotalus."

"I'm a fool?" said Fel-hoen as he entered the room swiftly with Niccola behind him. Startled, the four lords turned to him. "That kind of talk, Soaje, could be considered sedition."

"Forgive me, my king," said Soaje, bowing low. "There are so many rumors in the air that I have become confused. I spoke hastily."

"You always do. Please, my lords, sit down and let me tell you of my plans."

As each man took his place around the table, Tegmen cleared his throat apologetically. "Your Highness, the council is no place for a woman, no matter how beautiful."

Fel-hoen looked at Niccola. Beautiful? By the gods, she was stunning. Her dark looks smoldered, and Fel-hoen could sense the fires within her. He swore that he would yet make her queen. "This is Niccola. She is my new advisor."

A sharp intake of air was heard throughout the room, and it was several minutes before anyone spoke. To take a mistress was nothing new for any king, but to give her a position was unheard of . . . and dangerous. Tegmen at last found his tongue. "What happened to Solon?"

"He was found murdered in his bed. It is no matter . . . He had become useless to me anyway."

"But a woman, Fel-hoen? The gods forbid—"

"There is no god in Corigo but me, and I shall do as I please! Do you wish to withdraw from the kingdom? I can remove your lordship as easily as I raise my hand."

"There is no need for that, King Fel-hoen. I did not understand your position, and now I do. Please tell us what we can expect concerning war."

"There is to be war against Crotalus. He kidnapped my son and is holding him hostage for the ransom of my kingdom. I want my son back. King Jerome of Paduan has agreed to join with Corigo in riding against Crotalus. He has a strong army of his own as well as six lords and their armies at his command, although some of those armies are quite small."

Soaje turned to Niccola, unable any longer to ignore her presence. "Is this your advice to the king?"

"Yes," she said, unflinching even though his gaze was malicious. "Crotalus' treacheries are well-known. The only way we can hope to defeat him with minimal loss is with greatness of numbers."

"And it doesn't bother you that Andurin will be the first city to be destroyed by Crotalus?"

"I do not wish to lose anything," she said bitingly, "but loss in war is not new. If we attack first, we can lure him to a better place for us to fight."

"And do you think that you are intelligent enough to lure him?"

"I know his weakness. Once you learn a man's weakness, the battle is over."

"Then use his weakness now and avoid the war."

Fel-hoen, silent during the discussion, slammed his hand down on the table. "You are a fool, Soaje! You cannot see the opportunities that are blossoming under your nose. Think of the things we shall gain. We shall not only recover Prince Temrane, but acquire lands of which we have only dreamed. The Amil Mountains all the way to the sea that lies behind them have been feared by our people for years because of the wizards and witches that have populated them. Each of them was destroyed by Crotalus in his mad lust for power. We now have the chance to rid the mountains of all wizards and make them free for our people. Do you not think that is worth fighting for?"

No one stirred. Faces were stony, as yet unconvinced. Kies cleared his throat, and everyone looked at him. "Your Majesty, land is always worth having, but not that land. You have said there is no god but you, and I won't dispute that if that is the way you wish it. But your subjects, not only in Zopel but in all of our cities, still believe in the gods, and the gods have forbidden that land. You will have an internal rebellion if you try it."

Niccola shoved her chair away from the table. "There has been too much discussion. Get on with it."

"She's right," Soaje said. "There is no need for further discussion. I think it's plain how we feel. I vote that we do not go to war."

"Vote?" sneered Fel-hoen. "Vote? I do not intend to take a vote. I am king . . . I am supreme. We go to war! I shall send word to King Jerome of Paduan. If any of you do not join me in this, I shall label you as traitors and you shall be hewn down as surely as will Crotalus."

He stood up and with Niccola on his arm retreated from the room filled with speechless lords.

"He is mad!" Soaje spat out at last, breaking the tension.

"Perhaps," said Pelaro, "but that only makes him more dangerous. What choice do we have but to go along with him?"

"We can fight him!"

"What good will that do?"

"We can dethrone him and place one of ourselves on the throne."

"And be king of a dying land?" Kies asked. "As little as I like Fel-hoen's qualities, he is right. Crotalus must be stopped before the entire land is destroyed. Thank the gods, he has only attacked Zopel so far, but do not be deceived. He will attack the other cities when the time is ripe for him."

"Kies is right," Pelaro said. "We can think of dethronement once Crotalus is stopped. But we must first stop the wizard."

• • •

In the dark of night Soaje crept into Tegmen's room at the castle. The argument between the four lords had quitted only with the coming darkness, and no decision had been made. Soaje determined that he would make his own decision and the gods could take the rest of them. He found Tegmen waiting for him.

"They are cowards," he said.

"They are not cowards . . . only fools," Tegmen replied.

"Do we join together against Fel-hoen?"

Tegmen took a moment to think. "You realize that we fight not only Fel-hoen but the King of Paduan?"

"He's a fool for joining with Fel-hoen. Yes, we fight them all."

"We may yet have to fight Crotalus."

"I think not. He has a weakness. Fel-hoen's whore is right in that. I believe I know what that weakness is. We can bargain with Crotalus. He will be ready to bargain, especially if we give him Fel-hoen's head."

Tegmen laughed quietly. "All right . . . we join together."

"Rest now, Lord Tegmen. We shall need to leave before dawn."

Twenty-One

The lords of Paduan listened in respectful silence as Jerome put before them King Fel-hoen's request. Faces were grave, as war is not a matter lightly decided. At last Jerome was finished and the matter open to any discussion.

Lord Ulster was the first to speak. "I do not trust Fel-hoen, my king."

"Do you have any reasons or just a general feeling?"

"More a feeling than anything else, but there have been stories."

"We have all heard stories that are not grounded on fact, Lord Ulster. I won't tolerate a decision made on that basis."

"I understand, sire, but one fact I do have: King Fel-hoen made no pretense of rescuing his son until the public outcry was against him. It was then the story circulated that the prince had been kidnapped."

"All right," Jerome said, "I accept that as fact, and it does certainly show that King Fel-hoen has little true regard for his son. That does not change the fact of Crotalus' destruction of Zopel."

"What about the lords of Corigo?" Lord Sipple asked. "What do we know of them?"

"King Fel-hoen was to have a council with them upon his return to Zopel. He will send me word as soon as a decision is reached, but I have no reason to doubt that it will be war. The lords are four in number, but I know nothing of them personally. If anyone here knows different, please speak."

"I have an acquaintance with Lord Pelaro of Amick," said Thomas. "Our cities have often traded with each other, as we are both on the border. He is a loyal man and knows his mind. He does not chase fantasies in his head. He has often spoken of Lord Kies of Mandor. He is a very young man, in his early twenties, who would be very inexperienced in battle."

"Tegmen is perhaps the most fearful of the gods of the whole lot of them," said Diones. "I know him but little. He is most concerned with Derrich and what is best for it, even if it goes against the king. Since Fel-hoen has turned his back on the gods, Tegmen might very well turn his back on Fel-hoen."

"That leaves Soaje, Lord of Andurin," Falcon said. "He is a ruthless man, and his ambition makes him dangerous. He is the only lord who turned against the previous king to place Fel-hoen on the throne. I think we would be wise to be wary of him."

"What about the townspeople? Would they fight?" Thomas asked.

Jerome sighed. "Unfortunately, that cannot be hoped for unless Crotalus is lured from his castle. The townspeople believe their gods have forbidden them to set foot in the mountains. They will not further risk the gods' anger."

"It would be best if we could lure Crotalus from his castle. His potents and powers are strongest there," Falcon said.

"Then have we decided to definitely go to war?" Jerome questioned.

Lord McIlree glanced around the table. Each lord seemed to be waiting for some kind of inner guidance, some hunch that would add further weight to their knowledge. He was the first to speak. "It is imperative that Crotalus be stopped. I vote yes."

"Wait," Jerome said. "There is one further piece of information you must have before the final decision. Falcon will not fight this war. There is a private battle he must face alone. Palmer will ride alongside me."

McIlree turned to Falcon with a look of quiet surprise. "I will not question your private matter. I leave that to you. But one question I would like to ask, and it is not meant as a personal affront to Palmer. Is Palmer expert enough to handle six armies?"

"He is more proficient and knowledgeable in the use of arms than I am. I am fully convinced that he would make a better leader of armies than me," Falcon answered.

"Then why is he only second in command?"

"Where friends are concerned, he has a soft heart and no selfish ambition. However, there is no one more capable of riding alongside our king to defeat an enemy."

McIlree nodded. "Then I repeat my earlier vote—Yes."

The vote went around the table: eight votes for war, none against.

• • •

Crotalus raged in silence against the theft of his apprentice. The men in his army knew him well enough to stay far away if they could. Some, of course, were not so lucky. A soldier had been summoned by Crotalus to bring him a sword. The soldier was beheaded with it moments later.

Crotalus rotated the sword in his hands, watching the sunlight glint from the steel and then become slowly covered over by the dark blood of the soldier. He delighted in its darkness.

As he thought over the matter, he saw only three possible explanations. Fel-hoen could have stolen the boy, but he was a cowardly man who quaked at the name of the wizard. He could not have crept into the mountains and entered the castle fearlessly to rescue his son. He would plan war, of course. Crotalus expected that. He knew the townspeople would be outraged at Fel-hoen's treachery, and it would be only by a lie that Fel-hoen would keep his crown. He would appear as the broken-hearted father, weeping for his son, heaping curses on the wizard. War was the only possible outcome.

The second possibility was that Temrane left the castle of his own accord. This the wizard dismissed almost immediately. The boy would have had to escape on a horse to be gone so quickly, and none of Crotalus' own horses were missing. In addition, Temrane was too young to bribe anyone into helping him, and he did not know his way out of the mountains.

But then who had the boy?

He didn't know how it had happened, but he was sure that Falcon Jaqeth had Temrane. There was no one else who would dare oppose him so openly, defy him so brazenly. As he had mesmerized Rafaela to lure her away, so he had captivated the prince and had stolen him. If he didn't hate Falcon so much, he might almost admire him for his cunning and his spells.

A plan was beginning to form in his mind to trap Falcon, but it wasn't developed enough yet. He wanted something that would not only destroy Falcon in the end, but would humiliate him at the feet of the wizard before his death. Crotalus believed he knew how to do that, but details still needed to be worked out. And now, if Falcon did indeed have Temrane, more care would need to be taken.

He strode over to the headless soldier lying on the floor. He lifted the bloodied sword high above his head and brought it down in a sweeping arc into the body. He cackled as the sun sank below the horizon. "Darkness!" he howled. "Falcon, I shall not only bring death to your body, but darkness to your soul. It shall be mine!"

• • •

"Come," Batakis said to Cand. "We will walk today. Devona says it is time to regain your strength."

Cand readily agreed, and as the two walked through deeply green fields that Autumn would not touch for another month yet, Batakis felt his spirit lighten. There was no need to doubt his God, nor his faith in the Redeemer. True, his faith was still growing, but that in itself was a reason for rejoicing.

"You asked me several days ago why I was right about my God and you were wrong about yours. Do you still wish an answer?"

"If you have an answer for my deeply troubled soul, I will gladly listen."

"I cannot give you a full answer, for even I don't fully understand. Menon is filled with mystery, and perhaps there are things that can only be revealed by Menon Himself. But I can tell you what I know for certain."

"What is that?" asked Cand with a smile for this young man who spoke with such earnestness.

"My God gives me peace. Your god gives you turmoil."

"How does your God give peace?"

"I have only begun to search these things out, so tell me if I do not make sense. Turmoil comes from sin, and when man sins he is far from his God."

"That is true."

"Then how is man restored?"

"By making sacrifice to the god."

"How do you know if the sacrifice was large enough?"

Cand was silent for a moment, his anguish making it difficult to speak. "I don't know. I thought I knew, but I was wrong."

"And what happens if you sin again? Another sacrifice is made. And so it goes on forever."

"Devona spoke one time to me of one ultimate, final sacrifice. Tell me of this sacrifice."

"A very, very long time ago we used to sacrifice the blood of animals and the fruits of our harvest. This was to cover over our sins and restore us to God. But the sacrifice had to be offered over and over again because the sacrifice could not change us. It was just an animal – innocent, yes, but just an animal. Perhaps a man could have been sacrificed, for man is not merely an animal, but then the innocence would be lost. But what if a god sacrificed himself?"

Cand's very first vision flashed before him: the lamb on the knoll, the knife descending into the image of Hoen, the lack of blood. He understood now, in his darkness of despair, what that lack of blood meant. Hoen was lifeless, an image made by man. It could no more give life than a stone. He sank down to his knees as his world crumbled and threatened to crush him.

A later vision was recalled: the lion who became the lamb with blood flowing from its side. Hoen was defeated by this living sacrifice.

Cand doubled over in pain that ripped through his stomach. It had been weeks since he felt this pain, since the Calli-kor. He had thought at that time that Hoen was punishing him.

Batakis knelt down beside Cand and placed a tender hand on his shoulder. "Can I get you anything?"

Cand looked at him, but the commonplace question gave way to a burning need of Cand's. "How can an immortal die? Tell me, if you know."

"I do not know. It is a wondrous mystery, but perhaps a mystery that no mortal can understand until he understands all things."

"Tell me of your peace. Why do you feel peace?"

"Because the sacrifice has been made and accepted. I do not need to wonder if my sins are forgiven. They are. I am in fellowship with Menon, a bond that nothing or no one can break, including me. Why should I not feel peace?"

"How old are you, Batakis? Thirty years? You are still a babe as far as the world's reckoning goes. Your sins cannot have been very large, nor your pain very great."

Batakis laughed a little and helped Cand into a sitting position. Then he too sat down, his back against a tree. "Even the smallest sins separate us from the True God. In His eyes there is no such thing as a small sin. And as for pain, who can say? I have carried a great weight of pain, but compared to someone else's it may seem small. It doesn't matter. My God is large enough to handle my great pains, and yet not so large that He does not cry with me."

For an instant Cand saw who Menon must be: a God who feels pain, rejoices in companionship, laughs, cries, and calls mortals friends. "It is too much," he said to Batakis. "I have heard many things today, some wonderful, some terrible, all mysterious. And yet somehow my soul says they are true. I need time."

Batakis nodded. He understood, for he had disclosed things to Cand that he had never uttered before. He felt himself swept up into the love of Menon. He also needed time.

• • •

Kreith stood rigid before his father, Palmer, and Falcon. The other lords had long since retired, and these three alone discussed strategies and tactics. Kreith had come in silently but quickly, and now stood in a warrior's stance at the table, waiting for his father's recognition. Falcon suppressed a small smile. He knew what Kreith had come to ask, and he felt a surge of pride and love for the boy he was helping to raise to manhood.

At last Jerome looked at him and nodded his assent for Kreith to speak.

"Your Majesty, I wish to be part of the council."

Jerome did not laugh, nor did he wonder at the formal declaration. "I think that would be wise. As you are to be the next king, you need to be a part of the decisions made in this room."

"Thank you, Your Majesty. I also wish to ride into battle with you."

"That I cannot allow. You have not even seen your eighteenth year yet."

"But during war everyone who can fight, does. It would not be right for me to remain here while others wage war."

"It would not be right for the country to be without a king should both of us be killed in battle."

Kreith knew he had no answer to this, and his rigid stance relaxed. "Father, please hear me out," he pleaded.

Jerome sighed. "What is it about this battle that everyone is begging me to be in it? First Falcon and now you. Perhaps Alexandria will be next. Very well . . . Falcon, Palmer, please leave us, as we obviously have weighty matters to discuss."

Kreith waited until both had left the room, although he had not minded their presence.

"Tell me your heart."

"It's Merry. She is to be my wife, but she lies under a spell put on her by Crotalus. It just doesn't seem right for me not to fight for her."

"Do you know that Falcon is not fighting?"

"Yes. He told me this afternoon."

"Did he tell you why?"

"He only said it was a personal battle he faced."

"That's true. Everyone fights the battle in his own way. Not everyone fights with swords against the enemy. There will be plenty here to do."

"Like tending the wounded? That's women's work!"

"Kreith, tending the wounded is a special gift that not everyone can do, and its importance is never questioned. You have made war into something glorious and grand. It is not. It is bloody and frightening. Sometimes in order to stop a greater evil, fighting must take place, but it is not the supreme will of Menon."

"I know that, Father . . . Forgive me. I know caring for the wounded is important and a great part of battle. I just feel helpless and frustrated because I want to fight for Merry."

"I understand, but you would better serve me and ultimately Merry herself by fighting the battle here. I believe that Batakis is planning a trip to Zopel the day after tomorrow to see what can be done for the people. Why not go with him? Perhaps you will find some sphere of usefulness to ease your restlessness, and you may even see Merry while you're there."

Kreith smiled. It was not as pleasing a prospect as fighting heroically for the woman he loved, but it was better than remaining behind.

• • •

McNyre scrutinized Duncan at every opportunity. There was no doubt that he was seriously wounded. His face was ashen, his lips pressed tightly together in pain. His eyes were glazed as though he were feverish, and McNyre noted that they rarely focused on him. He slumped over in his saddle as if it were too much effort to sit upright.

"He is not well," Temrane said, seeing McNyre watching Duncan. "We should get him help. We are traveling between Mandor and Amick. We could turn to either city."

"No . . . It is too risky. Crotalus has men everywhere who are too afraid to do anything but his bidding. We must continue on."

And yet he did not know if Duncan *could* continue on. In another day they would reach the borders of the Wastelands. Duncan, in coming to Andurin, had left the Forgotten City and traveled south immediately, leaving the Wastelands in a few days. He had traveled west then. It had been a long way to go, but most of his journeyings were through cities. This time, McNyre thought, they were going to enter the Wastelands miles from the Forgotten City. McNyre judged that it would take two weeks to get there and that through heavy sand, blistering winds, and little shelter.

"McNyre!" McNyre turned at Temrane's shout and saw Duncan slide from his saddle onto the ground. McNyre leapt from his horse and hurried to Duncan's side. Temrane had already dismounted and was kneeling by him, his eyes filled with worry. "Is he — "

"He is unconscious," McNyre said. "Find me the water jug." Temrane ran to the horses, while McNyre ripped his tunic into rags. He took the rags, wet them, and placed them on Duncan's forehead. "Wake up, Duncan," he whispered. "This is your mission, not mine. I do not even know where we be going."

"We could tie him to his horse," Temrane suggested. "Or build a bier to pull him."

"The trip is too long. He would never survive. God of Duncan," he said, lifting his face to the sky, "if ye be a real god and not like the gods of my country, don't let Duncan die here. What do we do?"

McNyre sat for a moment as though listening, but there was nothing to hear. "The heavens be silent."

"Perhaps they have always been silent," Temrane whispered.

"This old man did not think so. I have never heard a man speak of the gods as this one did. Not even your priests in Zopel."

"You speak blasphemy! The gods will punish us!"

"Ach! I have heard that for many years. My blessings and my punishments have not come from the gods. Duncan did not speak of punishment and blessing. He spoke of love. It was love of his god that sent him out to find ye. Do ye love your god?"

"I don't know any more," the boy said softly, a tear forming.

McNyre immediately regretted his harsh words. "Well, there ye be. A man who doesn't believe and wants to, a boy who does believe and doesn't want to, and the only one of us who knows for certain is unconscious. We be a sorry lot."

Temrane smiled, his first smile in days.

McNyre returned the smile. "That's better. I don't know why, but it is. I say we head for Amick. It is dangerous, I know, but I love this old man too much to let him die here."

• • •

"Now what?" asked Temrane as he and McNyre viewed the edge of the city.

"Ye stay here with Duncan, and I will try to find a healer who will not talk much."

Temrane watched McNyre disappear over a hill and then turned back to Duncan. He wet the rag again, mentally making a note to fill the jug with water before they left Amick. He did not want to run out of water in the Wastelands.

As the cool rag touched Duncan's face, he opened his eyes. Temrane was glad to see they were clear. "What happened?"

"You became unconscious and fell from your horse."

"Where are we?"

"On the outskirts of Amick. McNyre went to find a healer."

Duncan wanted to argue, but knew it made no difference. He could not go on to the Forgotten City. Death would claim him quickly if he tried to cross the Wastelands.

"Are you afraid to die, old man?"

"Is that what you think I am doing?"

"Yes."

"I am not dying. If McNyre finds a healer, even a bad one, I will not die. But to answer your question, no, I am not afraid. I'm not quite ready yet — there are things I have left unfinished, people I would wish to see again. But then, I suppose no one is ever quite ready. But I am not afraid. And if the Redeemer chooses to let this body rest, so be it. I shall rejoice to see His face."

"You are not afraid to see his face?"

"No."

"Is he not a fearsome god?"

Duncan smiled. "Very. But I am His child. I have no cause for fear."

Temrane sat silently, washing Duncan's face, watching over him as he slipped back into sleep. He thought about Candy and wished he could be with him, speak with him. They used to have good talks.

Temrane wished he could go back to the days when he was a servant of Hoen and his future was laid out like a road map. There was no confusion then.

Something about Duncan's speech, his talk of the Redeemer God, made Temrane yearn for something he could not name. He longed for the love of which Duncan talked. He craved the security of resting in the god's arms. He wanted to be someone's child.

He lay down next to Duncan, his head resting lightly on his shoulder. He wept out of great loneliness at the loss of his god, his uncle, his father. "Please don't die, Duncan," he whispered into the sleeping man's ear. "I need you."

Twenty-Two

Farrel Jaqeth, in his lucid moments, knew he was going to die. But his lucid moments were only like pinpricks of starlight in a forbidding darkness. As Devona had said, when the end was near he would be more rational, and that time was now. Thanking the Redeemer God for His providence and for the mind that had at last cleared, Farrel called his children to him.

They came and sat on his bed, Ivy near his heart where she had so often been, and Falcon behind her. "The days grow short, my children. Tonight, I feel, will be my last night on this earth."

Falcon opened his mouth to protest, but choked back the words. He would not utter meaningless lies on his father's deathbed. He laid his hand over Ivy's, which already held their father's hand.

"There are so many things I would say to you . . . things I have wanted to say all my life and yet did not have the words nor the perception.

"First, I commend you both to the Redeemer's care. He is your first breath in the morning and your last thought at night. Seek Him before all things. Never doubt His love for you."

Farrel placed his hand on Falcon's head in blessing. "Falcon, you are getting ready to undertake a journey that for you carries great joy. Be happy in the going, and rejoice in Menon. Remember that it is He who gives you love to share with another. Bear Him always before you so that you are not tempted to put another in His place.

"Continually put your hatred of Crotalus into Menon's hands. Your battle with him is not done; nay, it has not even begun. This final struggle will be fought, not with swords and lances, but with honor and truth. Keep your heart on both and you shall prevail, although it may seem as if you have lost.

"War becomes you, Falcon, as it did me in my youth. But no man should feel comfortable with war, as we have. It is an evil circumstance, necessary at times, but not something in which to glory. You have the seeds of greatness in you if you can put your faults under the command of the Redeemer. When the battle with Crotalus is over, seek peace as diligently as you ever sought war. Learn more of Menon, and let His peace give rest to your soul.

"Finally, my beloved son, do not trouble yourself over my death. I go willingly and have few regrets in my life. My strongest regret is that you spent so much time raising my daughter. You did a commendable job. Do not delay your journey because of my death."

Falcon leaned over and kissed his father's bearded face. There was much he longed to say, but the tears hot in his throat blocked the words. He at last whispered through the tears, "I love you." His father's deeply brown eyes with flecks of green loved Falcon in return and understood the scarcity of words, although there was no lack of feeling.

Farrel cupped Ivy's face a moment in his hand.

"Ivy, you have become a beautiful woman. However, your merit does not lie in your beauty, but in your vitality. Your heart, through many trials, has become strong, and yet has not been hardened. Your love and concern for me has been unfailing, and Cleve Palmer will reap the reward when he becomes your husband.

"You are a rare woman. You are not satisfied with any thoughts or feelings that have been given you by another. You continually test things for yourself. You do not wish to simply have a husband and be happy with that. You demand your own fellowship with Menon and a life to yourself before you are willing to share that life with another. This is a strength more women would be wise to follow. However, be careful in this so that you do not exclude Menon in your zeal to be yourself. I have had the privilege to have known only one other woman with such great strength, drive, and love, and I now hold her up to you as an example. Go to Devona and watch her work . . . Listen to her talk about

Menon . . . Model your desires after hers. Then you shall not stray from Menon.

"As I told Falcon not to delay his journey, so I tell you not to delay your wedding. If, when the war is over, the time of mourning is not up, do not delay. Never concern yourself with the rituals men deem proper, but look to Menon instead as your constant guide of right and wrong.

"My children, death cannot separate us. The love of Menon is too strong for that. I go to be with Him. I shall no longer see dimly but face to face. A day is coming when we shall all rejoice together in His presence."

Ivy's arms went around her beloved father's neck, and she laid her head on his shoulder, her tears wetting the blankets. She let go with one arm and reached out for Falcon, holding the three of them together.

It was as they huddled there together on the bed that Farrel Jaqeth, the Dragon Slayer, finally ended his years of pain and breathed his last.

• • •

Temrane and McNyre gently lowered Duncan onto a bed in a small room in a very small house. The house was on the outskirts of Amick and was owned by a tight-lipped woman who gave the appearance of walking the earth before any other human. Her eyes were shrewd and took in every detail of the two men and the boy as they entered her house.

She watched as the older of the two men was laid on the bed. He had to be a foreigner. His clothes, although dusty and torn, were unlike any she had seen before. The boy, though, was the one who caught her attention and held it in a steel hand. He was dusty as well, his face smeared with grime, his hair in a hundred tangles. But it was his eyes that arrested her. Their color was ordinary enough, as was the shape, and for a moment she could not say what it was that was different. Then she realized it was his expression. A boy his age, which she guessed to be between twelve and fourteen, should have a liveliness about the eyes, something of the imp that could not be squelched. This young one's eyes had seen much sorrow and misery. There was no inquisitiveness, little trust, only a sobering grief.

"Do I know the boy?" she asked McNyre.

McNyre pulled a silver coin from his bag and pressed it into her palm. "The boy has never been here."

The line between her eyes deepened, but she put the coin in the folds of her dress and nodded. "The boy is not staying here, is he?"

"No . . . only the man. You said you could help him."

"Rest is what he needs, and that he shall receive. He cannot stay long. There are rumors of war, and it shall go very badly with me if a foreigner is found here during time of war."

"As soon as he is strong enough, he will leave."

The woman nodded again, scowling a little, and left the room.

"Such company you leave me with," Duncan complained.

"She will not give away your presence, and that is the most important thing."

"I should be going with you."

"Ye not be well enough. I considered all of us remaining here and then going on, but it would simply take too long."

"No . . . You're right. Temrane cannot be much longer in Corigo. It is better for him the sooner he reaches the Wastelands." Duncan looked at the boy slumped in the corner of the room. "Take him tonight."

"I will . . . as soon as it is dark. The woman won't talk, but nevertheless I don't want her to see in which direction we ride."

"Duncan, please don't make me go," Temrane pleaded from the corner. "I want to stay with you."

"Are you still afraid of McNyre?"

"Lad," McNyre chided gently, "there are plenty of things to be frightened of, but I am not one of them. I will see ye safely to the Forgotten City."

"It's not that. I trust you. You came back for us. It's just . . ." His voice tapered off.

Duncan nodded at McNyre. "Give us a moment alone. I think I know what's troubling the boy."

McNyre nodded and left the room, shutting the door quietly behind him.

"Come . . . sit beside me." Temrane did not hesitate, but hurried over to the bed and took the hand that Duncan held out to him. "You have a great loneliness inside."

"Yes!"

"Do you want to tell me about it?"

Temrane fought down tears. "I can't."

"I see. Then I shall tell you about it. Your father has done one of the most heinous things he could possibly do. He has betrayed you, and you don't know why. You wonder at times – I can see it in your eyes – what evil in you made him do this. You think that you must be a horrid person for him to turn his back on you. Am I right so far?"

Temrane nodded as a tear slipped from the confines of his eyelids and was whisked away by his hand.

"Shall I go on?"

"Yes."

"Your Uncle Candy is a man you love very much, and he loves you deeply. But he is also the high priest to the highest god, and that must come first. Somehow you offended the god. He also has turned his back on you. Because Hoen has shunned you, his priest must do the same or risk further retribution. So Candy has also let you down. You had hoped and prayed for Candy to rescue you, but he didn't. Your sin must have been very despicable indeed."

Temrane swallowed hard and balled his hands into fists.

"And now you feel that I'm turning my back on you."

"You were hurt because of me!"

"I would have gotten hurt whether you were there or not."

"But you wouldn't have left your city. It was my fault!"

"Temrane, let me tell you a little bit about my God. Like your gods, He does what He pleases. I don't often understand my God's ways any more than you understand yours. But my God loves me more than I can imagine, and everything He does is for me. He does what is best. I left the Forgotten City because He told me to. I cannot explain what His best is in these circumstances, but I know that He holds all things in His hand.

"My God says there is no sin He cannot forgive. And you, child, are very precious to Him. And because of that, you are very precious to me. I am immensely privileged to have you bestow your love on me. I shall never turn my back on you. McNyre, for reasons of his own, has decided to cast his lot with us. He is a man not used to loving, and I am immensely privileged to receive his love. Share your love with him. Perhaps between the two of you, the hurt you both carry can be done away with.

"Now, you have been holding back tears for the last half hour. If they need so badly to be released, then let them come."

At this kindly invitation, Temrane threw himself upon Duncan's chest, wrapped arms around his neck, and wept.

Duncan held him, stroking his hair, and muttered softly, "That is good, child. Bitter tears need to be shed before the healing of love can come in."

• • •

"I do not see any reason to wait," Ivy said to Falcon for the tenth time that night.

"It is a tradition," he replied, also for the tenth time. "There is a four-day waiting period, and then we have the Celebration of Journeys."

"It may be tradition, but it is not law. I even heard King Jerome and Father talking the other day about it. Jerome said it was a holdover from the ancient days, thousands of years ago, when our people also worshiped gods."

"What more did he say?"

"That they believed the soul left the body on the fourth day and then the body could be burned as a 'return offering' to the earth god."

"Did Jerome say that is why we now burn the bodies of the dead?"

"He said it was not an offering to any gods, but simply returning the body to the earth from which it came. The point is, Falcon, it was once law, but we do not worship many gods now, but the One True God, who does not bind us to silly laws. Father walks this very instant with the Redeemer God. He no longer cares if we celebrate his journey on the first day or the fourth."

"I believe that, Ivy, with all my heart. But why do you so much want to go against tradition?"

"Because you have a journey that needs to be started also. You had planned on going at sunup tomorrow, and I know that you will not go if we wait to celebrate for four days."

"Father told me to go."

"So do you wish to go and I will celebrate in four days?"

"No. You are right . . . I couldn't leave. We will celebrate tomorrow."

And so, as the sun rose high during the day and was at last casting an orange and pink glow in the clouds toward evening, the priest, bearing the funeral torch, Falcon, Palmer, and King Jerome led the procession toward the funeral grounds. They rode in full armor on armored horses to honor the man who had been one of Paduan's fiercest warriors. Behind them, two ceremonial horses pulled the funeral bier.

As they rode through the streets, people joined the procession on foot, people who loved Farrel—peasants and nobility, men and women, the old and the young, for Farrel did not discriminate in his life concerning who Menon brought to him. Even in his brief periods of lucidity, he had shared what he had with others. To some he told stories of the old days; others he taught how to slay a dragon. The patriarchs came to him to reminisce, the young ones for advice.

The song for the dead began as they walked and was picked up by various voices along the way. The song brought comfort to the grieving as well as hope, because this was a *celebration*. One of the ancient ones had said not to grieve as those who had no hope, and the people of Paduan took this to heart. If they wept, it was because they would miss Farrel and because they still dwelt in a place of shadows.

When they reached the funeral grounds, Palmer and Jerome lifted the bier onto their shoulders and bore it to the pyre. Falcon and Ivy, carrying red roses, walked to the mound. "He looks much different," Falcon whispered.

"It is because he is not here."

"He walks now in sun-drenched valleys with no pain and nothing between him and the Redeemer. His body lying here is nothing but a shell. Farrel Jaqeth is not here."

They both took the roses and laid them around Farrel's body, the sweet smell riding on the wind to remind them of earthly life. As they turned to leave, others came forward and laid roses on the pyre. The priest was last. He laid his roses down and spoke a prayer over Farrel's body, commending him to his eternal home in the presence of the High and Mighty God. When he finished his prayer, he touched his torch to the roses.

Falcon watched in worshipful silence as the smoke curled up toward the heavens and the shell sparked into flame. "Good-bye, Daddy," he uttered. "I shall miss you."

• • •

Duncan watched Temrane and McNyre from the windows of his heart, for his room held none, as they rode out of Amick. His heart was heavy for them, and he knew they traveled in deep danger. He yearned to go with them, not understanding why he had to be left behind, Menon's will totally incomprehensible to him and almost unbearable.

"Menon, I not only do not understand, but I don't like it. The boy needs me now. His heart is wounded, and I know in time I could heal it. He is just starting to respond to my love. And I do love him. And I love McNyre. And I am anxious to see Rafaela again. I am frightened for all of them. I know I drew maps for McNyre, but what if he still can't find the Forgotten City? And what of Rafaela? What will she think when a strange man and young boy show up at her door?"

Only then did he think of a note, and he wished he would have written a message for McNyre to give to Rafaela. "Ach! I am a stupid old man." And then he laughed, and the small chuckle turned into deep rumblings of mirth. "Yes, I am a stupid old man. It was a miracle to have found Temrane at all. Surely you are big enough to get McNyre and Temrane to the Forgotten City and to reassure Rafaela that everything is all right. This is not my mission, Menon, but Yours. I have begun to think I am too important. I am not healing Temrane's heart at all. You are. It is all in Your hands. Please forgive me."

Still chuckling a little, he uttered a prayer for the safety of Temrane and McNyre and then went to sleep, knowing that he needed rest in order to leave this place if it was Menon's will he do so, knowing that he had once again turned everything over to the Redeemer God who held it all securely in His loving hands.

• • •

Falcon held Ivy's hand as they listened to Bria and Alde clanging around in the kitchen. Bria had offered to make food for Falcon to take with him on his journey, and Alde was helping him make a pack and ready the horse.

"I don't want to go," Falcon whispered, squeezing Ivy's hand.

She smiled a little, a tear threatening to form. "You have to go. Rafaela needs you, and it has been thirteen years."

"But you will not have anyone here. I miss Father more than I can say, and you must feel his absence even more. You were with him much more than I was, and now he's gone. Your loneliness is going to be great, and I won't be here to help you through it. Palmer leaves soon, and then you won't have him either."

"But I have both of you in my heart, and the Redeemer carries you in His hand. Bria is going to stay here a few days. Please don't worry about me."

Falcon was silent. He didn't want to burden her further with his fears, but his heart would not be calm. He worried not only about Ivy, but about the war. Would he ever see Ivy again? Or Palmer? Perhaps he would return to find the war lost and the realm in the cruel hands of Crotalus. *I will fight then*, thought Falcon. *I will fight with every breath I have. I will fight until I too am dead and defeated.*

He stood as Alde entered the room. Together they walked out to the horse. "I'm glad you're not fighting in the war, Falcon," Alde said. "Do you go of your own accord, or does another send you?"

"Both," he replied shortly. He did not like Alde and wished to keep this conversation short.

"This is an evil war, Falcon, and all who fight in it will be tainted."

"All wars are evil. This one, however, is necessary."

"The war against Crotalus is necessary, I will grant you that. He should have been hunted down long ago and killed. The Redeemer God will not suffer to have one such as he live. It is not the war against Crotalus that is evil. But we should not be taking up sides with the Corigans. They are an evil, godless people. They will corrupt us with their ways."

"Crotalus is torturing those people, Alde. If he gains their realm, there will be nothing but endless suffering for them."

"It is no more than what they deserve for rejecting the love of the Redeemer God."

"Some of them have never even heard of the love of the Redeemer God. Others have not seen it."

"They have seen enough to turn! The Redeemer God is punishing them for their disobedience. We should honor Him by cutting ourselves off from such people. We should have nothing to do with them."

"Alde, you are forgetting where we came from," Falcon said. "We also were a godless people, worshiping many gods. We also were deserving of nothing but Menon's wrath, but by His mercy and loving-kindness we became His children."

"Exactly! We are His children . . . They are not. And because we are, we live in a certain way. I don't believe joining forces with pagan people is the way the Redeemer's children should act."

"Alde, I don't think there is anything in this world that you are unsure of. You think you understand Menon's will in everything. I don't believe you have ever doubted. Be careful, Alde," Falcon said softly. "Menon's ways are too high above man for man to understand all of them." He walked back into the house as Bria was walking out. He brushed by her, too upset to say anything.

"What is wrong with Falcon?" she asked Alde.

He shrugged. "Maybe he is realizing his mistake in leaving. His father has only been dead a little over a day, and already he is leaving. It isn't right, Bria."

"Alde, the Redeemer has given us freedom. We do what we do out of love, not mere duty. Let Falcon's freedom alone."

"He is not free to go after a woman who doesn't know the Redeemer. She was in love with a wizard, and most probably still is. Falcon should cut her out of his heart if he is to live in the will of the Redeemer."

Bria ceased the argument, for nothing she could say would change him. Instead she went into the house where Ivy and Falcon were preparing the last things for Falcon's journey. She crossed the room over to him and put her arms around him. "You are the one who best knows Menon's will in this matter. Don't let one whose heart is cold place doubt in yours. Go in peace, Falcon, and return in health."

She squeezed him briefly and then left. Falcon could hear as she and Alde walked down the road. "He is hard for me to bear," Falcon said to Ivy. "I don't know how she bears him so well all of the time."

"She has been wonderful, Falcon."

"It is going to be a noisy house with her and the children here."

"Father always liked it so."

"That is true. I miss him already, Ivy. And I miss you already."

They walked out to where Falcon's horse waited and saw Palmer waiting with it. Falcon turned to Ivy and swept her into his arms, lifting her from the ground. "Don't get married until I come back. I want to be there to dance with a full heart."

"I won't," she promised with tears in her eyes. "I love you, Falcon. Return soon."

"I will . . . I promise. I love you."

He turned to Palmer, and the two embraced. "Take care of her, Palmer," he whispered urgently. "If anything happened to her, I don't know if I could bear it."

"She'll be fine. I won't let anything happen to her. You take care of yourself. Return as quickly as you can. We may need your strong arm."

"Lead them well. I know they will serve well. My prayers go with you, as does my heart. Perhaps when we meet again the days will be brighter."

Falcon mounted his horse, and with a last look at the home that had grown immensely dear to him he rode off, grief an unwanted companion in his heart.

Twenty-Three

Winni walked heavily to the temple, misery marking every footstep. She carried Jasper in her arms, and as she walked she struggled to remain upright under the load of the eight-year-old boy. Her hands were under his neck and knees, his head hanging limply over her arm. One of his arms rested on her neck, although there was no pressure from it as there should be from a hug. His other arm dangled from his body as though the shoulder had no more use for it.

She climbed the temple steps, stumbled once near the top, righted herself, and continued through the door into a temple that seemed to her as lifeless as her son.

Galion, his eyes weary and wrinkled despite his youth, hurried to meet her. "What has happened?"

Winni laid Jasper at Galion's feet. "You promised us the god's blessing."

Galion did not reply, could not reply. All his years of service to Hoen had not prepared him for this. He deplored Fel-hoen for the crimes that had brought about this scourge. He detested Cand for thrusting him into the high priest role not with ceremonies and celebrations, but with anguish and death. And he resented this woman in front of him, perhaps the holiest in all Corigo, for reminding him of his impotence and failure.

"There is some sin," he said automatically but with little conviction.

"There is no sin. Drucker and I have made every sacrifice. We made the highest offering. You took my Kalei. You promised blessing."

"Winni, there must be a secret sin somewhere. Search yourself. There should have been favor upon you."

Winni smiled a little. "You know we have always made sacrifices and prayers. We have given money and pigs and blood. We have bought incense and gods. Always we have been blessed. Our crops have always been good, our pigs fat. Trouble has come upon the land, and so we offered the highest oblation: our daughter was accepted for sacrifice. And now our son's soul, the one we fought to save, has been taken. It is strange, is it not, that our crops are still good, our pigs growing daily, while according to you our livestock and harvest should falter. They do not. I do not know what to do any longer, Galion. There are no more sacrifices to be made, no offering higher than the one we already gave."

She stepped back to leave, her questions still unanswered, and then turned again to Galion. "Some speak of a higher god than Hoen. Perhaps there is war in the Dwelling-Places. Maybe Hoen will be overruled and his followers ground into dust."

"It is possible," Galion said hesitantly, envisioning a potential way out of this situation. "In that case your course is clear." He saw her eyes light and knew he was doing the right thing. "You must begin a search for this other god or goddess. It could be one of the gods already residing in Corigo or a different one. As soon as this god is discovered, Drucker, who is a holy man, must set up a temple to this god and become his priest."

Winni nodded her understanding, her face alight with enthusiasm.

"Go now, and take Jasper with you. Care for his body. Although his soul is gone, his body is not dead. When you have established a new temple, the god may choose to return Jasper to you or to take him as the first sacrifice."

Galion watched as Winni picked up her son and labored down the temple steps. He turned and went into the room that used to belong to Cand. He also stood in front of the god, much as Cand had done. Doubts he could not understand or assuage howled in his heart. "Kill me now, Hoen," he uttered. "I can bear it no longer."

• • •

Niccola eyed warily the man who had introduced himself as a lord from Paduan. "Which one?" she had asked. He had smiled and then replied in a raspy voice, clearly disguised, "As one who is ready to betray the kingdom, you can hardly expect me to answer that."

"Take off your jester's mask."

"Nay, my lady. My anonymity protects me."

"Perhaps you should speak with King Fel-hoen."

"No . . . You are the one who is intelligent enough to rule this country. Fel-hoen cares for nothing but his throne, and when he dies it dies with him. He is not far-seeing nor far-reaching."

"Tell me what you want."

"Not much . . . Just half the realm of Paduan when you come into power."

"When I come into power? I don't know what you are talking about."

"Please don't plead ignorance. I know that the lands of Paduan and Corigo are about to be united once Crotalus is defeated. That is a well-known fact. I suspect that the death of Jerome and then Kreith would not be far behind that. Perhaps you are even now planning Fel-hoen's death so you will be ruler over all."

Niccola stood up. "I do not need to listen to this. I shall call the guard and have you forcibly removed not only from this castle but from Corigo."

The lord smiled. "And have me tell Fel-hoen and Jerome who you are?"

Uncertainty stopped her. "Everyone knows who I am. I am Niccola, formerly maidservant of Queen Kenda and wife of a leatherworker, now mistress and advisor to King Fel-hoen."

"And Princess Niccola. I have known almost from the very beginning and have watched you, waiting to see when you would make your move. I had no doubt that you would make one. After all, you are your father's daughter. He was a ruthless man, and you bear his image on your soul."

"Even if what you say is true, to what good would you use it?"

"If Fel-hoen or Jerome knew, it would spring your trap before you are ready. Your prey would then escape without harm. The same would not be true for you."

She stood silent, frustration welling up in her like an overfed river.

"I am not an unreasonable man, princess. Give me half and you shall still have all of Corigo and half of Paduan."

"And what of Crotalus?"

"That is the best part, my lady. You know of his greatest desire. I know how to put it into your hands."

"Of what are you speaking?"

"Falcon Jaqeth."

"That is also a well-known fact. He is the king's highest knight."

"Yes, but he does not fight in this war. He has been sent away by Jerome. I alone know where he goes, thanks to my well-trained spies. If you agree to give me the kingdom, I will turn this piece of information over to you. You can then use it to destroy Crotalus in whatever way you see best. He is a formidable enemy, and you have no hope of beating him without wounding his weak spot."

She thought for a moment. "During the battle it shall be your arrow that kills Jerome. I shall deal with the boy later."

"If you wish."

"Give me the information."

• • •

Fel-hoen at first wouldn't give Kreith permission to be with Merry, but at last he had relented, the look of pleading in the boy's face too great to be refused. Kreith sat by her bed and held her hand in his. He had expected her hand to be cold, as in death, but the warmth of it made him wonder if she only slept. He stared at her face, waiting for, almost willing, it to move. There was nothing but stillness. Her body took in small breaths of air, just enough to lift the chest cavity a little, and then expelled them quietly. She did not sigh or cry out or smile or weep.

He wished he could fight for her. He wished he could kill whoever was responsible for this, whether it be Fel-hoen or Crotalus. There had been times when he had not understood Falcon's great desire to kill Crotalus, could not comprehend his hero's complete hatred of the wizard. Now he not only understood Falcon, but embraced the loathing and hugged it to him as Falcon had once done.

He stroked Merry's raven hair and then picked up a brush on her bed table. He brushed the long hair, first splaying it on the pillow behind her head and then down over her shoulders. Tenderness for her overwhelmed him and melted his bitterness toward Crotalus. He had seen Falcon turn away from his wrath, thus relinquishing his cherished dream of killing his enemy Crotalus. He had watched as Falcon became stronger and more of a lover to Rafaela than he had been when his animosity was so great. Menon was more honored by great love than great hate.

"I love you, Merry," he whispered into her ear. "As soon as the war is over and Crotalus is defeated, you shall be returned to me and we shall be married." With the tenderest of words he spoke to her through the day, somehow feeling that her soul, wherever it was, would understand and return the love.

• • •

All of Paduan seemed to be out in the streets of Beren to cheer as the king's army rode by with King Jerome and Palmer in the lead. The people knew in their hearts that not all would return, and yet none would have them turn away from the noble act of killing an evil wizard. A few, however, felt as Alde did, that they should not join themselves to the Corigans, but they were too few to subdue the festive mood.

The army would ride west and meet the other armies of Paduan in Alexandria on the King's Highway. They would then continue west to Zopel and join with Fel-hoen, who would lead them into the Amil Mountains. Jerome and Palmer hoped to enter the Amil Mountains without the knowledge of Crotalus, though both doubted this could actually be done. They wanted to press hard around the castle first and kill as many of Crotalus' army as possible before luring the wizard himself out of the mountains and away from his spells.

Palmer scanned the masses for Ivy's face and spotted it easily. He thought it would be hard to miss, for hers was easily the most beautiful face in the crowd. Indeed, the rest seemed plain beside her. Her eyes were a little red, but her countenance was smiling and he smiled back at her, for once regretting the fact that he had to leave. She put her right fist over her heart and he did the same, the traditional war signal between lovers that although they were apart their hearts would be together as one.

As he touched his chest, he remembered what lay beneath the armor. Ivy had made a shirt for him to wear to war, a royal blue shirt of soft silk. As other women gave their men treasures to take with them into battle, she had woven this with all her love. Tears stung his eyes for a moment. He did not know if he would ever return, and though this thought had often occurred to him before battle, it had never been as repugnant a thought as it was now.

He thought of Falcon already traveling north to the Forgotten City and Rafaela. Although he was happy for his friend, he missed him and wanted him by his side. He could not remember ever riding into battle without Falcon beside him. Palmer had no doubts about his ability to lead the armies, but if he had had a choice, he would have chosen Falcon.

Redeemer God, he whispered in his heart, *let us be victorious. Let us return in safety.*

"You look like a man who has just prayed for protection," Jerome said above the roar of the crowds, beginning to thin as they left the center of Beren.

"I have. I have asked for victory and safe return."

Jerome thought of Alexandria and her tears at his parting. She had been fearful for him, more so than his last battle. "I too regret leaving. I hope this is the last war I shall face. I am too old for such things."

"You, my king? You never grow old, and you are as fierce now as at the last battle and the battle before that."

"Perhaps. I am a man of war, but I strongly desire peace, Palmer. Let us fight fervently and return soon."

"Agreed."

Jerome rode in silence then, not mentioning to Palmer that he felt this unlikely. A cloud had covered his soul, threatening and violent. It chilled him to the very heart, and he wondered if the chill came from his grave.

• • •

Devona and Batakis comforted Lomeli as much as they could in his distress, the fact of his wife being with the king more than he could bear. He had shut his eyes to it as long as he could, but Niccola was so brazen in her intentions that he could no longer ignore it. The pain cut him deep.

"Come with us to Beren," Devona urged. "She will not turn of her own accord from this course she is pursuing, and it only hurts you to watch it."

"I cannot leave. I must wait for Temrane. If the war goes well, Temrane could be back very soon, and I am the only one who can lead him to Cand. It is the only way he will be safe."

"You do not trust Fel-hoen then?"

"No. He bartered his son before, and he will do it again when it is convenient for him. I must stay here."

"At least let us take Caldon, so he will be safe. We are taking as many children as we can into Beren where Crotalus cannot find them. We will be taking a wagonload tonight and then return for another. We will take any adults who wish to come as well. Will you let Caldon come with us?"

"I can't. Not yet. He is the only thing I have."

"It is dangerous, Lomeli," Batakis said. "He is of an age to be taken. Jasper was taken, and he is eight. Caldon is five. It is surprising he hasn't already been taken."

"I know. Let him remain with me at least tonight. Perhaps on the next wagonload."

"Very well."

Even as they spoke, Caldon walked into the room. He had wanted to see his mother and had ventured up the stairs to where she shared quarters with the king. He had only spent a few minutes with her, but it was enough to make his eyes shine with childlike adoration. Now he skipped across the room and bounded onto his father's lap.

Batakis and Devona rose to go. They had almost enough for one wagonload of children and wanted to get onto the King's Highway before it got dark. "We will be back, Lomeli. Please consider what we have said," Batakis entreated.

Devona bent down and kissed his cheek. "I shall pray constantly for Niccola. She is not so far gone that the Redeemer God cannot restore her."

Lomeli nodded and watched them go. He wished he could believe in a Redeemer God. His own god, Anok, was a thundering god, dwelling in places that other gods forbade. He was remote and indifferent to the toils of his people. "I would like to believe," he half-whispered. "But how can I be sure that this Redeemer God is different from any of the others?"

Caldon looked at him strangely. He didn't understand this talk from his father, but loved him just the same. "When is Mama coming home for good?"

"I don't know, Caldon. I wish I knew."

"She said she was going to give me a present in a few days. She showed it to me. It's a dagger that has jewels all over the hilt."

"What kind of jewels?"

"Reds and greens mostly, but a few are clear."

"Then it is not a dagger that belongs to her. She could not afford it. It probably belongs to King Fel-hoen."

"She said it was hers, but she was going to give it to me. I liked it. It was pretty."

Lomeli could never remember Niccola giving Caldon a present or showing any particular affection for him at all. Perhaps she was changing. "Maybe she will be home soon," he said hopefully.

"We love her a lot, don't we?"

Lomeli felt the lump in his throat, and he involuntarily looked upward to where Niccola even now was with King Fel-hoen. "Yes, Caldon, we do."

• • •

Niccola watched as Fel-hoen paced the room, his strides long and brisk. "What is troubling you?"

"Jerome's armies left this morning for Zopel."

"There is nothing wrong in that, Fel-hoen."

"No, but in a few days time we shall be engaging Crotalus' army in battle, and I know very little of my enemy. I do not wish to lose my kingdom, Niccola."

She smiled enigmatically. "You have lost it already, my love."

"What are you talking about?" He stopped pacing to face her.

"This kingdom was never yours. You are now king over soulless bodies. You have taken my advice simply because you could think of nothing yourself. It is not surprising. When you took the throne sixteen years ago, you had no royal upbringing. Your father was a priest."

Fel-hoen's ire was raising with her impudence, but he couldn't help but listen to her. She held him captive with her eyes. He wondered if she were a witch. "What are you leading up to, Niccola?"

She stood and walked over to him. She put her arm around him, caressing his neck with her hand, while with the other hand she pulled a long dagger with jewels on the hilt from the folds of her dress. With a practiced upward thrust, she slipped the blade between his ribs and punctured a lung.

"I am Princess Niccola, daughter of Lyca, true King of Corigo."

Fel-hoen's life began rushing out of him, but even in his panic he glanced at the door, wondering if he could escape this mad woman.

"You cannot escape," she said, reading his thoughts. "There is a guard outside the door who will not allow you. I bribed him. He is my first subject, Fel-hoen." She jabbed again with the dagger, impaling his heart. "Your kingdom is lost. I reclaim it now in the name of King Lyca."

Niccola pulled the dagger from Fel-hoen's body and stepped back as he slumped onto the floor. His hand reached out to her, imploring her for mercy, but it was only for a moment. She watched as life passed from him. He died much the same way he had lived, with no thought for anyone but himself and his kingdom, a greedy man dying a coward's death. There would be no great battles fought for him, no hero's songs; misery was his only legacy.

She swung to the wardrobe in the corner of the room. It was locked, but that would be no problem for her. She found the keys behind a secret panel in the wardrobe and began experimenting with the locks. She had heard Fel-hoen open the secret drawer once before and had listened carefully. Now she put all her concentration into recreating those sounds.

At last the drawer slid open. She passed over the jewels and crowns, searching for the orb. She found it in a special black velvet pouch. She removed the signet ring from her dress and placed it inside.

She held the pouch before her eyes. Here, contained in this bag, was the kingdom. Whoever held this pouch ruled, and now it was hers.

She went to the washbasin, rinsed the dagger, and placed it in the drawer before closing it, listening as all the locks engaged. She crossed the room and called for the guard.

"Someone has murdered King Fel-hoen," she said sarcastically. "Call for the queen . . . Bring her in here."

He nodded, snapped to attention, and left the room. He returned in a moment with Queen Kenda. She uttered a cry at the sight of her husband and dropped down beside him. Lifting her head toward the heavens, she wailed for the gods to take her life.

"Who has done this?" she asked.

"My lady, Anson the blacksmith was the only one in here," the guard lied. "When I heard my king cry out, I rushed in and Anson was escaping out the window."

"Find him and throw him in the dungeon. He shall not escape justice."

"Just a moment, guard," Niccola said. She held up the pouch for Kenda to see and opened it, revealing the orb and signet ring. "These are now mine. Strip this woman of her finery and royal clothes, and throw her in the dungeon along with Anson. Then come back and take care of the king's body. I am now the queen."

"Yes, Queen Niccola," he replied and grabbed Kenda by the arm, leading her from the room, too stunned by the turn of events to say anything.

Niccola sat on the bed that was now hers and thought about her kingdom. There would have to be a funeral for Fel-hoen, and she would have to meet with King Jerome. But before everything else was Crotalus. She could give Crotalus Falcon Jaqeth's location, and while he hunted for Falcon she and her army would slaughter his army. Alone, he would not be nearly so powerful. No doubt after killing Falcon, he would be in an expansive mood, careless. It would be little trouble for a beautiful woman such as herself to enchant and kill him.

She went to the wardrobe and again opened the secret drawer. She found the crystal ball, life pulsating within it, and withdrew it from the drawer.

Sitting in a chair by the window, she stroked the ball and called Crotalus' name. Within minutes a form rose from the ball, substantial and yet not wholly real. She wanted to shudder at the grotesque apparition but held herself in check. She dared not show any weakness.

"You have placed your life in grave danger by calling me," he said. "I have not given you authority to do so."

"I have not asked for your authority. Your servant Fel-hoen lies dead, killed by my hand. I am now the ruling power in Corigo. I have information about your enemy Falcon Jaqeth which may be useful to you."

She knew she had touched his weakness. His eyes narrowed, and he licked his lips. His greed for Falcon's death was evident to all. "Don't imagine that any information you can give me will mean I shall stop stealing the souls of your subjects. I still want your kingdom."

"I realize that, but getting rid of Falcon will also be to my benefit; he is no friend of mine. My army still intends to war against you."

Crotalus laughed. "I like you. You have fire and daring. It shall be a pleasure doing battle with you. Perhaps when my army defeats yours and I have taken control of the kingdom, I shall spare you and make you a sorceress."

"And perhaps when I defeat you, I shall make you into a plaything for my son."

Crotalus laughed. "No one has ever talked to me so. I rather enjoy your sparring tongue. Give me your information."

"Do you know of the Forgotten City?"

"No. Tell me of it."

"The only thing you need to know is that Falcon Jaqeth rides there alone. I know not what he seeks. It is located in the Wastelands, in the far northeastern corner. He travels north from Beren, riding up the coast."

"And you are certain he is alone?"

"Yes." Niccola could see the lust in his eyes, and for a moment felt pity for the stranger Falcon Jaqeth.

The image of Crotalus sank down into the ball, and just before he disappeared he said, "We shall meet soon, queen. I shall enjoy it." The ball went dark.

Niccola picked up the crystal and smashed it against the wall, slivers of glass covering the rug. She no longer had any need of it and did not want Crotalus to have access to her. The true war had begun.

Twenty-Four

"You love the old man a lot, don't you?" Temrane asked McNyre as they crossed into the Wastelands. It would be almost impossible for their enemies to track the horses here, so they had slowed their pace a little.

"Very much."

"How long have you been friends?"

"A couple of weeks. Why?"

"You seem to have known each other much longer than that."

McNyre studied the boy a moment. He was unusually talkative. Temrane had said few words to McNyre as they fled across Corigo, and now came this talk of Duncan. "I feel as though I have known him all my life. He has touched me in the deep places, as my people say. He is a peculiar man, Duncan is. From the first time I saw him, I felt he was different. I loved him almost right from the start because of his honesty and innocence, and yet it is immensely uncomfortable to be around him sometimes."

"Why?"

"Because my dark side is more exposed when I am with him."

"I haven't noticed a dark side."

"Ah, but it is there. I am the only one who knows of its existence, and I ignore it most of the time. But when I am with Duncan, I am ashamed of who I am. Ye would think that I would not want to be with him because of this, but his presence comforts me as well."

"What have you done that is so terrible?"

McNyre rode silently for a time and then at last said, "I cannot tell ye. The pain is too great. Perhaps sometime, but not now. Why so many questions about Duncan?"

"I miss him," the lad said simply.

McNyre did not reply. He also missed Duncan – more than he cared to admit. He could not explain the feelings in him toward the man. All he knew was that something in Duncan made him a better person, that he had left his home to wander with this odd man and now roamed the Wastelands with a boy because of Duncan, and yet Duncan was now gone. McNyre couldn't understand why he did not leave Temrane by the side of the road and go home. Two months ago that was exactly what he would have done.

Love. He loved Duncan, but it was more than that. Duncan loved him, and Duncan loved Temrane. McNyre felt himself extremely attracted to Duncan's God. He did not often question Duncan about this Redeemer God, but he saw Duncan's God in all his actions. He had none of the false piety of the priests, demanded no sacrifices. Duncan lived his life fully for the One he called Menon, and McNyre could not help but respond.

As they rode into a sky that was quickly darkening, howls could be heard in the distance. "What is that?" Temrane at last asked, unable to bear any longer the tension the sounds created in him.

"Wolves."

"I thought there were no wild animals in the Wastelands. Duncan told us those were just stories." His voice edged with panic.

"Well, I see two possibilities. Perhaps we are not yet far enough into the Wastelands to escape the animals. We still be close to civilization. Another possibility is that Crotalus suspects our destination and has sent them."

"He has power over animals?"

"He has domination over men, and some say he has power over the dead. Why should he not have power over the animals as well?"

"Do you think these wolves are from him?"

McNyre stopped his horse and waited as Temrane pulled beside him. "I don't think it makes much difference where they come from. They are headed toward us, and wolves be wolves whoever sent them."

"What are we going to do?"

The howls grew louder as the wolves moved in closer. "I don't know. There is no shelter, no cliffs, no mountains. We could turn and run the other way, but I have no doubt that the wolves can outrun the horses." McNyre looked into Temrane's eyes and saw that he had frightened the boy badly. The lad's eyes were as round as moons and his face as pale. McNyre smiled. "I've been in worse spots."

"Then you can get us out of this?"

"I don't know if I can, but we are going to give them a fight. I ran from danger once, lad, and vowed never to do it again. We fight them head-on."

"What do we do?"

McNyre removed his crossbow, loaded it carefully, then adjusted the quiver on his back in order to grab the arrows easily. He tossed an arrow to Temrane, who caught it midair. "Keep your horse as close behind mine as possible without tripping them up. I will kill as many as I can with my bow as they attack. However, some of them are going to get through and attack you. Use the arrow to stab at them."

He stopped and listened. The howls were loud, and McNyre could tell that these animals had smelled them. "Don't strike at the bodies because if ye hit bone the arrow will break. Stab at the soft parts—the open mouth, the throat, the nose, the eyes are best. If ye wound him bad enough, he will leave. Give him a mere flesh wound and he'll kill ye. When we break free, we'll turn north and go deep into the Wastelands. They will not follow where they do not smell water. The most important thing is, stay close. Can ye follow all that?"

Temrane was kept from replying by the sight of a pack of gray and brown wolves bearing down on them from the east. He tried to count them and could not, but he judged their number to be about fifteen. They loped toward them, and McNyre spurred his horse. Temrane did the same, staying close behind McNyre.

He watched as McNyre rapid-fired three arrows, killing three wolves. A fourth arrow was loaded and sped toward another heart, stilling it. Temrane began to feel that they might get away due to McNyre's superior skill with a bow. But even as he thought it, a wolf broke from the pack and came at him. As the wolf leapt high to knock him from the saddle, Temrane grasped the arrow and thrust it into the wolf's face. The wolf yelped in anguish and rage, but it did not rise again. Temrane saw he had stabbed it in the eye.

McNyre fought as fiercely as he could, spearing many of the animals, kicking others, punching one with his fist until his hand was bloody and the wolf vanquished. But he could not get them all, and more than he would have liked escaped his arrows and attacked Temrane. He could hear Temrane close behind him—could hear his cries of victory when a wolf was killed, his wails of fear when yet another savage beast attacked.

McNyre saw only five wolves left and pulled another arrow from his quiver. He shot one, but the remaining four divided and passed his horse to attack the horse behind him. He turned quickly with a shout and saw the horse with Temrane still on his back go down in a flurry of gray fur and bloody teeth. He launched two arrows into the fray, leapt from his own mount, and quickly pulled the two dead wolves away so he could see the others. One wolf turned from the horse he was mauling and jumped on McNyre. As man and beast rolled on the sandy ground, McNyre grabbed it around the throat, forcing the gnashing teeth away from his face. He remained like that a moment, unable to do anything more than hold the wolf at bay. The brute struggled, scratching McNyre's stomach with strong back claws. With every bit of strength he could muster, McNyre twisted the wolf's head until he finally heard a snap.

He heard Temrane's cries, muffled by the remaining wolf's growls, and he quickly loaded his bow for one final shot. The arrow whizzed through the air, burrowing itself deep in the wolf's neck. Silence then cut through the air like a sword, and McNyre realized how much noise there had been with the wolves' snarls, the horses' frightened neighing, and his own shouts.

He strode to the horse and pulled Temrane from it. They both sank to the ground and clung to each other in exhausted silence, neither willing for the moment to let go of the feel of another human being. At last the anguished whinnies of Temrane's horse drew McNyre's attention. The wounds were many and deep. Blood poured from his neck, soaking the dry ground.

"Can you do anything for him?"

McNyre shook his head. "I can only end his suffering." Matching his words with action, he withdrew an arrow and shot it hastily into the horse. The horse whinnied one last time and then grew still. Temrane slumped to the ground, soundless tears coursing down his face.

McNyre had lived alone and friendless for most of his thirty-four years. Oh, he had many acquaintances, and some even called him their friend, but none knew the real McNyre, where he came from or his story. He had refused to let anyone in that far. Duncan had seen a slight crack in the armor and pried it open a bit. But now, seeing Temrane's dejection, the armor broke, and with all tenderness McNyre reached out and laid his hand on the boy's head.

Temrane had only needed that small touch and he was again in McNyre's arms, sobbing as though he would never stop. He needed to give someone the love that ached inside him, and at last he recognized that McNyre would not only receive the love, but return it.

McNyre wept with Temrane, tears that came from deep within, from a bitter past that refused to be forgotten. The tears cleansed much of his hostility, leaving behind a better soil. What he planted was now up to him.

He hugged Temrane to him. Inside both of them, a great wound had begun to heal.

• • •

Both woke to a chill that sank deep into their bones, biting away all thoughts of further sleep. "No matter," McNyre said, "it is time to move on anyway." The full moon radiated in the dark sky, washing the Wastelands in silver. "It is a beautiful night for riding. A little cold perhaps, but it will be good to get miles behind us while it is cool. It will be blazing hot later, with no shade and little water."

As Temrane stood, he cried out in pain and dropped back to the ground.

"What is it?" McNyre asked.

"My leg. I can hardly move it."

McNyre bent down and tore away the remaining shreds of the pant leg, exposing the limb. Temrane's leg had been seriously mauled by the wolves. Dried blood and sand clung to the torn skin, but McNyre could see more blood beginning to flow from the ragged wound. McNyre took some water and poured enough on the wound to wash away the sand.

He then ripped off the bottom of his shirt. "I've already sacrificed one shirt for Duncan, and now another for ye. If we don't get to the Forgotten City soon, I shall have no clothes."

"Can't you use the pants you just tore up?"

"No. They be full of blood and dirt. This will do." He wrapped the strips firmly about the leg. "Ye should be able to walk a bit now. We will have to stop the horse every now and again for ye to exercise the leg. Always make sure ye can feel your toes. If they become numb, tell me and I will loosen the bandage."

Temrane helped McNyre retrieve his arrows and then clean them as best they could without the aid of water. Neither was willing to use more of the precious liquid on washing. McNyre replaced the arrows in his quiver and strapped it and the bow to his back. He helped Temrane onto the horse and then mounted behind him.

McNyre, setting a comfortable but brisk pace, turned the horse north.

• • •

After five days on the horse, Temrane was sick of the riding and the constant jogging of the animal. His wound had healed well, and he did not need the frequent stops any longer to exercise his leg. But he often longed to get down and just walk. When McNyre did stop the horse for a rest, it was usually during the middle of the day when the sun was at its zenith. It was too hot to walk at those times, and Temrane spent the time napping. Their nights were spent in riding. He looked forward to a time when he could again sleep in a soft bed with covers over him and nothing to wake him except the sun's morning light.

McNyre had been quiet the last few days. Temrane didn't understand, but he wished it was not so. He wanted the closeness he had felt with McNyre after the wolves attacked, but being shy he could not tell McNyre what he wanted or why he wanted it. He could not even put a name to his need. His mind replayed the events of the wolf attack, and something McNyre had said suddenly caught his attention. He leaned forward in the saddle.

"McNyre, when we were attacked you said you had run from danger once. I can't imagine you doing that. You're about the bravest man I know."

"I'm not a hero, Temrane, but a fool. And perhaps the thing ye call bravery is simply a dream of death."

"I don't understand."

"In many ways I am just looking to die."

"Why?"

McNyre did not answer, but stopped the horse. "We will let him rest a few moments. I think we be very near the city. The desert is not so desolate here."

He left the horse by a little patch of yellowed grass, tying it to a dead branch he had driven into the ground. He walked in the direction of the city with Temrane beside him. "It is so bleak. Being here has made me want to be home more than anything else could have done."

"In Andurin?" Temrane didn't think that Andurin was such a jewel either, not compared to Zopel with its rocky heights and crashing sea.

"No. Andurin is where I live, but it is not my home. I come from a country far from here . . . across the ocean."

"I didn't know there were such places."

McNyre lowered himself to the ground in the shade of a small bush. He closed his eyes in remembrance. "It is a beautiful country. Everything is dark green except for the sky, which ranges anywhere from a very pale to a vibrant blue. Meadows are filled with purple and yellow flowers. And in the very early morning a mist lies across the land, covering everything with a sort of haze until the sun burns it away."

"Why did you leave?"

McNyre looked at Temrane, and Temrane could see the pain in his eyes. "There was danger there and I ran from it."

Questions leapt to Temrane's tongue, but he could not ask them. His heart ached at McNyre's grief, and he wasn't sure any longer that he wanted to know.

"I have told this to no one, not even Duncan. I don't know why I am telling ye, except that maybe it is time for it to be told. I am a slave."

"You mean you are a servant to the king?"

"Something like that, except a slave cannot leave the king's service if he chooses and a servant can. A slave is told what to wear, what to eat and when, where to live, and whom to love. If ye rebel even a little, ye are beat. If the masters be bored, ye are beat. I watched many of my people die because they wanted to do something as simple as read a book and were not allowed.

"At a very young age a wife was chosen for me, and when I turned eighteen she was given to me. I was lucky. She was everything I would have chosen myself, and within a few years I loved her deeply. She became pregnant and bore me twins, a girl and a boy.

"At this time the emperor's wife took a liking to me, I don't know why. She called me often to her rooms, and it became obvious that she was trying to seduce me. I let her. Not because I wanted her or because she was beautiful, but because I saw in this a way I could escape. I gained her trust, and then one night I rode out. I have never returned."

Temrane could see the tears in McNyre's eyes, but he had to know and so asked, "Why is that so bad? You didn't kill her, and you could have. You just wanted to be free."

"I left my wife and children without any means of support. They were perhaps killed for my disobedience. I abandoned the only ones I ever loved to save myself. That price alone would have been too high, but there is something else. My father was a queer old man. He did not pay homage to the gods of the kingdom. He worshiped a god he called the Most High. The emperor was a cruel man who did not hesitate to kill traitors, and my father was put to death as an insurrectionist. I never saw any point in angering the emperor. I, after all, did not worship my father's god. I worshiped no god.

"Although Duncan calls his God Menon or the Redeemer and my father called his Most High, I know now that they worship the same God. This God has placed a call on my life. I knew it even back then."

"What was the call?" Temrane asked, fascinated.

"To free my people."

Temrane sat stunned. No wonder McNyre at times wished to die. He had not only betrayed a wife and two children, but an entire nation of people.

"I thought I had escaped, but I have not. Apparently this God's reach is very far. There is nowhere I can run that He cannot find me. And I now see that my only happiness will be in fulfilling His call on my life."

McNyre stood and walked back to the horse. "It is time to leave. I believe we shall reach the Forgotten City by morning. It may be difficult to find Rafaela."

Temrane, feeling anguish and love for McNyre, hugged him, wanting to say something, but being unable to speak.

McNyre hugged him back, grateful for his love, amazed that it should come to one such as he. "I am tired of running, Temrane. If the Most High Redeemer God will see me through this with you, and I live, I shall return to my homeland. I shall free my people."

Twenty-Five

Rafaela stood in the Home of Weaponry in front of the gold sword. She did not wear one of her customary dresses, but rather pants of soft white wool. The tunic she wore was the deep purple of royalty and was belted with more white wool. She had made this outfit years before and considered it her warrior's garb. She would not need armor, for when the time came she believed it would be to the death, and she was content with that knowledge. Her attire, and her practicing with the sword, were the only secrets she kept from Duncan.

She now lifted the glass lid of the sword case and removed the sword with an air of ownership. She swung it a few times in the air, liking the feel of it in her hands. It did not have a separate identity, but was simply an extension of her.

There had been a time, many years before, when war appeared glorious to her. It seemed a thrilling and noble thing. How she longed to be a man in those days! She had grown dissatisfied with tailoring and wished she could fight in a war.

She discussed this often with Duncan and came to realize that her romanticizing was due to the fact that she was very much in love with Falcon. She did not want to be a mere wife. That might have been good enough for other women, but not for her. She wanted to be a companion, a comrade in arms, perhaps the first woman knight.

She saw now that there was no such thing as a mere wife. Or a mere tailor, a mere knight, a mere parent. Life was too complicated for that. The Redeemer God had chosen to give each person an endless number of combinations of people they could be, and often were. Her duty to the Redeemer was to be the best she could be at whatever she chose.

In her quest to learn of the knighthood, and Duncan's desire to show her the truth of war, she read as many books as the Forgotten City contained on the final war of Menon's people. In reality it was not a war, for only one side fought. The Menontes were slaughtered by the thousands as they dwelt in the city.

The massacre had occurred during a supposed time of peace. The Menontes lived in a city whose name was wiped out along with the occupants. The neighboring cities tolerated their worship as long as they did not speak of their God. The Menontes could not accept that, and spoke often and eloquently of the love of the Redeemer God and His sole authority over humanity. Many people from those cities accepted this love and began to worship Menon as well.

The government feared the Menontes and their single-minded worship. They could not afford to have their own gods overthrown or to risk their emperors losing their influence. One night, while the Menontes glorified their strange God, enemies fell on the worshipers and butchered them. Some tried to escape, but were quickly captured. These were handed over to prison officials, who were given the job of extracting information in any way possible. After information was received, the captives were turned over to the executioner whose duty it was to "reform" the criminals. They were told to worship only the emperor and the gods he raised. One at a time, the captives were commanded to renounce Menon. If the prisoner refused, and most of them did, the executioner labeled him a lawbreaker, laid the offender's head upon a block, took up his heavy, golden sword, and brought it down upon his neck.

Blood flowed freely in those days, and only a few escaped and went into hiding. Duncan's great-great-grandfather had been one. The sword had been found when the ravagers left, and he took it, cleaned it, and cared for it. In his eyes this pagan sword had become a thing of beauty, for the martyrs' blood upon it had made it holy.

Rafaela saw the hideousness of the massacre, and of war in general. But her imagination had been sparked also. Would she have held strong or renounced? That question had plagued her for days. She longed to do something great for Menon, something worthy of His name.

She trained with the sword daily, readying herself for a battle she knew she must someday fight. The Home of Weaponry was too crowded a place for her to train, so she went each day to the Great Ballroom in the main castle. The walls were made of mirrors, and light filled every corner. The marble was cool on her feet.

She stood now in front of the mirror, thrusting, jabbing, parrying imaginary blows. She carried no shield. The sword was shield enough. As she swung the sword, she caught a movement in the mirror.

She watched warily as a man and young boy approached slowly, unaware of her gaze. She waited until they were in the middle of the large room and then whirled around, jumping in the air and landing a few feet in front of them. Another leap put her behind them, so she was between them and the door. She held the sword in front of her.

"Who are you?" she demanded.

The boy's eyes were wide, and the man for a moment was speechless. "Are ye Rafaela?" he asked at last, wishing the door was behind him and wondering how he could get to it.

Her eyes narrowed, and she pressed the sword closer to the man's throat. "State your name and your business."

"I am McNyre of Andurin, and this is Prince Temrane of Corigo. I have a message for Rafaela from Duncan."

Temrane watched the woman's face and saw no change in it. He could not remember a message from Duncan, but he was not going to argue with McNyre when a woman brandished a sword against them. She was wonderful though, he thought. Her hair was short and curly, something he had never seen on a woman. Although he had seen prettier women, noble women, this one carried herself as though she were different. She was not royal, for royal women did not wield swords, but neither was she earthly. Something in her eyes spoke of a painful immortality, as though she had tasted death and survived. He remembered Crotalus' description of her as a goddess and knew without a doubt that the woman in front of him was Rafaela, the wizard's obsession.

"I am Rafaela. Give me the message," she said without lowering the sword.

Before McNyre could speak, Temrane fell to the ground at her feet. "Please, goddess, do not slay us. We are your servants."

Rafaela faltered a moment and then lowered the sword. McNyre's shoulders sagged in relief. Rafaela laid the sword on the ground and bent down by Temrane. "Do not bow to me," she said softly, touching his hand and urging him to rise. "I am not a goddess. I am a worshiper of the Redeemer God."

"He said that if there were goddesses you would be one. He told me to worship you."

"Who told you that?" she asked quietly.

"The wizard Crotalus."

McNyre saw the sudden tears in her eyes, the paleness of her skin, her lips compressed in pain as though she had been pierced with her own sword point. "My lady, can I get ye anything?"

She appeared not to have heard him. "The temptations are still so strong," she murmured.

McNyre was about to question her again when she abruptly turned, picked up the gold sword, and walked toward the door. "Come," she said. "You have obviously traveled very far and are no doubt hungry. I shall prepare you a meal, and you shall tell me of Duncan."

Temrane cheered at the mention of a meal and followed Rafaela from the room. McNyre also followed, but he had seen much in the past few minutes upon which to ponder. Rafaela was nothing like the woman he had imagined. He remembered her with the sword in her hands, and he had glimpsed rivers of strength within her. Yet, she trembled at the name of Crotalus. She had been hard and unyielding at first, and then as tender as a mother with Temrane. And at one time she had been the lover of Crotalus. That was reason enough to be wary.

He listened carefully as Rafaela told Temrane about the city. Temrane had thought that Zopel was the most splendid city in the world, but his eyes were round with amazement as the wonders of the Forgotten City were laid out before him. As they reached the Home of Weaponry where Rafaela returned the sword, Temrane ran ahead, fingering this shield, longing after that sword.

Rafaela turned to McNyre and smiled at him. "I can tell that you do not trust me. No matter. I'm not sure how much you can trust me or how much I can trust you."

"I know I can be trusted, my lady. And though I be cautious, I have no reason not to trust. Duncan trusts ye, and I trust him with my life."

"Duncan is the finest man I have ever known. Please forgive me, McNyre. I have not been with anyone but Duncan in fifteen years. I have forgotten social courtesies and things such as polite conversation. We have much to discuss."

"There is much I wish to tell ye."

"The tour of the city will wait then. Let's leave Temrane here – he seems happy. He can join us when the meal is ready."

• • •

Crotalus sat quietly at his desk, his posture belying the tension that mounted within. Falcon Jaqeth was even now riding to the Forgotten City. The wizard had sketched maps according to Niccola's directions and had judged what Falcon's course would be. He would no doubt follow the eastern sea coast in order to gather supplies for himself in Chantey and Keffram. If he left three days ago on horseback, Crotalus judged Falcon would be in Keffram within another day.

He contemplated Falcon's reasons for traveling to the Wastelands and a place called the Forgotten City. Falcon was a warrior—why then did he not fight in the war? The answer had to lie with Rafaela. Only she could keep him from battle. Niccola did not mention the boy being with Falcon, but perhaps Temrane had told Falcon of Crotalus' dream of restoring life to Rafaela's body. Maybe Temrane and Falcon had thought of a way to revitalize her flesh. That would mean Rafaela was in the Forgotten City.

He picked up a bottle from his desk. It was light for its size, very thin and fragile, cut from crystals, yet big enough that he needed two hands to hold it comfortably. The pieces were beginning to fall together in his mind. He could dispose of Falcon, punish Temrane, and find Rafaela all by following Falcon into the Wastelands. He didn't want to attack Falcon before reaching the Wastelands, for then he would still be in Paduan with armies and allies accessible to him. But in the Wastelands he would be cut off from everyone. And if Crotalus could reach Falcon before he came to the Forgotten City, no one could be summoned to come to the knight's aid.

Crotalus looked up as his captain knocked on the door and walked in. He stood unswerving before his master.

"What do you want?"

"Forgive the intrusion, master. There is a lord from Corigo who desires to speak with you. His name is Soaje."

The final piece of the puzzle fell into place in Crotalus' mind, and the plan became as clear as the bottle in his hands. "Send him to me, and see that we are not disturbed."

Shallis nodded curtly and removed himself from the room.

Crotalus did not need his many years of wizardry to tell him the type of person Soaje was. He could read his personality the moment he walked in. His swagger spoke of fear, the close eyes of greed. This was a man who would do anything to further his own interests. His presence in this room meant betrayal.

"I believe you are the Lord of Andurin. Am I correct?"

"You are."

"Your king is about to do battle with me. Do you betray him?"

"I do not believe that he has Andurin's best interests in mind."

"And you think I do?"

"I think you can be persuaded."

Crotalus laughed, feeling in an expansive mood now that Falcon's downfall was near. "Persuade me."

"I have no doubt that you will win this war. All I ask is that Andurin be left alone and under my lordship. Lord Tegmen of Derrich asks the same."

"And what do I receive in turn?"

"Two things. First, our loyalty. We will fight alongside your army."

"Your loyalty means little to me when I see how loyal you are to Fel-hoen. But no matter . . . You said two things. Name the other."

"I know your greatest enemy . . . I have had dealings with him in the past. I can place him in your hands."

"Everyone is so anxious lately to put him into my hands. He seems to have become a great bargaining tool."

"Who else has offered him?"

"Lord Soaje, you have made your offer too late. I already know where he is and what his business is. In fact, I know some things about Corigo that you perchance have not yet heard."

Soaje kept his face stony, although his heart constricted. Things had not gone as he had planned. "Tell me."

"Fel-hoen is dead, murdered by a woman who calls herself Niccola. Do you know her?"

"Yes. She killed Fel-hoen's advisor and took his place. I am not surprised that she has killed Fel-hoen. Has she taken over as queen?"

"Of course. And she still intends to lead the army into war against me. I sense she has a great deal more authority and courage than Fel-hoen. The only thing I regret is that I was not there to see his death."

Soaje did not reply. He saw the lust in Crotalus' eyes and was terrified at it. His own destiny was clearly controlled by Crotalus.

Crotalus sensed the surrender of Soaje's will, and his thin lips smiled as his glance grew harder. "You have offered me nothing that I can use. I could kill you right now and feed you to my men to make them stronger." He watched as Soaje's eyes bulged. "But . . . I am in a generous mood today. I shall deal with you on my terms."

"What are your terms?"

"I want two people. The first you will bring me this very day. I want a knight. Not a very high knight, nor very intelligent. Just an ordinary soldier. You will bring him to me and then release him forever into my care." He fingered the glass jar lovingly, its part soon to be played.

"It shall be done. Who is the other?"

"Niccola. You, Tegmen, and your armies shall remain in Andurin and fight along with my army, but your priority—and Tegmen's, because if you fail I shall kill you both—is to capture Niccola. She has great power—I can sense it, and I desire to feed on her power."

Soaje shuddered as Crotalus spoke the word "feed." His voice had been cold and animalistic, a consuming greed that stopped at nothing. Soaje did not want to deal any longer with Crotalus. He felt he had underestimated the wizard, but he could not extricate himself now.

"It shall be done."

• • •

Duncan no longer felt safe in Amick with the old woman. She had cared for him faithfully, and he felt himself growing stronger. But many times lately she had frowned when she saw him, a look in her eyes that measured his worth. He knew she was poor and wondered if she was thinking of trading him to someone for food. It was not unlikely. So with money McNyre had left him, he bought a horse and headed south.

At first he had wanted to ride straight for the Forgotten City, but the desire to go south was so intense he could not deny it. His plan now was to ride into Zopel, find Cand-hoen, and take him to the Forgotten City. Temrane would be overjoyed, and Duncan looked forward to giving him that happiness.

Thoughts of Temrane and McNyre flooded his mind, and loneliness filled his soul. They had probably reached the Forgotten City by now and were with Rafaela. He longed to be with them, to feel their close companionship, to hear their voices.

Ah, Menon, he thought, *I will not be satisfied with solitude again.* But it was not a sad thought. The joy of humanity had filled him. There would still be times of solitude, as there must be to commune with Menon, but how better to reach the people than to live among them, breathe with them, to celebrate, suffer, and die with them.

His ancestors were not wrong in separating themselves from the world, and for years he had not been wrong. There had been a glorious heritage to uphold. It was important for someone to know of the Menontes and the people they had been, of their city and their destruction. It was vital that the rapturous music, the great literature and books of learning, the works of art and architecture all be preserved and studied.

But that period had passed. He had studied all his life, but now it was time to pass that knowledge on to others. He recognized that knowledge without a pupil is like water poured on the ground. He was spilling vast quantities of life itself onto a rocky and barren soil when it begged to be absorbed by others. Although McNyre had tried to hide it from him, Duncan could see the thirst in McNyre. Temrane needed instruction about a multitude of things. Duncan hoped that when he found Cand-hoen he would find a questing and willing mind.

He liked the prospects of the future and was anxious to be started. It was time to teach.

• • •

Gilreth shook with fear. The stories he had heard had not truly prepared him for the awfulness of the wizard in front of him. The hair that hung to Crotalus' waist looked like vipers, and the scaly skin and hooded eyes added to the image. Gilreth was convinced the sorcerer could tear him apart with a simple word.

"Do you fear me?" Crotalus asked.

Gilreth was unsure of his answer. He wanted desperately to know what Crotalus wanted. That would determine his every reply. "You are deserving of my fear, my lord."

"I see you have some intelligence." Crotalus walked behind Gilreth and placed his hands on Gilreth's face. His long nails and powerful fingers caressed his cheeks. "You have no need of fear, Gilreth. I do not intend to harm you. Do you see that jar on the desk?"

"Yes . . . It is very beautiful."

"Yes, it is. I am going to take your soul for a brief period of time and put it in that jar. This will not hurt you—unless, of course, something happens to the bottle. But don't worry. I will take very good care of it."

"What will happen to my body?"

"It will stay right here, in my protection."

"I'd rather not."

"Well, Gilreth, you don't have a choice. It is what I will to be done, and my will is sovereign. But perhaps when I release you again, you shall serve me in other areas. I like you."

Gilreth forced himself into stillness, ignoring the hands on his face.

"Therlig eb ereth tel, therlig eb ereth tel, therlig eb ereth tel."

As Crotalus repeated the words of the spell, Gilreth could feel his strength sapping away, his essence flowing out of him. With the last bit of strength he had he opened his eyes and saw a gray vapor pouring into the jar. He followed the trail and saw that it came from his chest. He thought his life was ending.

Crotalus put the stopper in the jar and swirled it around, watching the gases merge together and separate. It was not all gray; there were a few streaks of black and a few white, but most of it was ashen, dingy, neutral gray.

"Here it is, Falcon," he whispered. "Here is your downfall."

Twenty-Six

The two remaining lords of Corigo, the lords of Paduan, King Jerome, Palmer, and Malcolm, the king's knight of Corigo, sat at the council table in the Great Hall awaiting King Fel-hoen. Rumors had filled everyone's ears about whether the king lived or not. No one knew for sure. Some had seen him, others denied it, still others supposed that Crotalus had destroyed him in the most gruesome manner possible.

Niccola put an end to all rumors when she swept into the room. All eyes were upon her, and she gloried in their stares. She wore a burgundy dress of rich velvet. Strings of pearls adorned her waist and neckline; diamonds glittered on her ears. Her hair spilled softly onto her shoulders and reflected all the lights of the Great Hall. No one could miss the thin circlet of gold resting on her head. Each man felt that she was easily the most stunning woman he had ever seen and that she wore the mark of nobility well.

"Gentlemen, thank you for your patience. There is much that needs to be decided upon. First of all, King Jerome, lords and knights of

Paduan, I welcome you to Zopel. I wish it were in happier circumstances.

"I am sure that you have heard many rumors. I wish to put them to rest. Several weeks ago King Fel-hoen made me his advisor upon the death of Solon. In trust, he gave me his signet ring. Last week he was murdered by a townsman who believed he was freeing his people from a curse. He is now in the dungeon. The signet ring gave me the right to the orb and to rule Corigo. Are there any questions concerning this?"

Lords Kies and Pelaro remained silent. Both wished to retain their lordships no matter who sat on the throne. Jerome, although he suspected much, could not say anything against her. "What of the war?" he asked.

"It was Fel-hoen's wish to go to war. Crotalus needs to be stopped. Therefore, come morning, I shall ride out of Zopel with Malcolm."

"You can't do that!" Malcolm said.

"Why not?"

"Because you are a woman! Women don't belong in battles!"

"I can ride and am as skilled as any man with a sword. I have also learned to use my sword from the back of a horse. It is vital for the townspeople to see me as their leader."

"I agree with Malcolm," Pelaro said. "It would weaken the troops to have a woman leading them. They wouldn't stand for it."

"But I am the queen! If they want to remain in Corigo, they're going to have to stand for it!"

"Queen Niccola, may I say something?" Jerome's was the voice of calm.

"Speak."

"In the early wars of my country, women fought alongside men and it didn't weaken either of them." Jerome glanced around the table at each of his men and at the lords of Corigo. "However" — he looked at Niccola — "I agree that you should not fight this battle. You have said that you are the queen, and it is true. The king or queen is the backbone of the country; your strength is their life. But you have no advisor and no children able to take the throne if you should be killed. It is inexcusable to leave a country without a ruler."

Niccola looked at him in surprise. It had been a long, long time since anyone had spoken to her with such deference. "Thank you, King Jerome. Your point is well taken, and perhaps I can earn the respect of my people if I remain here. If you have no objections, Malcolm shall lead my army."

"I have no objection."

"May I make a suggestion, Your Highness?" Palmer said.

"Yes?"

"I gather that you have great military knowledge, and although I agree with my king that you should remain in Zopel, I also hate to waste your wisdom. I suggest that there be continuous messages sent between our camps and Zopel. We shall detail for you our plans. Of course, they will be put into action by the time you receive them, but you would be able to discuss the next steps and share your ideas with us."

"I like the idea. Thank you, Palmer. I will pick the swiftest messengers I have. There are a few other items we need to discuss. The first may be the terms of the agreement between yourself and King Fel-hoen. I was the one who advised him to seek your aid. In regards to the marriage of Prince Kreith and Princess Merry, I want to say that it will take place when the war is over, just as it would have had Fel-hoen lived. Although Merry no longer has any legal right to the throne, she also has no one to care for her. I have placed her in my own care, and she will be as my daughter."

"That is most generous of you, Queen Niccola. I again accept these terms for my son and my country," Jerome said.

"There is a more serious thing to discuss, and that is the treachery of two of my subjects. The Lords Tegmen and Soaje have abandoned us and have apparently joined with Crotalus. Their cities, Derrich and Andurin, cannot be expected to join us. They will follow their lords with few exceptions."

"How did you learn of their disloyalty?" Palmer asked.

"Since taking the throne I have had scouts in the mountains watching Crotalus' castle. One of my scouts saw Soaje enter the castle alone and spend about an hour there. He left, and several hours later his army and that of Tegmen entered the castle. They have not returned."

"May I offer a suggestion then, Your Highness?"

"Of course."

"Zopel is too far away from Crotalus' castle to be a good base. I suggest we go into Derrich and then Andurin and take them by force. The people have no protection if their lords and armies are with Crotalus. The ones that swear fealty to you will live. The others will be put in the dungeons. This will open these cities to us for our use, putting us that much closer to Crotalus."

Malcolm nodded. "And the destruction of their cities would almost certainly lure Tegmen and Soaje out of the mountains."

"I can see no flaw in this. King Jerome?"

"I think it an excellent plan. It would help us swell our ranks before fighting Crotalus as well. I suggest that we separate the armies, half going to Andurin and half to Derrich."

"Agreed. Palmer will lead Kies, Diones, McIlree, and Thomas into Andurin. Malcolm will lead Pelaro, Sipple, and Ulster into Derrich."

Niccola watched as each man around the table nodded his agreement. She had done well. "Let us then end the council."

• • •

Cand stood before Hoen. He knew he had the power in his hands to push the image over and destroy Hoen, but he could not make the decision.

He heard a roar behind him and turned. The lion was leaping through the hills, growing larger. As he cleared the last grassy hill, he sprang in the air above Cand's head and landed on Hoen, knocking him to the ground. The lion's hot breath touched Hoen, and Hoen crumbled into dust.

The lion turned to go, but Cand could not bear it. "Wait!" he shouted. The lion stopped, but Cand could not speak. The lion roared, and the roar became words. "You are Mine now. I have sought you from the very beginning. Come with Me."

Cand took a step toward the lion and then another. The lion's massiveness terrified Cand. He was more the size of a horse with his head slightly above Cand's. His teeth were sharp and white, his claws mighty. Without knowing why, he climbed on the back of the lion, clinging to the black, silky mane. The lion leapt through the air and Cand saw the hills becoming flatter, the meadows rushing by, the Conmia Rivers flowing endlessly to the sea. The lion landed at the spot just between the borders of Corigo and Paduan where the Conmia split in two, his feet landing gently between the three rivers.

Cand slid from the lion's back. He didn't like being at this place. This had been a fearful place for him all his life. Everywhere he looked was water. The large Conmia came from the west; the two smaller but still powerful rivers cascaded over rocks, creating holes that a boat could be lost in. He felt his stomach lurch just watching the torrent.

The lion plunged into the spray, bounding into the middle of the three rivers. Cand gasped, sure that the lion would be swept downstream. But then he saw him standing in the middle of the river as though he stood on glass. "Come in with Me," He invited.

"I can't."

"You can."

"I can't swim."

"I am not swimming."

"I will drown."

"I would never let that happen to you."

"If You wanted me in the water, why didn't You just take me in when I was on Your back?"

"Because it is your decision. This is My river. I created it, just as I created the land, the skies, and the stars. The whole universe is Mine. If I tell the river to hold you up, it will."

Cand felt the water rushing by his feet. One step forward and he would get wet. "How can I be sure?"

"The only way you can be sure is to come in. Don't you trust Me?" the lion chided.

"Who are You?" Cand challenged. "Is this a vision or a dream?"

"Perhaps it is neither. Perhaps it is reality. As to your first question, you know who I am. You have sought Me for several weeks now; you have questioned. I am the Redeemer God."

"But You are a lion."

"That is a symbol. I am also a lamb, an eagle, an ox, a fire, a mighty wind. They are but symbols to help you understand. Come to Me, Candy. I am waiting anxiously for you."

Cand took a step forward and felt the cool water on his feet. He suppressed the urge to yank them back. "What if the water doesn't hold me? I would drown."

"That is true. But you must make the decision. I am offering you life – it surges all around you. Drowning would be a joy compared to the death you are in if you stay on the shore."

Cand could not argue with that. Ever since his discussion with Batakis about the sacrifice of the Redeemer God, he could feel the battle inside him between life and death. Hoen and all the other meaningless gods represented death.

But the lion had destroyed death.

Suddenly he could not bear being without the lion, without life. He ran into the river, feeling the water swell around him, lifting him up. He was being borne not downstream, but to the lion. He threw his arms around the lion's neck. The lion lifted him with giant paws and threw him into the air, catching him as he came down.

The lion played a game of rough and tumble with him, much as Cand had done with Temrane and Merry when they were small. His head went under the water numerous times, but he no longer cared. He had nothing to fear.

At last Cand was exhausted and lay across the lion's back. The lion swam back to the shore. "You must rest, for you have much work to do."

"What work, Menon?"

"You have spent your life convincing people of the reality of the gods. It is time to correct your teaching. I want you to go to your people and tell them of Me. There are many whom I have prepared to hear. You will also meet a man whose name is Duncan. He is My friend. Go with him."

Cand could not keep his eyes open any longer, and lying on the ground, his head resting on the lion, he closed his eyes. But before sleep overtook him, he heard the lion singing him a lullaby.

• • •

Niccola was ecstatic about the council. There had been a little fighting, but she had expected much more. King Jerome had with a few words shown her how a ruler should act, how to command respect. She admired him for that and thought about how difficult it would be to kill him. At least it would not be by her hand. She had only given the command to Jerome's lord; he would do the rest.

She went into her room thinking about the speech she would write to tell the people about their new queen. She wanted something to impassion them, to raise them from despair, to persuade them to fight in the war against Crotalus for her.

Caldon lay on her bed. She smiled as she saw him, thinking he had probably come about the knife. He wanted a present and she wanted to give him something with jewels, bright and shiny, something every boy would want. Her smile faltered and then disappeared as she approached the bed.

Caldon did not move. She spoke his name, but noted no response. Sinking to her knees, she gently patted his face, rubbed his hands between hers. She forced the tears back, not willing to admit that Crotalus had stolen her son.

She noticed a scrap of paper on the pillow beside Caldon's head. She picked it up and read its only sentence: "A present to make our meeting more interesting." She crumpled the note and threw it to the floor. The tears then would not be denied and gathering Caldon into her arms she wept over his still body.

A sound at the door made her turn, and she saw Palmer there. "Forgive me, My Lady. I did not mean to intrude. Is there anything I can do?"

Grief overwhelmed her, and she could not speak, but slowly shook her head.

"Please forgive the interruption," he said and turned to go.

"Please don't leave me," she said. "I don't want to be alone."

Palmer crossed the room and knelt beside her. He stroked Caldon's face. "Is he your son?"

She nodded. "I have not been a very good mother and always thought that I would have been better off without a child. But now I cannot bear the fact that he is gone." She looked into Palmer's face and searched his eyes, finding them compassionate and sensitive.

She handed him the paper she had crumpled. He spread it out and read it, his jaws tightening in anger. The pain this wizard had caused filled him with wrath. So many children gone, so many parents desolate, Rafaela hidden away, and his best friend's heart achingly wounded.

"Find him for me, Palmer. I love him. Crotalus . . ."

"There is no need to say anything further, My Lady." He held her and stroked her hair as she cried.

Niccola stayed like that a moment and then was struck with the impropriety of it and pulled away. As she did so, she noticed that Palmer was a very handsome man, more her own age than Fel-hoen had been, and certainly more attractive than Lomeli. "Please stay here with me tonight."

"I cannot, My Lady."

"No one need ever know."

"But I would know." He smiled at her. "You are one of the most beautiful women I have ever known, and if circumstances were different I would no doubt be tempted. But I belong to a woman whom I love and admire very much. I will not betray her."

"But I need you."

"My Lady," he said gently, "you also belong to another. I can see in your eyes that your love for him has grown cold. But his grief over the loss of your son will also be great. Share your pain with him and you might be surprised at the depth of your love."

She watched as he left the room. Her passion was sorry at his leaving, and yet he also spoke to her with consideration. He did not treat her as a harlot, but as a woman worthy of his esteem. Jerome had acted the same way. She did not understand why the men of Paduan treated women as equals.

She wanted to go to Palmer and speak with him about this, but did not want him to misunderstand her intentions. If she wanted to earn his respect, she would take his advice and seek out Lomeli. He probably did not even know yet of Caldon. She would find a few moments the next morning, before the armies rode out, to speak privately with Palmer.

She found Lomeli in his workroom, mending a saddle, no doubt in preparation for tomorrow's battle. He looked up as she walked in, and a cautious delight diffused his face. "Niccola, you are beautiful."

"Do you really think so?"

He simply nodded, tears wanting to form, for he could never offer her things such as she was wearing now. He did not blame her for leaving. A beautiful woman like Niccola deserved better than a leatherworker.

"Lomeli, come inside the house so we can talk."

He followed her and looked at her questioningly when they entered the house. He marveled to see tears in her eyes. "What is it, Niccola?"

"It's Caldon. He's been taken," she said as the tears spilled over her lashes and ran down her cheeks.

Lomeli sank to the ground, stunned by this revelation. "Are you sure?"

"He is upstairs on the bed. I am very sure." She dropped next to him. "I am so sorry, Lomeli. It is all my fault."

He watched in amazement as she cried for the son he had been so sure she did not love. He carefully put his arms around her and drew her to him, and was further surprised when she did not refuse him.

"Crotalus has done this to me because I taunted him. I am now the queen, and he wanted to let me know that he is more powerful and will have this kingdom."

"He would like you to think that, but it is not true."

"What *is* true, Lomeli?"

"Batakis and Devona are taking children with them into Beren. They asked to take Caldon, and I would not allow it. I have been lonely and selfishly wanted Caldon with me. If it is anyone's fault it is mine."

"I cannot bear it! I have treated him so badly, and now he is gone. I am very sorry, Lomeli."

"He is only gone for a time, Niccola . . . We must hold on to that. The armies will fight Crotalus, and all the children will be restored. And I promise you that Caldon will be the first!"

She rested in his arms, more content than she had been in a long time. Perhaps Palmer was right. Perhaps love could yet be restored.

Twenty-Seven

Falcon had assumed when he learned Rafaela had not died that his extreme hatred of Crotalus would dissipate. The fact that his wrath grew stronger, and harder to give over to Menon, tested his faith. Misgivings flourished as abundantly as summer weeds. As soon as one was uprooted, two more would sprout.

His search for Rafaela and his knowing the war was being fought without him – these refused his mind any rest. It had been thirteen years since he had last seen Rafaela, and much had happened in those years. He was a different person now – more mature, less headstrong; there was gray in his beard and possibly in his heart that had not been there before. He loved Rafaela with an intensity that overcame immense obstacles and, at times, common sense. But would he still love her when he finally found her?

Falcon had spent last night in Keffram with friends of his father's. They were simple people, fishermen by trade, fond of gardening and children. Falcon shared a bed with the young grandson, his two chickens, and a rabbit. The old man, Shuest, had talked of the old days with Farrel, the days when war was noble and dragons terrorized the land.

Now war was fought for trifling things, the dragons were tame, and men no longer cared.

Falcon felt a sly depression creep over him as he pondered the old man's words. He kept them in his mind long after the boy had slept and the chickens had quieted. He had known Shuest all his life. The last time he had seen him, ten years ago, Shuest had been cheery, laughing, affectionate with Deanna, his wife of thirty years. Now he seemed a bitter old man, the affection replaced by a biting sarcasm, the laughter by sighs. Something had changed him in ten years.

Had Rafaela changed? Falcon had not remained the same—why should she? Would he like the changes in her or she in him? They had not been together for thirteen years. Could their love surmount the transformations? Of course, he thought. Their love had endured much. Or had the anger and the search for her become the true passion?

Then there was the problem of the war, he thought as his horse jogged up the seacoast toward Melram. He felt he had abandoned his men. It was true Jerome had sent him, but the nagging feeling remained. His best friend was fighting against an enemy who was wicked beyond any imagining. Falcon still believed he could have lured Crotalus away from the castle; killing him would then be very little trouble.

And there it was. The base of all his doubts came to a pinnacle with Crotalus. He still craved Crotalus' death. And it was not good enough that Palmer might kill him, or Malcolm, or even Jerome. He did not want just the death of Crotalus, but to be the agent of it. He had imagined for thirteen years the various ways he might bring it about, and now it was ripped from his hands.

Falcon jumped from his horse and began walking, his anger needing a release. *It is not too late, even now*, he thought. He could turn west, and though it would be a long trek he would not be too late to join the battle. However, it would go against the direct orders of his king.

I don't care if I disobey, he thought. *Jerome had no right to keep me from this.*

Against this he placed the thought of Rafaela. He remembered her dark eyes, her inquisitive spirit, the laughing love he had shared with her. He thought of Menon and his loyalty to Him. Menon demanded total allegiance, a devoted servant. Killing Crotalus was not in His plans. Harboring hate toward Crotalus meant refusing Menon His absolute rule in Falcon's heart.

It's worth it, he thought. *I would give up Rafaela in order to murder Crotalus.* His heart beat faster. *I would give up Menon*, he thought, and his heart thudded painfully in his chest.

As he walked, an idea stole into his mind that, once lodged there, was almost impossible to remove. He could call Crotalus to him. It was so simple. He didn't know exactly how to do it, but he was sure he could.

But he wouldn't. Calling Crotalus would involve dark arts such as wizards used. Such action would be wrong; it would deny everything he had ever learned of the ways of Menon.

He stopped. But he had just said he would give up Menon. He stood as still as a rock as the decision dangled in front of him. It would be so easy.

"Stop!" he screamed as loud as he could, falling to the ground, doubled over as though in great pain. "Menon, I made my decision once . . . Why must I make it again? Stop torturing me! If You will not let me kill Crotalus, then take away the desire! Grant me Your peace!" He hammered the sandy ground until his fists were bruised and his eyes stung from the flying grit.

He slowly remounted his horse and pointed him toward Melram. He did not feel peace, only a tiredness that sapped his vitality. But he would continue on. If Menon chose to torment him, so be it. Falcon was a servant and would continue to be one until Menon brought him home.

• • •

Niccola observed the men from her window as they prepared the horses. War was in the air. She could smell it as well as hear it. The shouts of tense men filled the castle yard, and the horses caught the mood. The smell of horse sweat, different in war than at any other time, was pungent.

She had given her speech to the townspeople just after sunrise. At first they had been suspicious, skeptical of her and of her ability to rule. But as she spoke of banding together against Crotalus and returning their children, she saw the fire of her message leap from one heart to another. She, too, had lost a child. That made her one with them, and they responded to her with an admiration seldom shown to Fel-hoen.

She watched now as her servant gave the message to Palmer that she wished to speak with him in her quarters. He gave one last command to a knight and turned toward the castle. If he had any apprehensions about her reasons for wanting to see him, he did not show them.

He entered and bowed. "Queen Niccola, I have received your summons."

"Thank you. Please sit down." He sat in the chair across from hers, and she was amazed at his lack of awkwardness. How sure of himself he was! She took a deep breath and released it. "Palmer, I want to apologize for last night."

He shook his head. "There is no need for apology. You were understandably distraught."

She smiled a little. "Not so distraught that I didn't know exactly what I was doing. I am not used to being around men who do not give me what I want. And you were right about my husband. I have never loved him, but last night I saw glimpses of what might be."

"I am very glad."

"I would like to ask a favor of you."

"Anything I can give you, I will."

"I have never had a friend, Palmer. When I was growing up, I was a princess and not allowed to play with the peasants. I have never made a friend. Would you be my friend?"

Palmer smiled and took the hand she held out to him. "I would consider it a privilege, My Lady."

"Do not call me 'My Lady' or 'Queen Niccola,' just Niccola."

"As you wish, Niccola."

She stood and walked to the window. Palmer joined her. "The men will be expecting you to speak with them before they ride out."

"I shall be glad to. Did you hear my speech this morning?"

"Yes, I did. It was very good. Did you mean everything you said?"

"Of course. What did you think I didn't mean?"

"Nothing in particular. There are times when a ruler says things simply to stir a certain response in his people. I am just wondering what kind of ruler you are."

"A very good one!" she retorted and then felt a stab of guilt. She had murdered twice to gain this throne and had planned the murder of this man's king to retain it. "Do you always talk to people this way?"

He smiled. "No . . . just to the ones I call friends."

"Then you must not have many friends."

"No," he admitted, "I don't. It is a responsibility I take very seriously."

"A responsibility? I have never heard it described as such."

"My duty to my friends, and my friends' duty to me, is to hold them to a right path."

"What do you get out of this? You and your king are so different from my people, from any people I have known. What is it that drives you to do this?"

"I live and die for Menon, the Redeemer God. He is the only reason I need."

"You're serious?"

"Very serious."

She felt suddenly uncomfortable in his presence and squirmed under his gaze. "You can go now," she said at last. "I don't believe I want you for a friend."

He walked to the door, but turned before walking through it. He smiled at her, and she was again struck by his handsomeness. "It is too late, Niccola. You have made your choice and must abide by it. I intend to abide by mine. Like it or not, we are friends."

• • •

The city of Melram was too far inland to be a seaport or to sustain a large fishing trade. Therefore, when the people moved south to the fishing towns of Keffram or Chantey or west to the farming communities of Yartenn, Eschay, or Vierne, the city died and stayed on the map as simply the northernmost point of Paduan. A few of the buildings remained as testimony to the city, but they were as old and worn-out as the men who remembered a young Melram.

Melram had been deserted for as long as Falcon could remember. He had never known a time when it flourished, nor known anyone who had. His father might have, but he had never spoken of it. Melram was simply full of the ghosts of things that might have been; its few prospects were heavy with impossibilities.

Although Falcon did not fancy spending the night in a town that spoke of melancholy, he was too tired to try riding any further, and he liked even less the thought of sleeping in the open. At least on the north side of Melram he could find an abandoned building to sleep in and be protected from the night.

He tied his horse in front of a building and walked inside. The night outside had been dark, but at least there had been moonlight and stars.

Here there was nothing. Frustration welled in him. He couldn't wander around this building in utter darkness; floorboards had perhaps rotted away, there could be fallen beams, or he might jar stones loose. He couldn't risk being hurt in this place; that could mean a slow death for him.

He opened the door as wide as possible to let the moonlight in and saw that he was standing at the doorway of a very large room. In the middle of the room was a staircase. Its top was concealed by shadows, but that did not matter to him; he was not going to investigate it. Looking around the room, he saw a window hidden by a cloth of some sort. He crossed to it and yanked it from the window, sending several large spiders scurrying for cover. At least now there was more light.

He removed his pack from the horse and laid his blankets by the doorway. He got as comfortable as possible and pulled the blanket over his head, trying to shut out the abandoned city, the ominous building, the recurring temptation to summon Crotalus.

Falcon had slept only two hours when a sound awakened him that was entirely inconsistent with his surroundings. *He had heard a child laugh.*

He pulled the blankets down and sat up, alert for any noise. But the harder he listened, the more the sound eluded him. At last he decided that he had been dreaming. He lay back and pulled the cover over his head, only to hear it again.

This time as he listened he could hear not only laughter but children talking. It was coming from upstairs. He watched the stairway for what seemed like hours, but whoever was upstairs was not coming down.

As the sounds continued, Falcon slowly stood, casting aside the blanket. He could not let the laughter go on without knowing who caused it. He made his way to the staircase. He glanced above, but the light from the window did not reach up that far.

Testing each step before he put his full weight upon it, he cautiously moved upward. The stairs creaked loudly, but Falcon did not care if he was heard and in fact was sure he would not be, for the children's laughter and singing drowned out all else.

As his head ascended into the darkness, he stopped and waited for his eyes to adjust. He felt upward with his hands and counted three more stairs. After these his hand encountered a door. There was a small amount of light escaping from the top of the ill-fitting door, promising him vision if he could open it.

He went up the remaining stairs. Though he could not find a knob, he pushed the door gently and it swung open. Light broke over him as he saw a large undivided room with three of its walls made of unbroken glass. Moonlight was streaming in.

He glanced over the entire room from the doorway, but saw nothing. No furniture, no staircases, no other doors, nowhere for children to hide. Yet the laughter went on, surrounding him. "Where are you?" he said, his concerned voice sounding unnatural amid the childish glee.

"Shhhh! He hears us!"

"But he can't see us!"

"How can he hear us?"

"Because he's in the same room with us! Now be quiet!"

"No," Falcon said, "don't be quiet. I like hearing you. Where are you?"

"We're all around you, but you can't see us."

"Why not?"

"Because we don't have bodies anymore."

"I like not having a body. I can fly!"

Falcon felt a finger brush his hand. "Are you here to help us?"

"Do you need help?"

"I want to go home."

Falcon could not see them, but he sensed them closing around him. He reached out a hand, instinctively trying to comfort them. "Do you live in Zopel?" he asked.

"Yes," said a boy's voice. "I am the oldest . . . I'm ten. Some say the princess doesn't have a body anymore either, but she isn't here with us or else she would be the oldest."

"Do you understand what's happening?" Falcon said.

"No . . . Are we dead?"

"No . . . Your bodies are still alive, but an evil wizard has taken your souls and placed you here. We are fighting him now, and soon we'll be able to put you back in your bodies so you can go home."

"Will you stay with us until then?"

"I can't. I must leave in the morning, but as soon as I can, I will return and take care of you until the war is over."

"When will you come back?"

"Can you count the days?"

"Yes . . . We can see the sun coming up and going down."

"Then count ten days. I will be back by then, maybe before. Don't leave this room, all right? I don't want anybody to get lost."

"We can't. We tried on our first night here. The man who put us here said some funny words to keep us here."

"Why are you awake? You should be resting."

"We don't sleep," the child said. "And we don't get tired."

"Well, I'm very tired and I need to sleep."

"Please stay here and sleep," said a very young girl's voice. "We'll try and be real quiet."

"All right." Falcon laid on the floor. He felt as though his head was resting on someone's lap. He felt numerous "fingers" stroking his hair, rubbing his forehead. With a feeling of complete contentment, he fell asleep.

As sunbeams struck his eyes, he awoke to a morning that was as quiet as an empty room. He was beginning to wonder if he had dreamed it all when he felt a slight tickle in his ear. He brushed at it and heard a child giggle.

"Ssshhhh! You'll wake him up."

"He's already awake. Aren't you?"

"Yes, I am."

And the noise burst around him as though it had been bottled up for hours: laughing, many talking all at once, playing a game of tag, clamoring around him.

"I have to go," he said reluctantly, almost wishing he could stay with these delightful children.

"But you'll be back," one said cheerfully. "We'll wait for you. What's your name?"

"Falcon. What's yours?"

"Lis."

"Well, Lis," he said, "I will be back in ten days. You count the days, and don't be sad while I'm gone."

Falcon went back down the stairs, avoiding the ones that looked rotted, marveling that he hadn't killed himself last night treading on them. He packed up his blankets and put them on his horse, who acted skittish at all the noise.

He waved at the window, certain they all watched him leave, feeling their good wishes go with him.

"Thank You, Menon," he uttered. "You have restored me and refreshed me." There was a purpose in his going to the Forgotten City that extended beyond his finding Rafaela. He had also found the children. When Crotalus died, as Falcon knew he would, the children would be free, but they wouldn't know how to get back to their bodies. Falcon would be the one to lead them. He couldn't think of anything he would rather do.

Twenty-Eight

Although many children had to help their parents with the fishing trade or farming, Queen Alexandria taught them whenever they were available about the world beyond Paduan, about history, about the Redeemer God and His dealings with humanity. She now found that this schooling kept the children of Corigo from boredom as well.

Devona and Batakis had brought in one wagonload of children, all over the age of eleven. These were children who were at least for the time safe from Crotalus, children who could be returned to their parents when the war was over. Although Devona and Batakis tried to urge parents to come as well, most would not leave. Business needed tending, life had to go on, a few of the men were needed to prepare for the battles. Most of the people of Zopel felt they could not be taken – their gods would protect them. There had been a reason why their neighbors' children had been taken; perhaps some sin had been unconfessed or some sacrifice kept from the gods. But *they* were holy people, and they would be safe. But just in case, their children were sent to Paduan.

Alexandria would not hear of the villagers in Paduan taking on the children – most could not afford another mouth to feed. So she opened the castle not just to the children of Corigo, but those of Paduan as well. She felt that the children could ease each other's loneliness. They played all morning in and out of the castle, around the town, making friends. And in the afternoons, when it was too hot to be outdoors, Alexandria held school.

Batakis and Devona wanted to leave immediately for another load of children. Devona desired to talk with Lomeli again, hoping to convince him of the urgency of the situation so he would let them take Caldon. Before they left, though, Batakis went home along with

Devona to speak with Cand. Hopefully Cand would know some way to speak to the people so they would release their children to them.

"I do know of a way," Cand said, eyes bright and lips curving gently. "I will come with you."

"Absolutely not! It is much too dangerous."

"Time has passed, my friend. The hatred has no doubt cooled somewhat. They are my people."

"They also tried to kill you," Devona said softly.

"That is true, but there is something you do not know that I must tell you before you can refuse me. If after I tell you you still refuse, I shall submit to your will."

They watched him, and Batakis could see the impish look in his eyes, the mirth that bubbled inside him, and he knew what Cand would say.

"I have been with Menon," he said simply. "I am His."

Batakis let out the breath he had been holding and beamed at Cand. "I cannot tell you how joyful that makes me."

"I think I can guess. Batakis, I have done much damage to Menon's name, although I did not know it at the time. But I know it now, and I must undo what I can. I need to talk with my people. If it is dangerous, He will be with me. If it is His will for me to die by their hands, then it shall be done. I can no longer remain here. Menon commands me to go."

Devona nodded briskly. "Then you must go. I too am concerned about your going, but the will of Menon is supreme and must be obeyed. As you say, He will travel with us, guiding our steps and preparing our paths."

• • •

Niccola heard that Cand was back in Zopel. Some said he had been resurrected from the dead and now preached a new god. Others said he talked about the strange god of the Paduans. She heard enough to wonder, and desired to talk with him. If he knew of this Menon, she wished to be taught. Foreign emotions were raised in her when she thought of what Palmer had said: *I live and die for Menon.* But before she could speak with the ex-priest, affairs of the kingdom demanded her attention.

Malcolm, leading his armies, had ridden into Derrich and found it almost deserted. Most of the townspeople had gone to Crotalus' castle along with Lord Tegmen, or so the people who remained said. Malcolm did not believe this. These were religious people who would not have willingly taken up residence with a wizard, not even to protect their children. He felt that Tegmen had slaughtered the people who refused his lordship over them; the people who remained now had been in hiding. Tegmen had undoubtedly moved the willing people into Andurin. This made Andurin a stronger fortress and put Palmer and his army in more danger.

Malcolm sent a messenger to hurry ahead of his army to contact Palmer and Jerome. The message said simply to remain where they were and to not attack Andurin until Malcolm could join them. He then sent word to Queen Niccola that he was returning briefly with subjects who recognized her queenship. Then he rode with the people of Derrich back to Zopel.

Niccola agreed with Malcolm and would give sanctuary to the people of Derrich until they could safely return to their homes. If that time never came, they would be offered land in Zopel and could work as servants of Niccola. She ordered her servants to prepare places for these subjects. While she waited for Malcolm, she would speak with Cand.

Lomeli sat with her in the throne room, self-conscious amid the fine trappings, but happy that Niccola's acceptance of him had lasted this long. He greeted Cand, Devona, and Batakis warmly and then felt the peace that can come when a sorrow is shared with others as he told them of Caldon.

"He will return," Devona said.

"I hold on to that," he said. "I only wish I would have listened to you and sent him to Beren."

Niccola watched Cand's face and saw no fear there. She saw a peace that she had seen deep in Palmer's eyes. But what impressed her more than this was a gaiety in his manner that had been lacking before. This was a former high priest in front of her, and yet the seriousness of that office was gone.

"You are right, my queen," he said when she mentioned this to him. "For me, the True God is no longer angry and vengeful, because I now stand before Him as His child. A child has no need to fear."

"And you do not fear me?"

"Why should I fear you?"

"I was instrumental in trying to accomplish your death. Your brother is dead, and many say it was by my hand."

Cand smiled sadly. "You could kill me now, Queen Niccola, and it would not change me. My life is bound up in Menon, and no one can sever that tie. My brother is dead, and my heart grieves. I never thought I would be sad when he died. There was no love between us. But Menon has changed my heart. I wanted to talk with Fel-Hoen again, to make things right, but it is too late. And so I only hope to make as many things right as I can with the people who still live."

The queen heard Palmer's words—"I live and die for Menon"—wrapped around Cand's words. "And you say your sins are forgiven?"

"All of them."

"Without a sacrifice?"

"The sacrifice has already been made. I could never make a sacrifice sufficient to make me clean. But the Redeemer God has done that for me."

"But perhaps there is a sin so large that the sacrifice would not cover it."

Cand remembered his time with Menon, the water that had been like glass, the Sovereign God governing all life within His hands. "No," he said simply, for there was nothing else to say.

Lomeli sat silently, watching his wife's face. He could see her struggle with ideas and emotions, and he wondered why. She had never given the gods any thought before. When she had sinned, he had offered sacrifice for her. She had never been to any of the temples. Yet she was changing, or something was changing her. He at last cleared his throat and asked, "Why did you come to me two nights ago?"

"I am your wife."

Lomeli laughed. "You have not truly been my wife for the entire time we've been married, and yet now it is different. Why?"

"I had been talking with a man from Beren . . . He's my friend . . . He talked of Menon." She began to cry. "I don't understand what's happening. I want this peace that you have, Cand. I want to live and die for Menon. Tell me of Him."

Cand told her what he had experienced and what he knew, looking often to Batakis or Devona for confirmation. Niccola listened intently, her eyes never leaving his face. "It is good," she said at last.

Her maidservant appeared at the door and told her that Malcolm awaited her. She stood and walked to the door. She turned and smiled at them, belief being born in her heart, responsibility for the things she had done trying to smother it. "I must go and make things right," she said and left.

Lomeli looked after her with astonishment. "This is beyond my understanding," he said. "She has altered so drastically." He looked from Batakis to Devona. "When you were nursing Cand back to health, you talked to me often of the Redeemer God. I listened because I was fascinated, but I didn't believe. Your god didn't seem very different from mine. But now I believe. I can see that he doesn't just ask for the blood of animals – He wants hearts. More, He changes hearts. Niccola is right – it is good."

• • •

Niccola listened as Malcolm described what had happened and what things he had done. Then she instructed the servants to find places for the people of Derrich. "Come with me, Malcolm," she said. "There is something you must do for me before you ride to Andurin."

He followed her into the dungeons where she had placed Kenda and the blacksmith Anson. There was not much light, but he could see what she was doing as she unlocked the chains that held Anson.

"You are free. You have been found innocent of any wrongdoing. Please forgive me for the wrong that has been done. Queen Kenda will see that you receive ample compensation for the work you have lost."

Anson rubbed his wrists where the chains had been, bowed briefly to her, then stumbled up the stairs. Niccola watched him go and then released Kenda. She took the crown from her head and handed it to Kenda, who took it hesitantly. "My Lady, I have also wronged you and do not expect to be forgiven. Malcolm shall inform you of the war that is being fought."

She turned to Malcolm. "Malcolm, as your last service to me as queen, I command you to chain me to the wall where Queen Kenda was. I have committed murder and treason and shall remain here."

"My queen, please don't ask me to do it!"

She smiled at him. "You have been a loyal subject, but I am no longer your queen. Put the chains on me."

Malcolm reluctantly did as she commanded. "What shall I tell King Jerome?"

"Tell him Kenda is back on the throne. Nothing else need be said."

"Yes, my lady."

"Go now . . . Jerome's army awaits you."

As they left and the door banged shut, Niccola was left in complete darkness. She could hear rats scuttering on the floor, sweeping past her feet.

"Forgive me, Menon," she prayed awkwardly. "I have done so many wrongs, I don't know if You can forgive me. I know that even if You do, I have done things that the people will not forgive. Please accept this as a gift of remorse. I have done too many wrongs to ever right them. I cannot bring back the dead. Forgive me."

As she felt a rat brush against her leg, she prayed to die. She had no right to life when she had murdered. A slow death seemed a just punishment for her.

• • •

Malcolm rode hard through the day, pausing for nothing, feeling that the destiny of his homeland rested on his reaching King Jerome by nightfall.

He found Jerome's camp two hours past nightfall. The camp was only a few hours ride from Andurin, close enough to send scouts to watch and yet far enough away to not be seen. He stumbled into the tent Jerome had set up, interrupting a discussion between Jerome and Palmer.

"Please, King Jerome," he said breathlessly, "you must help us. Zopel will be destroyed . . ."

"Calm yourself," Jerome commanded. "Tell me what has happened."

"Niccola abdicated the throne."

"What!"

"I don't know why. She said she had committed murder and treason. She released Kenda from the dungeon and gave her back the crown."

Jerome thought a moment. "That is surprising . . . But why will Zopel be destroyed?"

"Your Highness, understand that I hesitate to speak ill of a woman, especially my queen, but Queen Kenda is not a leader. She was the wife of Fel-hoen, but she cannot lead a country. She cannot hold the people together while their fathers, brothers, and husbands are fighting a war. Niccola could. You saw the people when she gave her speech. She created a passion in them that has not been there for a very long time. They will lose hope without Niccola. Can you do something?"

"We cannot tarry here another day. The armies of Soaje and Tegmen are in Andurin. They expect battle, and battle we must give them or we will lose too many of our men. Yet, a country must not be without a leader."

"Sire, let me ride to Zopel and speak with her," Palmer suggested.

Jerome looked at the knight. "For what reason?"

"She is a friend of mine, and I can convince her to hold the throne until the war is ended."

"You are certain of this?"

"Yes. You are needed to lead the armies. Malcolm will lead his. If I leave now and ride without stopping and then back the same way, I can strike any men who escape your attack."

Malcolm gave thought to an idea and then said, "There is a shortcut from Zopel to Andurin that lies in the mountains. If an army were to wait for Palmer at that place, he could come back through the mountains and come in on the west side of Andurin."

"I know the place you speak of," Jerome said. "It comes dangerously close to Crotalus' castle."

"But I need not take my men through there," Malcolm went on. "They can wait for me at the junction. If Crotalus is alerted at that time, we will make a strong frontal attack on him and hold his army off until you arrive. It may confuse our numbers. It might be just the illusion we need."

"What men do you want?"

"My army and that of McIlree."

"You have them. I shall tell them of our plans. Palmer, you have no time to waste."

Palmer nodded, left the tent, and hurriedly prepared his horse for the ride. As Malcolm had done earlier, so he now rode without stopping, pressing the horse forward with an urgency that could not be denied.

When he reached the castle in Zopel, dawn was a faint light in the east. The town was quiet, and Palmer was thankful that at least riots had not broken out yet. Perhaps few knew of Niccola's resignation and he had come in time. He demanded passage through the castle gates and the massive front doors. He found a groggy-eyed servant to lead him to the dungeon and then commanded him back to bed.

He found the key hanging on the wall and released the chains that held Niccola. She put her arms around his neck and cried. Palmer had worked up a good anger at her on the way to Zopel, but as he held her his anger left. "Niccola, why are you doing this?"

"I want to know Menon, Palmer. I am purging myself."

"That is not necessary, Niccola, and you are causing unrest in your people."

"They are not my people, Palmer. I am not the queen any longer."

"Niccola, listen carefully to me. There is nobody who wants you to know Menon more than I do. But this is not the way. You are not purging yourself. You are running away from something. What is it that you are fleeing?"

"Perhaps the things I have done wrong."

"All of us have done wrong things. Confess your wrongdoings . . . Don't flee from them."

"Can I confess them to you?"

"Do you know that Menon forgives you for them without telling me what they are?"

"Yes, but I need to talk to someone, and there are things that I need to ask your forgiveness for and have your help in setting them right."

"All right . . . Tell me."

She sat down on the cold floor of the dungeon, and he sat beside her. She could not bring herself to look at him for a moment, but then boldly looked into his eyes. "What I have to say will probably end our friendship."

"I am not that easily frightened off, Niccola. And if Menon forgives you, then I can do no less."

"I seduced Fel-hoen so I could eventually become queen. Toward that end I murdered Solon, Fel-hoen's advisor, in order to take his place. I then killed Fel-hoen and stole the crown. I blamed the death on an innocent man and had him and Kenda locked down here."

"These things have been suspected all along, Niccola. Menon forgives you for them, as I do."

"Because of these things, the throne is not morally mine."

"That is true, but the people need you right now. Kenda will lose the country, as she is not a leader. You must continue to rule at least until the war is over."

"Is that what Menon wants?"

Palmer sighed. "Honestly, Niccola, I don't know. His plans are so far above mine that I wonder at times that I know Him at all. I do know that you are needed, that Menon is not being served by your locking yourself in a dungeon. When the war is over, let the people or Kenda decide your punishment, or turn yourself over to Jerome. He is the most just man I know."

"There are two other things, Palmer, things you may not forgive me for. I need your help to correct them."

"What are they?"

"Do you know a man in Jerome's army who is the hated enemy of Crotalus?"

Palmer felt a sick thud in his stomach. "Yes . . . Falcon Jaqeth."

"I wanted to be able to attack Crotalus' army without Crotalus there. When he returned, my army could then attack him alone and he would be defeated."

"Go on."

"I told him that Falcon was riding to the Forgotten City."

"What!" Palmer jumped to his feet, the sick feeling within him growing.

Niccola said nothing, knowing that she deserved whatever he said to her, wanting to cry out because she valued his friendship too much to lose it.

"You told Crotalus where Falcon could be found? Do you not understand how evil Crotalus is? Do you know how much he hates Falcon? He will spring on Falcon now without warning, and Falcon will not be able to fight against it!"

He leapt toward the stairs. "I must warn him."

"Palmer, wait! You would never get there in time! Your army needs you too."

"I love Falcon! He's my best friend. I can't stand by and let him die!"

"There's more you need to hear."

"I don't want to know anything else!"

"You have to! I must tell you where I got my information."

He stopped and, breathing hard to control his emotions, sat back down. "Tell me."

"One of the lords from Paduan betrayed him. He is also going to kill Jerome."

"Why? . . . Which lord?"

"I don't know. He wore a mask and disguised his voice. He blackmailed me. He wanted half of Paduan when the war with Crotalus was through. I told him he could have it, but it would have to be his hand that killed Jerome."

"You commanded him to kill Jerome?"

"Yes," she whispered. She expected him to leap up again and scream, but he did not. She could hear his labored breathing, could see his fists clenching and unclenching as he struggled for balance in his mind.

"My first loyalty is to Jerome," he said at last. "Although I want to go after Falcon, I must not leave my king undefended. I will go to him and warn him. I have scouts even now who are watching Crotalus' castle. If they see him leave, then we shall do our best to kill his army and then him. I will have to leave Falcon in the Redeemer's care. If Crotalus has not left the castle yet, then God be merciful to him, for I shall not be."

"What do you want me to do?"

"First and foremost, lead your people. I don't think Kenda will put up a fight at this point for the crown. Take it back and be queen. Second, contact Kreith, the Prince of Paduan. Tell him of the betrayal and to be ready to assume his father's duties if we cannot find the betrayer in time."

"Kreith is here, in the castle! He has been with Merry."

"Summon him quickly. He shall ride out with me. I must go now. I shall send a message to you as soon as I can about Crotalus."

Kreith was summoned, and when he heard of the betrayal he lost no time in dressing and preparing his horse. His mind jumped over the lords, weighing this one, judging that one, but he could come to no conclusion. Fear was a cold clamp on his heart.

Niccola watched Palmer mount his horse. She saw the tears in his eyes. "I cannot tell you how sorry I am to have caused you pain," she said. "I do not expect to keep your friendship, and I am also exceedingly sorry about that. When this war is over, I shall submit myself not only to Jerome but to you for punishment. Good-bye, Palmer."

He could not speak and left in silence. Tears coursed down Niccola's face as she watched Palmer and Kreith ride away. Palmer's sincerity in their brief friendship touched her deeply, and she wept that it could no longer continue. She walked sorrowfully into the castle, trying to prepare herself to again serve as queen.

Twenty-Nine

As Palmer and Kreith sped over the hills on their way to the shortcut where the army waited, Palmer pondered Niccola's words. One of Jerome's lords was a betrayer. He prayed that it might be McIlree, for then he would have unknowingly foiled his plans by removing him from Jerome's presence. But even as this hope was born, it died. McIlree had been friends with Jerome for far too long, fighting side by side with him in the early Freedom Wars. Some people said he hesitated taking a lordship because it would separate him from Jerome.

Ulster had come from Corigo originally and could possibly have known something about Niccola with which to blackmail her. Yet, he had never been known to be particularly ambitious. He enjoyed his lordship and the privileges that came with it, but had never aspired to the crown.

Thomas had youth and energy, but the great passion of his life was music. Because of him Vierne had become culturally rich. But Palmer could not imagine him wanting to usurp the throne at Beren in order to spread more culture.

Both Diones and Sipple had risen from peasanthood to become lords. Both, Palmer felt, had ambition enough to try for the crown, but he didn't consider either of them capable militarily of capturing it. Diones had known Alexandria when she was young, serving under the lordship of her father. He had been instrumental in putting Jerome before Alexandria as a suitor. Sipple, on the other hand, had been a knight in the army of Jerome's father. But when Jerome declared war on his father, Sipple had been persuaded to join them and had been touched by the love of Menon.

Palmer could not imagine any of them being a traitor or killing Jerome. Maybe Niccola was mistaken. Perhaps it was someone simply calling himself a lord of Paduan. But that didn't help Jerome—there was still someone who planned to kill him. The only thing Palmer could do was warn the king.

They reached the junction sooner than Palmer thought possible and immediately sought the scouts. "Has there been any movement?"

"None."

"Has Crotalus been spotted?"

"No. If he was in the castle when we started watching, he is still there."

McIlree came up to them. "Kreith, what are you doing here? Palmer, I sense urgency in your voice. What has happened?"

Palmer hesitated. "I have need of Kreith. Falcon has been betrayed. It is likely that Crotalus will leave his army behind to attack Falcon."

"Do you want someone sent to Falcon?"

Palmer's heart skittered in his chest like a caged animal. "I would like nothing better than to go to him myself, but it is impossible. Although we know his destination, there are many miles between Beren and the Forgotten City. Crotalus could meet him anywhere along the way. We simply do not have the time or the manpower."

"I'm sorry, Palmer . . . I know that is a hard decision for you. For me too. Falcon is a friend of mine as well."

Palmer considered telling McIlree of the plot against Jerome, but decided against it. He would not mention it to anyone until he was sure who the betrayer was. Although he trusted McIlree, he could not be sure.

"Do we attack the castle?"

"Not unless we're spotted. We will remain with the original plan and join with King Jerome."

"But if Crotalus is still in the castle, we can save Falcon."

"Crotalus is not that easily destroyed. We had planned all along to lure him from the castle. Inside his domain he is too dangerous and has too much access to his spells; our men could be bewitched into killing themselves. We can't take that chance."

"We could wait here until we see him leave and then fall upon him. His mind would no doubt be upon Falcon, and there would be two armies against him."

"We don't even know that he's in there. He could already be in the Forgotten City. We can't watch his castle forever." Palmer wanted to scream out to the skies. They were trapped. Whichever way he turned, someone would die. "Await my command," he said to McIlree. "Kreith, let's talk a moment."

He could see that McIlree was confused at this, but he did not hesitate to go stand by his army. *He is loyal*, Palmer thought, *but I wish he were the betrayer*. "Kreith, you and I are the only ones who know Jerome is in danger. I have given the matter some thought, and this is my plan. If you think it a bad one, say so. Don't look at me like that . . . I know you have never served in battle before, but you have trained under Falcon Jaqeth. That alone is worth more than a few battles.

"The main objective of this war is to stop Crotalus. We are in the best position to do that right now. On the other hand, we have a duty to our king. But we do not know where his danger is coming from, and without knowing that our protection of him is worthless. He has six armies with him, and they are even now attacking Andurin with her two armies. Does that sound like a fair summary so far?"

"Yes, but I might add a few points. We don't know that Crotalus is in the castle, and we don't know that my father is not already dead."

Palmer knew the effort it took Kreith to say this and patted him on the shoulder. "That is why I am sending you to Andurin while I remain here. If something has happened to Jerome, the armies will need leadership immediately or the betrayer will simply step in and take the crown. You are the only one who can assume that role. McIlree and I will make a brief attack on the castle to determine if Crotalus is inside or not. If he is not, then we shall raze his castle to the ground. As soon as you have defeated Andurin, join us."

Kreith nodded and leapt on his horse. Without a word to anyone, he spurred the horse and with dread pressing on his heart raced toward Andurin.

Palmer turned toward McIlree, who watched him with an expectant air. "McIlree, prepare for a frontal attack."

• • •

The castle at Andurin was well defended, and though Jerome and his armies far outnumbered the armies of Tegmen and Soaje, Jerome was losing many men because of its position. The castle was built into a mountain of rock and could not be approached from the back. He had sent men to the north side of the castle and the main body of his troops to the east. To the south was the Andurin River.

"I am open to suggestions," he said as the lords gathered around him. "They are beginning to launch fire from their catapults. So far we have been able to put out much of the fires with a small loss of lives, but soon we will run out of water. We can take it from the Andurin River, but that will take time."

"Can we scale the castle walls?" Kies asked.

"A few of us could, but not many."

"But if even a few of us did, we could throw the catapults from the walls."

"Their archers would pick you off the wall like flies," Malcolm said. "You would have to immobilize the archers first."

"We could launch catapults to do that."

"But we would have to launch the catapults even while you were on the wall. It would be a tremendous risk to your life with very little gain if you should survive."

"What about the river?" Diones asked.

"We cannot sail up it."

"But a troop could go into the hills south of the castle, walk up the mountains to a place on the river above Andurin, then sail downstream and have easy access to the castle. The back of the castle is much less defended than the front because of its inaccessibility. We could easily dispatch of the men there, and then we would have an entire troop of men within the castle."

"It is too dangerous," Ulster said, and others agreed with him. Diones began to argue with Ulster.

Jerome held up his hand, silencing tongues that wished to speak. "It is dangerous, but the benefits are high if we succeed. We are losing many men now. The only other course we have is to surround the castle and wait for their supplies to give out. That could take us months, and I for one don't think we can wait that long. I know Crotalus won't. I will take a troop upstream."

"No, Your Majesty," Sipple protested. "Because it is so dangerous, let someone else go. You are needed too badly in the frontal attack."

"I appreciate your concern, Sipple, but my place is where it is most risky. If I will not do this, I cannot expect my men to either. Who will come with me?"

"Sire, I am the one who should come with you," Diones said. "It was my idea, and if it fails I should not want to risk any lord's life but mine. My troop will accompany us."

"Very well. Kies and Pelaro, continue the northern attack. Sipple and Ulster, start the eastern attack as soon as we leave. Draw their attention to you. Thomas, cover the river below us in case there are those who try to escape. As soon as we gain access into the castle, I will signal you from the wall. You will then cease your attack and storm the castle to assist us."

The men leapt to the commands, Diones preparing his troop for the trek into the mountains. Jerome looked up into the sky and saw the light being bled out of it. Darkness descended quickly in the mountains. *Menon*, he thought, *grant us success.* Peace was far from his heart.

• • •

Kreith raced into the camp, startling Thomas, who was intent on trouble coming from upriver, not from the south. "Kreith!" he whispered so he would not give his position away. "What are you doing here?"

"Where's my father?" the boy asked urgently.

"He is going upriver. What's wrong?"

"Who is he with?"

"Diones and his troops."

Something triggered in Kreith's mind, but he couldn't quite identify it. "Where are the other troops?"

"The Corigan troops are on the north front – Sipple and Ulster are on the east."

"Why are they going upriver?"

"Diones had an idea that they could sail down the river, coming in from behind, and gain entrance to the castle."

Kreith slowly shook his head. "Diones and his river. He has wanted to try that tactic for some time now. I must find my father. Did they leave long ago?"

"Not very. They could not have reached the mouth of the river yet, and they were on foot. You could easily overtake them."

Kreith nodded and pulled his horse's reins around to travel up the mountain. So Diones had finally gotten a chance to try his river theory. Of course Kreith had known for years that Jerome was not as conservative a fighter as he would be or even as Falcon was. He had not gained the throne from his father by playing it safe. He had taken enormous risks and would not stop at one now.

Kreith suddenly stopped his horse, a memory pushing through. After the mock battle, he had asked Falcon about Diones' suggestion. Falcon had said he wouldn't try it.

Kreith spurred the horse again, urging him a little faster, the dread becoming stronger. Falcon wouldn't try it, but Falcon was not as unconventional as Jerome. He had heard his father describe Falcon more than once as headstrong and obdurate. Falcon himself had told him many times that when he became king he would need to watch headstrong soldiers who thought they knew everything. Kreith had long felt that Falcon knew all there was to know.

He goaded the horse again, even though he was skittish about the hills and rocks underfoot. Kreith was not sure he would get there in time.

"You, as king, would have most certainly been killed." The words Falcon had spoken leapt in Kreith's mind as clearly as though Falcon were with him. ". . . certainly been killed . . ."

The horse wheeled around as Kreith pulled up hard on the reins. He sped down the mountain, not caring any longer how much noise he made, hoping Thomas would realize it was him and not shoot him. As he neared Thomas, he shouted, "Pull Ulster off the front lines and come with me."

Thomas did not wait for an explanation, but kicked his horse until it fled to where the Paduan troops fought violently. Jerome had commanded them to draw attention away from the river and this they were doing. Catapults of fire were screaming down on them; arrows filled the air. Thomas ducked and ran to the front where he saw Ulster.

"His Highness requires your troops," he shouted over the din.

"I have not seen him at the castle yet," he hollered back.

"Not Jerome . . . Kreith."

Ulster signaled his troops, and they followed Thomas to where Kreith waited. Ulster, Thomas, and two armies on horses looked anxiously at him, anticipating his command, and the thought crossed Kreith's mind that this was not a mock battle. This was horribly and frighteningly real.

"Diones has betrayed King Jerome," he shouted. "I want Diones killed as soon as he is spotted. We may have to do battle with his men, but not yet. They may not know what Diones has done, and I want no innocent men killed. Follow me!"

In minutes hundreds of horses were pounding up the mountainside.

Where his horse had felt slow before, Kreith now felt that he had wings. The mountain rushed by him in a blur of brambles and mountain grasses.

He stopped. He didn't want to go all the way to the mouth of the river on this path. If they had already left, Kreith would miss them. "We go off the path here," he shouted back. "Watch the river for any sign of them!"

He walked his horse more slowly now up the river, but the footing was slippery and he finally abandoned his horse. "Thomas, have your men dismount and follow me. Ulster, you stay on the path and travel upward. I do not want him to escape." His orders were followed without question. *Father*, he thought, *I may be able to order them and they obey me, but I am not ready to take command. Don't die!*

"There they are!" Thomas whispered.

They were coming down the river on five large rafts. King Jerome was on the front raft, Diones directly behind him.

"Stand back," Kreith ordered. "I don't want anyone seen." They moved back, and Kreith drew an arrow from his quiver. He aimed at Diones and hesitated. What if he were wrong?

He hesitated too long. Diones lifted his own bow, aimed directly in front of him at Jerome. As Kreith saw Diones raise his bow, he let his arrow fly seconds before Diones let his go. Kreith's arrow struck his arm, and it jerked upward just a fraction. But Jerome was hit.

Kreith could not see his father any longer, nor Diones, as they were surrounded by men. He shouted to the rafts as loudly as he could, "This is Prince Kreith. I am now the acting sovereign. Abandon your rafts and pull them to the riverbank. If you refuse, I have two troops of men waiting to do battle with you."

He waited what seemed like a long time but could only have been seconds before men started rowing furiously for the shore and then jumping into the river to pull the rafts up. Kreith drew his sword and led his troop down the side of the mountain to the shore. He first looked at Diones, whose eyes were filled with wrath and scorn. "Thomas, have your second in command bind this man in chains and send him to Zopel. Tell Niccola to put him in the dungeon until further notice."

"Yes, Your Highness," Thomas said, grabbing Diones' good arm and handing him over to Sheridan.

"Thomas, order these men to swear fealty to my sword or they too shall be sent into the dungeons to await judgment."

While Thomas and his men received their vows of loyalty, Kreith went to his father. King Jerome was pale from blood loss, his hair damp and lank. He smiled weakly at his son. “You did exactly right.”

“Sshhh, don’t talk . . . Save your strength.” He examined the wound without pulling the arrow out. Thankfully it had missed the heart. Hitting Diones in the arm had proved a good decision. But the arrow had still gone very deeply into the left shoulder blade. “I dare not remove the arrow. Can you survive the trip to Zopel?”

“I’ll have to. There’s not a doctor here.”

“Thomas, have your men get King Jerome to Zopel as quickly as possible. Send word to Queen Alexandria.”

“It shall be done, but I have bad news. About half of Diones’ men escaped to the west. Should we go after them?”

“Yes . . . I’ll be ready in a moment.” He grasped his father’s hand. “I wish I could go with you.”

Jerome shook his head. “Never leave your men without a ruler.”

Thomas’ men gently lifted Jerome and bore him to a bier they had quickly fashioned. “I love you,” Kreith whispered into his ear.

“I love you too. It is not over yet, Kreith. We shall again be together.”

Kreith held back tears as he watched them descend the mountain. There would be time to cry later. “One more thing and then we shall go,” he said to Thomas. “Send a messenger to Palmer, who is at the junction leading to Crotalus’ castle. If he is not there, he is at the castle. Tell him Diones has been stopped, Jerome is wounded, I am in command.”

• • •

Palmer received the message regarding Kreith gladly, although he wished for more details. He briefly questioned the messenger, who told him a little about Kreith’s exploits. Palmer longed to hear how Kreith knew it was Diones, but knew that would have to wait until later. For now he was content that Jerome had not been killed. “Prince Kreith took to that leadership role like he was born to it,” the messenger said. “And in a way I guess he was. Falcon would be very proud of him.”

The mention of Falcon brought to mind the battle at hand. Crotalus had not appeared, and yet Palmer was sure he was in the castle. Crotalus’ army fought recklessly and savagely, one man taking down a score of his enemy before dying. Palmer's losses were heavy. But still Crotalus had not shown himself. Palmer was convinced that the army would not fight so insanely without the fear of their master driving them on.

"Retreat!" Palmer called and gathered his men and those of McIlree around him. "We are losing too many men. Our enemies fear Crotalus too much to simply die by an arrow wound."

"It is more than that, Palmer," one of his knights said. "I buried an arrow into the throat of one. He plucked it out like a bee stinger and kept coming at me. A spell has been placed on them."

McIlree sighed. "I fear it is true, Palmer."

"But he can't regenerate dead tissue."

"No, but these men just keep fighting. It takes an enormous effort to stop them."

"We can't fight that alone. We must wait a time for reinforcements from Kreith. And perhaps if we stay still long enough, our enemies will be lured from the castle and away from Crotalus. Perhaps even the wizard himself will come out to greet us."

As the men settled down on the ground to wait, some sleeping, others watching the castle, others quietly talking, Palmer kept his eyes on the castle, not daring to blink, sure that Crotalus was waiting for a slip on their part so he could leave.

Two hours later there was movement in a window high in the castle. Palmer squinted his eyes, but only saw a black dot against the light of the window. "What is that?" he asked McIlree.

"I can't tell, but it's getting larger."

Palmer kept watching. "It's not getting larger, it's getting closer."

"It's some kind of a bird, I think."

Palmer drew an arrow from his quiver and slowly stood up, his eyes never leaving the bird.

"It's a falcon," McIlree said.

Palmer grunted. "He has a macabre sense of humor." He aimed the bow carefully and as the bird flew overhead, he let loose the arrow. The falcon seemed to sense that he had been shot at and whizzed down at Palmer's head. McIlree ducked, but Palmer refused, and though he tried to load another arrow quickly, by the time it was done the falcon was gone.

Palmer looked to McIlree. "We can enter the castle. Tell your men to slaughter the enemy. It will be gruesome work, for a simple arrow in the heart won't do it. Cut off heads and arms; use swords as well as arrows. They must be totally destroyed."

"What of Crotalus?"

Palmer looked in the direction of the Forgotten City, the direction he had seen the falcon fly. "He has left. May our friend be protected by Menon."

Thirty

Batakis and Devona sat with the bodies of Lis and Anne. Devona cradled them as though they still contained souls, sang to them, washed them and fed them. They had considered taking these two to Beren with them, but Farni so far had refused. He could not leave Zopel because of the fishing business, and he felt Velad demanded that he stay and his children remain. Cand spoke with him quietly in the corner, telling him of the Redeemer God, urging him to let go of belief in the sea goddess.

"Come and walk with me," Devona said to Batakis. "I have been sitting long and need stretching." Batakis accompanied her outside.

"Tell me what is on your mind, Batakis. I can see that you wrestle with some great thought."

"It is not a great thought, and I feel petty at times thinking it."

"What is it?"

"I have longed for a vision of Menon, Devona. What child of His hasn't? Why do the people who have served Him all their lives not receive a vision?"

Devona silently contemplated Batakis' face. "You have fallen into the mistake of supposing that receiving a vision is better than not."

"Isn't it?"

"Not always. Tell me which takes greater faith—believing in Menon although He is silent, or holding to Him because of a vision?"

"The first, of course."

"A vision is not a reward, Batakis. Although you doubt your faith, it is much stronger than Cand's. There will come a time when Menon masks His presence with Cand and demands that Cand follow Him for Himself alone."

"Then why did Menon give him a vision at all?"

"He is a man who has dealt in divinations and omens all his life. Menon bends to our needs in order to draw us to Him. You see how Cand speaks to the people that know him. He was a high priest, and they demanded visions of him. Well, now he has one to give them, a vision of the Redeemer God."

Batakis sorted through this in his mind. "Why then doesn't Menon give visions to all of them? They would turn to Him quickly."

"That is not His way. That would overpower them. They would not have a choice. The choice must be made to either love Menon or reject Him."

"Is that what happened with Cand?"

"He made the choice. Menon has been pursuing Cand all his life. He arranged circumstances to place Cand in the position he is in, and when life is over, Cand will look back and say there was never any time that Menon was not with him, urging him to doubt the lifeless gods, wooing him with love. You have seen the impact Cand has already had on the people in Zopel. Lomeli has turned, Niccola who never had any use for the gods has turned, Farni is even now changing. The people are listening, and lives are being transformed."

Batakis smiled. "In some ways, I suppose, witnessing this is more exciting than a vision. Is Farni believing?"

"Farni is a rather special case. Niccola turned because she suddenly saw the wickedness of her life. Lomeli turned because he saw his wife change. But look at Winni and Drucker. They are devout people, filled with the rules and laws of their gods. Cand talked with them yesterday, and they almost killed him because of his blasphemy. They will not convert.

"Farni, though, has always had a bit of rebellion in him toward the gods. He had been told that his daughters were punishments for a life of disobedience, and yet he loved them anyway. He should have sacrificed them to purge himself, but he wouldn't. He has followed the goddess because he was told that was right, but he has never had the heart for it and at times has seen the cruelty of his religion. I think Farni is another one Menon has been preparing for a very long time. He was half-believing before Cand even came to the door. Come . . . It is time we were back inside."

"Thank you, Devona. You always know the right things to say to lift my heart."

"I couldn't do any less for one who has given me so much."

"I love you, you know."

Devona smiled. "Don't start with your foolishness now. There's too much work to be done."

• • •

Niccola had commanded the most skilled doctors to treat Jerome, and although they had removed the arrow, he was still in much danger and would require constant nursing. Niccola took his care upon herself, hovering over him anxiously, meeting his smallest request with great pleasure. There was nothing she didn't do for him.

Queen Alexandria, though she desperately longed to be with her husband, could not leave Beren. Her duties as queen held her to the throne as constantly as did Jerome's, and she would not leave her people, especially in a time of war and bereavement, without a leader.

Niccola respected this attitude and wished she could know the woman who was Queen of Paduan. In deference to her, she sent daily accounts of Jerome to Alexandria and vowed within herself that if Jerome worsened, she would urge Alexandria to come and would take upon herself the ruling of Paduan if necessary.

Jerome's health, though, did not decline. Rather, he continued to become stronger, the color returning to his face, although there was still too much pain to sit up for very long. He questioned Niccola often about the war, and since she received reports from Palmer as well as Kreith she kept him well-informed and watched him fight the enemy with military strategies in his mind.

Niccola bided her time until Jerome was strong enough to converse with her longer than a few minutes. She then went to him, knelt at his bedside, and with tears marking her face confessed to him her part in Solon and Fel-hoen's murders, her treachery toward Falcon, and his own betrayal.

"I am not now seeking your forgiveness, sire. I know that may be long in coming, and I do not deserve even that. I am placing myself in your hands. I have injured many people and have put your country in jeopardy through my ambition. I renounce all rights to this country. It is yours. Do with me and it as you see fit, my king."

Jerome laid his hand on her head, deeply touched by her submission to his authority. "I forgive you with my whole heart, Niccola.

Although you were conscious of what you were doing, you had no knowledge of a higher way. You now have the love of Menon within you. He has shown you your wrongs, and you have repented of them. He forgives you willingly and entirely. I now do the same.

"You have great strength in you, Niccola, strength that I much admire. You have used your gift to ill purposes in the past. I now urge you to put them under Menon's hand to rule this country."

"I have no right to it. Kenda is the queen."

"Kenda came to me last night. She has no desire to continue as queen. She asks only that in recompense for the loss of her husband she be allowed to live in the castle under your care with her daughter, Merry. Will you meet that condition?"

"Gladly, Your Highness, but I am not worthy."

"Nor am I. Niccola, no king has a right to his country. He is an undeserving ruler, and this fact, if remembered, makes him a great ruler."

"Do you still wish Kreith and Merry to wed?"

"Yes."

"Then, if you so desire, I shall rule this country under your guidance until the time when Kreith and Merry ascend to the throne."

Jerome smiled. "That is what I desire."

"I shall leave you now, as I know you need rest, but I could not find peace until I had placed myself under your authority." She paused and then asked suddenly, "Did Palmer tell you about this?"

"No. He said you were friends, but he did not say anything else."

She smiled. "He's a good friend. He told me to come to you, but I am astounded that he said nothing to anyone else about the things I had confessed."

"Palmer is a good man and a fast friend. If he thought it your responsibility to confess to me, he would have said nothing. Develop your friendship with him, Niccola. He is a man who will keep you true to yourself and Menon. I have had few friends such as he and Falcon Jaqeth. They are rare. So if you have found one in Palmer, do not let go. It is painful sometimes, but friends like that are few, and you cannot afford to lose them."

"Thank you, my king. I shall remember."

She left him then, feeling cleansed and possessing a new sense of purpose. She pledged to win back Palmer's esteem and keep it. She promised to be the kind of leader Jerome and Alexandria believed her to be.

• • •

Duncan walked with amazement into the capital city of Zopel. He had expected large, beautiful buildings, summer greenery, and gentle, likable people. Never had he seen such grime. The buildings were large, and he supposed that in normal circumstances they were beautiful. But now they were covered with dirt from the streets, masking the richness of the city. This was not the squalor of poverty but of apathy, and even the people were touched by it, having been turned into savages by their grief.

He heard the cries of people, peaking and then descending, only to crescendo again. It was a mourning that exposed their innermost pain to the gods. More, it was the wail of a people abandoned by their gods.

Though he walked through the entire city and then back again, Duncan found no children. They had been abundant in Amick and Andurin, their voices rich with life. But here . . .

Duncan gathered from snatches of conversation he overheard that Crotalus had stolen the children. In time Amick, Andurin, Derrich—indeed the whole world—would all be childless. The world would die.

Duncan regretted that he had not spent more time talking with the old woman in Amick. He had heard rumors of a war against Crotalus, but assumed it was only to recover Temrane. Crotalus was obviously interested in more than just the boy.

He came to the temple of Hoen and walked inside, wrinkling his nose at the smell of burnt flesh and spilled blood. *Ah, Menon*, he thought, *if I could only show all of them how unnecessary this is!*

"Can I help you?"

He turned and faced a young, solemn-looking priest in a long white linen gown with gold braiding on the cuffs and hem. "I am looking for the high priest."

"I am Galion, the high priest to Hoen. How may I serve you?"

"I must be mistaken. The priest I am looking for is named Candhoen. Do you know him?"

Galion's eyes were frosty steel balls in an impassive face. "He is no longer a priest. Why do you wish to see him?"

"I have something belonging to him which I wish to return. I am a stranger in these lands and have not heard of his decline. Why is he no longer of the priesthood?"

"He lied to the god and turned his back on him. He loved a mere mortal more than Hoen. I have heard that in the last few days he has returned to Zopel and preaches in the streets. He is a mad heretic!"

"As I said, I wish to return something to him. Do you know where I can find him?"

Galion turned to go, distaste for this visitor mounting. "Listen in the streets for talk of a god called Menon."

Duncan left the temple in wonder. Had Menon indeed grabbed hold of the high priest, wrenching him from death, and was now holding him in His hands?

He wandered the streets and took Galion's advice, listening intently at the fragments the wind brought his way, and soon found himself near the castle by a small hut. He debated whether to knock, but before he could announce himself to anyone a man was pushed through the doorway followed by angry voices: "We don't want to hear anything from you, blasphemer! You should have died in your mother's womb!"

The man sprawled on the ground, and Duncan hurried over to him, holding out a hand to help him up. The man grasped it gratefully. Duncan grinned at him. "I have been looking for you, my friend."

"A number of people have, not all as friendly-looking as you. Are you sure it is I whom you seek?"

"Are you Cand-hoen?"

"I used to be, but now I am simply Cand. Who are you?"

"My name is Duncan. I have much to tell you, but not here in the street. There are too many others who might be anxious to hear what I have to say. Can we go somewhere more private?"

"The queen of the city has graciously given me a room in the castle with my friends. We can go there."

• • •

"I want to go home," Temrane told McNyre, who was struggling to wake up.

"What time is it?"

"I don't know, and I don't really care. I want to go home."

McNyre sighed. "I know, and as soon as Duncan returns we will talk of getting ye home."

"You don't understand. I want to go now."

McNyre touched Temrane's hand and felt the boy jerk it away. "Another dream?" he asked.

"Are you going to take me home, or must I go by myself?"

McNyre was confused at Temrane's sullen anger. In the time they had been together, they had grown closer, sharing sorrows, being able to laugh at one another, able to dream. Then the nightmares had started. Temrane would not say what they were about, but McNyre felt intuitively they were about either his father or Crotalus. Gradually Temrane was slipping away from him. He longed to pull the boy to him, but that would only drive Temrane further away.

"Temrane, can I at least light the lamp so we can talk face to face?"

"No!"

There was such panic in the lad's voice that McNyre knew he had to look at Temrane. He turned on the lamp, repressing a sudden shudder as he saw the boy's chest and hands covered with blood and feathers.

"What happened?"

Temrane's eyes were wide with fear. "I want to go home!"

Although McNyre was repulsed, he knew he needed to touch Temrane, to break through the barrier Temrane had erected. He reached out, but the boy turned from him. Not easily discouraged, he got out of bed, walked to Temrane, and pulled him into his grasp. Temrane struggled only a moment before collapsing against McNyre. McNyre could feel the slime of blood against his bare stomach and quelled his rising nausea.

Temrane pulled away. "I'm going to be sick!" he said and dashed to the washbasin, vomiting just as he reached it. McNyre stood beside him and stroked his forehead and back as Temrane was sick again in the basin. A third bout finished it.

McNyre wet some rags and cleaned Temrane's face. He then washed his chest of the blood-soaked feathers, laid Temrane in his bed, and sat beside him. "Do ye wish to tell me what happened?"

"I had a dream, and when I woke up I was holding a dead bird to my chest."

"Did this happen in your other dreams?"

"No."

"Tell them to me."

"In the first one I dreamed I was in the mountains by Crotalus' castle again, and my father was standing over me with the Calli-kor knife. He was going to sacrifice me so he could become a man. In the second one I was with Crotalus and we were performing some spell, but I can't remember what, something about raising the dead. The one tonight, though, was the worst. I dreamed I killed my father. Crotalus told me to kill him, and I did. I woke up, and I had killed a bird." He started crying, and McNyre wondered how much longer the boy could hold his sanity. "I want to go home, McNyre. My father's dead, and I want to go home."

"Your father isn't dead just because ye dreamed it."

"He's dead. I can feel it."

"There is a war going on. He might be dead. I'm not going to lie to ye. But he isn't dead because ye dreamed it. If he's dead, it's because someone killed him or he fell down the stairs or his heart stopped."

"I don't want to go back to sleep."

"I'll stay here with ye until you fall asleep."

"But I'm afraid I'll hurt something else."

"I won't let ye, Temrane . . . I'll be here."

Temrane at last quieted, and McNyre sat until dawn watching him sleep, praying to Duncan's God to protect him, wishing he could ease the demons that pursued the lad in his mind.

• • •

Rafaela found McNyre cleaning the bird from Temrane's room. "What happened?" she asked.

"Nothing," he said lightly, refusing to look at her. "I think a bird must have crashed into the window or something."

"McNyre, the glass isn't broken, it isn't even open for a bird to come in, and by the looks of that bird it has been crushed. If there is some reason you don't want to tell me what happened, then just say so. My feelings won't be hurt, and I won't press you to tell me."

He looked at her a moment, wondering where her core of strength came from, for she looked so fragile. "I'm sorry. I want to talk with someone, but I'm not sure ye be the one."

"Then perhaps you should wait for Duncan. He must have started back by now."

"It can't wait that long." He looked at the broken body in his hands. "I'm afraid for Temrane. He's . . . I don't know . . . slipping away. I'm losing him." He looked at her boldly, ready to say to her words he had not even admitted to himself. "I love him, Rafaela."

She was touched by the tears in his eyes as he spoke of his love for Temrane. "McNyre, I long to help you and Temrane, but I can't if you won't trust me."

"I will trust ye. Let me finish cleaning this, and then we'll talk in some bright and shiny place where darkness cannot hide."

She helped him remove all traces of the bird from Temrane's room, and then while McNyre washed she went into McNyre's room to look at Temrane. He lay still in the bed, barely breathing. Though one less observant might say he slept soundly, she could see the skittering eyelids that looked as though they might fly open at any time. She also saw what no one else could see: the slight shadow covering his face.

McNyre and Rafaela went to the kitchen to talk. As soon as McNyre walked in, he could feel the sunshine slipping into his soul as it cascaded through the large windows that covered every wall. Rafaela made a drink from mint and tea leaves and then sat down with McNyre at one end of the large wooden table.

"He has started to have nightmares, three of them so far—all having to do with either Crotalus or his father leaving him. After the first nightmare, he crawled into bed with me, we talked a few minutes, and he slept there the rest of the night. The next day he was distant and cross. I assumed it was because he hadn't slept well. The next time he again got in bed with me, but didn't say a word, and then he wasn't just cross, but angry."

He stared into his cup, his heart aching. "Last night he came in and demanded that I take him home. I lit a lamp and saw him covered with blood and feathers. He told me he had dreamed of killing his father. When he woke up, he had killed the bird."

Rafaela closed her eyes a moment, and McNyre realized she was listening and praying. He had seen Duncan do the same.

"You are right to fear for him, McNyre . . . He is in grave danger."

"From who?"

"Crotalus."

"It's impossible. Duncan and I were very careful about getting him here without his knowledge."

"Crotalus doesn't know yet that he is here."

"I don't understand."

"Don't underestimate the power of Crotalus. He is perhaps the most powerful wizard our world has known. Years ago the Amil Mountains were filled with witches and sorcerers, but the greatest fear a wizard has is a wizard with greater control than his. They cannot live together without feeding off one another. Crotalus' lust for food was stronger and greater than the others, and they perished until only Crotalus was left. When they died, he received their power."

"We know he is powerful. What does that have to do with Temrane?"

"Crotalus has the power to mark individuals, and the shadow of his mark is on Temrane. He sends his creatures to do his bidding, and they search out the mark. He sends dreams to haunt the one with the mark."

"So, is this only to torment Temrane?"

"I wish it were, but each time the wizard makes connection he draws a little closer to knowing where Temrane is. That is his real purpose – to find Temrane."

"Then Temrane is not safe here?"

"He is not safe anywhere."

McNyre struggled with the frustration and fear building in him. "Did Temrane kill that bird?"

"Yes . . . at Crotalus' bidding."

"Then we are not safe either."

"Crotalus would not hurt me. And I believe that Temrane's love is strong enough for you that he would not hurt you."

"Can he break the mark?"

Rafaela's eyes filled with tears. McNyre saw her clutch her hands together in fists, fighting for control. Her hands then relaxed, and she wiped away a tear that had rolled off her lash onto her cheek. "It is not always so easy, McNyre."

McNyre before had wondered about her unusual strength, and now he saw that if she had not been made strong through her trials, she would have been crushed under their weight. "Are ye still marked, Rafaela?"

She laughed – a small, shaky sound. "No. Little by little Crotalus was forced to let go of me as Menon took my life into His. I am no longer marked, but the desires still reside in me, more forceful of late. I fear sometimes that I will go back to Crotalus, the yearnings are that great. But I am strong, and I fight them with everything I have. A day is coming, I feel, that I will meet Crotalus face to face. My own strength cannot fight that, and I only pray to have strength enough to turn to Menon and ask for His strength.

"That is what I fear for Temrane. He does not know Menon. His gods are lifeless and helpless, and he is only a boy. I don't know if he is strong enough to fight."

"He has to be! I shall be strong for him!"

"It is his own battle, and he must make his own choices."

"Rafaela, ye can help him! Talk with him. Ye understand—ye have the yearnings that he must feel inside. If your Redeemer God hears ye, beg for the salvation of Temrane."

"That I can do," she said and rose from the table. McNyre followed her, his heart heavy with grief and a longing to bear this burden for Temrane.

Rafaela walked into McNyre's room and sighed heavily. McNyre passed by her into the room, but the bed was empty. Temrane had departed.

Thirty-One

Falcon hummed a song he had learned from his father about the Redeemer. The day was bright and warm, with no hint yet of Fall. He felt uplifted by the children, and life seemed wonderful. As his horse trotted closer with each step to the Forgotten City, Falcon was not content any longer with humming, but burst into song. He sang gustily and loudly of his love for Menon and his yearning for fellowship with Him, and the birds and animals he traveled with seemed to sing with him. But as he drew closer to the Wastelands and at last crossed into them, life became scarce until finally he was again singing alone.

Except for a large falcon above him. He kept an eye on his namesake, wondering why this bird should follow him into the Wastelands.

He slid from one song into another and then into another, not caring where one left off and the other began. As he started an unusual song he made up, he heard a chuckle. He stopped singing, halted the horse, and listened, but the noise had gone. As soon as he set off, he heard it again. At first he thought that perhaps one of the children had followed him, but this was an adult sound and lacking in innocence. It was not the first time he had heard that laugh.

"Show yourself," he said at last, stopping the horse. "Or do you intend to ambush me as the coward you are?"

The falcon swooped down to the ground and transformed into the laughing wizard. "I have no desire to ambush you. I would much prefer that you kill yourself."

"That is unlikely."

"Not as unlikely as you think perhaps. But is this any way for old friends to talk? We have not seen each other in thirteen years, Falcon. Have you taken a wife?" he hissed.

Falcon felt his anger surge, and he ground his teeth together. He knew that Crotalus was intentionally goading him, and he hated the fact that he responded so easily. He remembered a time, not so long ago, when Devona had offered him advice: *Don't let your weakness be your undoing.* He smiled a little, the anger easing. "I did not need to take a wife. I had a woman's love. You were the one she scorned," he said in a friendly tone.

Now it was Crotalus' turn to blacken with rage, and Falcon watched as he also grappled for control. As the battle was won, Crotalus smiled at him, showing Falcon that he had plans yet to be revealed. "Where is the boy?" he asked at last, his voice again laden with feigned friendliness.

"Which boy?"

"The boy you stole from me . . . my apprentice."

So Prince Temrane had somehow escaped. Why did Crotalus think he was with Falcon? "I have no idea what you're talking about."

"I have tracked him this far and sense he is very close."

"I pray to Menon that he escapes."

Crotalus' face darkened. "You are a fool for still believing in your sham god. If he is so powerful, let him come to me here and slay me."

Falcon laughed. "You have not changed, Crotalus."

Falcon's laughter infuriated the wizard. "Enough!" he hissed. "I have had enough of this bantering."

"I also magician," Falcon said scornfully, jumping from his horse and drawing his sword from its sheath. "I have waited thirteen years to kill you. Let us get it done with." He took a few steps toward Crotalus, who stood before him smiling.

"Wait!" the wizard said suddenly, grinning insanely at Falcon. "Before you slay me, I have something for you."

Falcon stopped and watched as Crotalus removed a jar from the folds of his robe. Upon seeing the jar, Falcon felt a thud in his stomach, wondering what it contained, almost certain he knew.

"Do you know what this is, Falcon Jaqeth?"

"I don't know *who* it is."

"Ah, but you have surmised that it is a soul. Very good. You have lost none of your intelligence. But what's this? I see fear in your eyes, Falcon. Is it Palmer? It could be. Or what about your sister? That could be interesting, although I think I could find better uses for her than stealing her soul."

"You evil, godless dog!" He lunged toward Crotalus, sword raised, intent on severing his head from his loathsome neck. But before he could reach him, Crotalus threw the bottle up in the air. Falcon stopped as though a giant hand had been placed in front of him and watched the bottle with dread fascination as it spun in the air, dropping until Crotalus caught it.

"Don't do that again, Falcon. I might not catch it next time. Let me tell you a little about this bottle, and then I'll tell you about the soul in it and the bargain I have for you."

"I do not bargain with blackguards!"

"Not even for the life of this soul? Don't be so rash! This bottle is very special. It is very thin crystal. I made it myself. It is so fragile that I could have shattered it just by catching it too tightly in my hands. If I dropped a heavier bottle here in the sand, the sand would cushion it and it would not break. But if I were to drop this one, it would be destroyed. Without the protection of the bottle, the soul would go out into nothingness, to be lost forever. Do you understand me?"

"Completely."

"I hope you are enjoying this, Falcon. You have waited for this for thirteen years, as have I. I am having a marvelous time. How about you?"

"Who is it?"

"That is the real question, isn't it? I can see that I will interest you on no other point until I reassure you just a little bit. It is not Palmer, and it isn't Ivy. But I want you to bargain for this life."

"What kind of bargain?"

Crotalus smiled. "A delicious one, Falcon. I have waited many long years for this moment. Just let me ask you a question first. Is there anything in this world you would rather have than my death?"

"I can't think of anything at the moment."

"Good. Likewise, it is my fondest desire to see you not only dead, but crawling in humiliation."

"I will not crawl in front of you . . . ever."

"Maybe not in front of me, but it shall happen. This is my bargain: I will let you kill me. You can make it as slow or as quick as you choose."

"What price will you exact?"

"The life of this soul. If you kill me, he will die. It is that simple."

"And if I choose not to kill you?"

"Then I will kill you. It is a beautiful bargain, is it not?"

"But if I kill you, you will have lost."

"It may seem like it, but I shall really have won."

"Why?"

"Because in that instant you will have renounced Menon. You will be saying that your life is more important than the life of this person. And you always told Rafaela that wasn't true, that in Menon's eyes all were equal. So prove it now, Falcon Jaqeth. Prove your words and prove your god . . . let me kill you."

"So either way you win, is that it?"

"Yes . . . in essence. But I don't want to just kill you. I want you to renounce Menon. I want you to suffer through life knowing that you were the cause of this man's death, and that you said you were more important than your god."

Falcon felt the sun bearing down on his head. "Tell me who it is."

"Does it matter?"

"No. It is just curiosity."

"I'm glad you asked, Falcon, because I long to tell you all about this person. That is part of the beauty of it. My first impulse was to take Palmer. Two things stopped me. The first is that he is protected, as you are. I can kill him with arms, but not with the arts of darkness. The second thing was the fact that you would be only too willing to die for Palmer. The same held true with Ivy or Jerome. I didn't want to make this an easy choice for you."

He chuckled and held up the bottle. "Look at it, Falcon. This is a man's soul. It is not light and airy, nor very black with dark deeds. It is gray. It is almost nothingness itself trapped inside a bottle.

"His name is Gilreth, and you do not know him. He is not of Paduan, but of Andurin in Corigo. His lord, Soaje, is a traitor to the throne at Corigo and at this moment is fighting against your army. Gilreth is a knight, but not a very high one. He is simply a soldier. He has done no noble deeds, no magnificent feats. Compared to the great Falcon Jaqeth, son of the great Dragon Slayer, he is nothing. He is a traitor . . . a stupid, worthless traitor. It would be easy to kill him, wouldn't it?"

"Shut up!"

"Do you need time to think it over? Go ahead . . . I have plenty of time. After all, what are a few minutes between friends?"

Falcon didn't want to think it over—he wanted to act immediately, snatching the bottle from Crotalus' hands and letting Crotalus kill him. But he hesitated, his mind sounding warnings within him, going over the choices again and again.

What did it matter? This Gilreth was not even a believer in Menon. But Falcon was, and Menon commanded him to give up his anger, his lust for revenge, his ravenous desire to slay the wizard.

He grasped the hilt of his sword tightly, stilling his hands that wanted to shake with rage. What of Rafaela? He didn't want to die now that he was about to hold her again, and in killing Crotalus he would be protecting her. The death of Crotalus would mean safety for the Forgotten City, for the prince, for Rafaela, for all of them.

Yet, supreme love demanded he protect this one also.

Don't make me choose, Menon, he prayed. *I can't. Send down fire from Heaven to consume Crotalus. Or let the earth open up and swallow me. Don't make me choose! The desire to kill him is so strong, and although I know what You command me, I don't think I'm strong enough to obey.*

Falcon could feel the battle raging between the man he had been and the one Menon had redeemed. Tears sprang to his eyes—tears of frustration, of pain, of a longing to be who Menon wanted him to be.

"Choose, Falcon!"

"I can't! You have placed an impossibility before me. You have set something before me where I have no hope of winning."

"Then you lie, Falcon Jaqeth, and your god is a mockery! You spoke of this life being a prelude to real life with Menon. If you believed that, you would not hesitate. You do not need to kill me for me to win. I have won already. Crawl before me!"

Falcon looked at Crotalus and was repulsed. The waist-long hair snaked around his head as though it lived; skin flaked from him like snow. He tried to look at him through Menon's eyes and failed. He could not see anything lovely about him. *I will kill him*, he thought, *and let Menon have His vengeance upon me.*

"I will not crawl," he whispered and raised his sword. He took a step toward an eager Crotalus, lifting the sword high in the air, ready to bring it whistling down on Crotalus' head. And then he stopped, Menon's love halting him, causing him to think one more time, to place himself under Menon's authority. He closed his eyes and focused on the Redeemer. *Menon, grant me peace . . . Grant me power to resist that which I have wanted for so long. I have nothing, but in You I have everything.*

Falcon opened his eyes and saw the rebellious creature in front of him. He threw the sword to one side.

"Have you then chosen death?" the wizard hissed.

"By the grace of Menon, I have," he whispered.

"Then die, Falcon Jaqeth!" Crotalus shouted victoriously, dropping the bottle to the ground.

Receive me into your arms, Menon, Falcon thought as he lunged for the bottle. His hand closed around it a bare inch from the ground, and in the same instant Falcon felt a searing in his right shoulder as Crotalus' fangs sank deep into the skin, filling him with poison.

Falcon's sight darkened almost immediately, but he heard the maniacal laughter of Crotalus as he transformed into a bird and flew away. Falcon lay still, waiting for the death that was sure to come. He felt a wonderful peace and contentment steal over him, and he felt he could reach out and touch the face of God. He closed his eyes and let the darkness overtake him.

Thirty-Two

Temrane walked south, not knowing where he was going, not caring. He had overheard a little of McNyre and Rafaela's talk. He had heard that he was marked. As far as he could tell, he had four choices. The first was to go home. Since his father was dead, and he had no doubts about that, he would be safe there. And Candy was there. He didn't know if Candy would want him, but he had to see him. Against this, he put the mark Crotalus had placed on him. He would endanger too many by returning. He had killed a bird; he could possibly kill a person.

He could go to Crotalus. Everyone else would be protected then, and perhaps the war would cease. If Crotalus wanted an apprentice, then he would be a good one. Crotalus would be much kinder to him as an apprentice than as an escapee. Something in him yearned to do this very thing, to place himself in Crotalus' hands and let go. But the love inside him held him back. Rafaela was Crotalus' obsession, and Temrane would not risk Crotalus using him to hurt her or to force her to leave the Forgotten City. He had seen the pain come over her face when she talked about Crotalus, and though he knew she had loved him once, and might still, he also knew that she served the Redeemer God and that this was a stronger love.

His third option was to remain with McNyre and Rafaela. He would have rather done this than anything, for he liked being with Rafaela. Although she was not as beautiful as his mother, she was kind to him, and he felt comforted just being in her presence. His thoughts swung to McNyre, and tears stung his eyes. Against all his judgments, against his will, and even against McNyre's warnings, he had come to love McNyre like a father. He was jealous of his attention and longed for his recognition. He was impatient when he could not be with McNyre. His anger after the nightmares was not directed to McNyre, although Temrane knew that McNyre had wondered if it was. It was not anger, but rather fear that he might kill McNyre. He would rather die than hurt the man he had come to love so much.

And so he came, at last, to the only decision left open to him. He must die. He had left the Forgotten City with no food or water; he did not even take a horse. He would walk until death overtook him, and if Crotalus found him before that happened, he would take a knife and, although the gods forbade it, still his own heart.

God of Duncan, he prayed, *let my passing be peaceful, and if Hoen will not or cannot receive my soul, then take it to Yourself. God of Duncan, be my God.*

• • •

Rafaela prepared food and water for McNyre to take while he impatiently paced the floor waiting for it, and when he snapped at her to please hurry up, she was not angry. She understood from where his emotion came. Her own heart felt tight; her lungs couldn't seem to take in enough air.

"Which way will you go?" she asked.

"South."

"Why south?"

"He wants to go home, and south is the easiest way to get there. Rafaela, isn't that enough food?"

"I'm making extra for Temrane when you find him."

McNyre stopped pacing and looked at her. "Are ye saying he took no food with him?"

She couldn't look at him, didn't want to see the grief in his eyes. "I didn't want to tell you. He didn't take any food, and as far as I can tell he didn't take water. He wants to die, McNyre."

Although this truth blazed brightly in his mind, he crushed it down, refusing to give it credence. "Why should he want to die? He's only a boy. All of life is stretched out before him."

"All of life running from Crotalus? He sees no other way out."

"Do ye?"

"Yes," she said softly. "Crotalus must die."

"There is already a war being fought for that purpose."

"Crotalus is not that easy to kill. We shall talk of possibilities when Duncan returns."

"Will Temrane and I be here when Duncan comes?"

She smiled and shook her head a little. "I am not a prophetess, McNyre . . . I cannot see the future."

"Will ye come with me to find Temrane?"

"No . . . I can best serve Temrane here. I intend to enter into prayer as soon as you leave, and I will not rest until you return."

"I don't like leaving ye here alone."

"That is an odd thought. I was here alone when you were with Duncan. There were also many times I was alone when Duncan was here. Sometimes I didn't see him for days. I am used to being alone."

"It's not that, Rafaela. I fear for ye. Ye said Crotalus is drawing nearer. If he were to find ye when no one else was here . . ."

"McNyre, you have a bothersome knack for taking responsibility on yourself that doesn't belong to you. If Crotalus were to come here, it would be best that everyone was gone."

"But who would protect ye?"

"It is best to leave it in Menon's hands. Crotalus would not harm me."

"Ye said that before. But I worry that ye will not be able to hold out against him."

"I worry about that sometimes myself, but that too rests in Menon's hands. Your presence here even now cannot hold me if I choose Crotalus. You have enough to concern you without burdening yourself with my cares."

McNyre sighed deeply, wanting to stay, knowing he had to go, wishing he could foresee the end of all this. "Will ye pray for me also, Rafaela?"

"Continually."

"And when I return, will ye tell me about your God?"

"Gladly. I pray that Duncan will also be back by that time."

"My heart yearns to see him again." On impulse, he leaned forward and kissed her cheek, love for her welling inside him. She was possibly the first woman he had loved for herself alone and not to fulfill his needs. And because he did not desire her, but loved her anyway, he felt suddenly the loneliness he had not felt for a long time for his wife.

Rafaela helped him put the pack she had prepared on his back and then walked with him to the edge of the Forgotten City. She laid a hand then on his head. "Go in the peace and protection of Menon. May He grant success to your search and guide you safely back here. Be enveloped in His love and mine."

She turned back toward the Forgotten City.

"May your God also protect ye, Rafaela," he whispered as he mounted his horse and began moving south.

• • •

Rafaela went into her rooms, built a fire in the hearth, although the day was warm, and unlocked a small door in the closet that she had not opened in a long time. She removed a box and sat it on her lap. She sat contemplating the box for several minutes before releasing the lock. She opened it and stared at the three things it contained.

"Menon, You know I wish to ask You about Temrane and McNyre. I care for them, and I know You do also. But before I can meditate on them, I must be cleansed by You.

"Redeemer, You know these are things I have held on to for a long time and I have not allowed you access. I will no longer follow You because I fear Crotalus or because I love Falcon. My communion must be with You alone. Therefore, I hold these things before You. Advise me."

She removed a crystal ball from the box. Crotalus had given it to her at the beginning of their days together. When she held it in her hands, she felt warmth and remembered how simple life had been then. They had talked of wizardry and joining together in ruling.

"Why do I hold on to this, Menon? Is it because it came from Crotalus, or am I holding to my past life? If I wanted to, I could summon Crotalus with this. Do I cling to it so I can easily go back with him if I desire?" She looked into its rainbow surface, so delicate and filled with illusions, as their love affair had been.

"My life is now based on the rock of Your love. I no longer need a fragile piece of glass." This said, she cast the crystal ball into the fire, shattering it. She imagined Menon destroying that part of her along with it.

She reached into the box again and pulled out a packet of letters, bound with a black ribbon. Although they were memorized long ago, she opened them now and reread them, reliving the emotions they had once stirred. There were seven letters, all from Falcon. They did not speak of love for her but of love for the Redeemer God. They had been written before their special love for one another was born, merely from friend to friend. Rafaela remembered that when the last letter was delivered, she had realized she was in love with Falcon and wanted to know more of his God than what he revealed in his letters.

"I do not want my love for You based on someone else's relationship with You. It must be a personal bond between You and me. I have found You and have enjoyed fellowship with You in Your presence. I no longer need someone else's experience." She cast the letters into the fire. She watched as the flames devoured them, and felt herself consumed by the pure and holy fire of Menon.

She drew out the last item in the box and held it tightly in her hand before releasing her grip and staring at it. It was a simple gold ring, a mere circlet of metal. She twisted it toward the fire and watched as it caught the flickering light.

Tears, normally under check, flowed down her cheeks and into her hands, wetting the ring. This was to have been her wedding ring. Falcon had given it to her, and life at that moment had never seemed sweeter. Only hours later Crotalus shot at Falcon and, missing him, hit her. Her life had ended on that day.

"But I have been resurrected," she whispered. "I have new life in Menon."

She started to cast the ring into the fire, but something held her back. She listened carefully for Menon's voice, but where it had seemed imperative to destroy the ball and the letters, there was no such directive here. She slipped the ring onto her finger. "Falcon and I were getting ready to begin a new life together. That life was cut short. I will keep this as a memorial to the new life I have that will never end. Perhaps, Menon, in Your infinite goodness You shall allow us someday to be together again."

The box empty, she tossed it to the flames. She walked up the stairs to the tower and sat by the wall that looked south. She could not see McNyre, but she would stay here and watch for him and Temrane, and perhaps she would see Duncan as well.

"Menon, You have raised me into new life, You have cleansed me and healed me. May Your Spirit understand my longings, even if I cannot speak them concerning McNyre and Temrane."

• • •

McNyre rode hard, his eyes constantly scanning the vast expanse of sand for movement. The sun was well on its course across the sky when he finally spotted a black form in the distance. Thanking Duncan's God, he spurred the horse and trotted quickly toward the boy.

When he reached him, Temrane did not turn, but kept walking. McNyre dismounted and, leading the horse, walked beside Temrane, not speaking, content for a time just to have found him. At last the boy could not stand the silence. "Go away," he said. "It is dangerous for you here."

"'Tis more dangerous for ye, lad. I have food and water."

"I don't want food and water."

"Ye will get extremely hungry and thirsty without them."

Temrane stopped and looked at McNyre in exasperation. "I am not going back with you."

"I did not ask ye to. If ye are determined to head south, then I shall go with ye."

"I might kill you."

McNyre pondered that a moment, wanting to laugh and cry at the same time. "Would ye?"

Tears trembled on his lids. "I don't want to, but I might."

McNyre started walking again. "I'll take my chances."

"You're a fool."

McNyre turned and looked at him. "Ye be right there . . . I am a fool. Temrane, I have been all over this country and back with ye. I have fought off wolves, told things to ye that I have never said to anyone, and I even sacrificed a perfectly good shirt to bind your wounded leg. Do ye really think I would just let ye wander off and die?"

"I'm doing this because I don't want to hurt you."

"I love ye, lad! I would rather die here in the desert with ye than be safe and secure without ye." He strode over to Temrane and clasped the lad's head to his chest. Temrane put his arms around McNyre and cried, wondering if the tears he carried inside would ever be dried up.

"Do ye love me, Temrane?"

"I love you more than anything, except maybe my Uncle Candy."

"Then ye will not harm me. Love is stronger than that. Through whatever happens, we will be together. And if Crotalus comes searching for ye, he will have to kill me first."

Temrane smiled at him, daring for a time to believe that what McNyre said was true. "Do you have anything to eat?"

McNyre laughed and dropped the pack from his back. "Rafaela packed enough to feed us until the world ends!" He handed Temrane the jug of water and watched as he took a long pull from it, then handed him a chunk of cheese. "After we finish this little picnic," he said, "where will we go?"

Temrane looked longingly toward the south and then to the north. "I don't know."

"Why don't we go back to the Forgotten City? Rafaela is watching for us . . . I know she is. And Duncan will be back soon. Don't ye want to see Duncan again?"

"Yes . . . a lot."

"Duncan told me to take care of ye. What is he going to say if ye aren't with me when he returns?"

Temrane smiled. "I'll come back."

"Good! And we will talk with Duncan about getting ye to your uncle. I promise."

"What about Crotalus?"

"His days be doomed, I feel. Rafaela speaks of his death. And if ye be worried about the nightmares, I will watch over ye at night. He will not get to ye, Temrane. I will make sure of it."

Temrane stood up and brushed cheese and bread crumbs from his pants. "I'm ready."

They mounted the horse, and Temrane took one last look behind him to the south. "Wait!" he yelled suddenly.

"What is it?"

"I see something back there!"

McNyre swung the horse around and peered in the direction Temrane pointed. "I cannot see anything. What do ye think it is?"

"I don't know. It's not moving. Maybe it's just a dead animal or something."

McNyre frowned and spurred the horse. "It may be," he agreed. "Or it could be something important. There aren't many animals dead or alive this far into the Wastelands. Let's go see."

It seemed to take a long time to reach the form. McNyre was ready to give up and turn north when he could finally make out that it was a person. A horse stood beside him. McNyre goaded his horse and flew across the sand.

He jumped from the horse and ran to the man, who lay as if dead, face turned toward the sky, hands clutching a bottle. "Do ye know him?" he asked Temrane.

"No, but I can tell he is a knight. That sword next to him is not a common one, and the horse looks like a warrior's mount."

McNyre knelt beside him and listened at his chest. He discerned a faint heartbeat. "He's still alive!"

"Is he dying?"

"Yes . . . He will most assuredly die if we don't get him to the Forgotten City."

"Why isn't his horse dead?"

McNyre stared at the horse. Temrane was right. If this knight was dying of thirst, the horse should be also, and yet the horse looked as though he had had a drink not long before. "Look in the saddle, Temrane, and see what's in there."

Temrane opened one side and then the other. "Food and water . . . plenty of both. There is also some cloth . . . nothing much else."

Plenty of food and water. McNyre looked at the man. Why was he dying? He looked him over carefully. His face was unmarked and seemed exceptionally at peace. McNyre gently opened one of his eyelids and looked at his eyes. They were green with specks of blue, oddly intense even near death, but they did not register McNyre's presence.

Temrane had also knelt beside him and now pointed underneath him. "There's a little blood on his shoulder."

McNyre tried to remove the bottle from the man's hands so he could roll him over, but his hands refused to loosen. He held on to the bottle as though it were his life. McNyre rolled the knight gently on his side, careful not to crush the bottle beneath him.

Temrane was right again – blood spotted the man's shirt on the right side. McNyre lifted the shirt, revealing the shoulder. Two small puncture wounds were visible just below the shoulder blade. "What do ye make of that?"

Temrane stared at the holes. They were eerily familiar, but he could not say why. "They look like a snake bite," he offered weakly.

"Tell me what's on your mind, lad. Ye obviously think it is more than a snake bite."

"I don't know. It seems like I've seen it somewhere before. But that's impossible. I know I don't . . ." His voice faded off, his eyes growing wide.

"What is it?"

"Crotalus."

"This is the work of Crotalus?"

"Yes."

"How can ye tell?"

"I don't know . . . I just feel it."

"That's good enough for me. Can ye tell if he has been marked or not?"

Temrane stared hard at him, not sure exactly what he was looking for. "I don't think so."

"Well, one thing's for certain. If this is Crotalus' work, we cannot lose any time in getting him to the Forgotten City. Hopefully Rafaela will be able to counteract this magic. Help me take that bottle from him and get him on his horse."

"What do you think is in the bottle?" Temrane asked as he pried the knight's fingers loose, allowing McNyre to take the bottle.

"I can't say, but it is important to the man. Take it and put it in my saddlebag. We will guard it carefully for him."

Temrane did this and then helped McNyre lay the man over his horse. They mounted McNyre's horse and headed north.

Neither of them saw the tear that slipped from between the man's eyelids, dropping to the arid ground below him.

Thirty-Three

Rafaela knelt by the tower wall, her eyes straining to see through the darkness. She had been here at the wall for hours, waiting to see McNyre return with Temrane. Though she longed for sleep, she would not abandon her vigil. She somehow felt that Crotalus was close and that her prayers were needed to protect Temrane. *And me*, she thought. The time was drawing nearer when she would have no choice but to take up the sword against Crotalus.

As dawn began breaking over the land, her eyes welcoming the coming light, she saw movement in the distance. She waited impatiently for what seemed like hours before they drew close enough for her to see clearly. She rejoiced at the sight of Temrane riding in the saddle behind McNyre. They pulled another horse, and she could discern a man's figure lying across it.

She ran down the tower steps, through her rooms, down more stairs onto the main level of the castle. She had set up a room as an infirmary, but had never used it until she looked at Temrane's leg when he first came. She made sure the bed was set up and checked her medical supplies quickly, although it was too soon to tell what she would need.

Assured that the room was ready, she ran outside just as McNyre and Temrane arrived. Temrane jumped from the horse and ran to her. She opened her arms wide for him and held him, stroking his hair, seeing that the mark on him was still present, but was no worse. "Please don't do that again," she rebuked, full of love.

"I'm sorry I worried you."

"It wasn't me that was most terribly worried, although I did fear for you. I don't know what McNyre would have done without you."

Her arm still around Temrane, she walked over to McNyre and

wrapped her other arm around him. "I thank Menon that you have returned safely. Whom have you brought?"

"A knight we found in the Wastelands. Temrane thinks he has been poisoned by Crotalus. He still lives, but not for long, I fear."

"I have readied the infirmary. Can you carry him inside? I will look at him immediately."

As McNyre lifted him from the horse, Rafaela caught sight of the man's face and though she gasped, her heart lurching in her chest, she said nothing. McNyre looked at her.

"What is it?"

"Nothing . . . I wasn't sure you had a good hold on him." *Falcon*, she thought, *my Falcon has been killed by Crotalus.*

Rafaela and Temrane led the way into the infirmary, where McNyre laid Falcon on the bed. McNyre helped her remove his shirt, exposing the two punctures. She then busied herself searching for medicines and herbs, considering one and then selecting another instead.

"Can I stay and watch you?" Temrane asked.

"No . . . not this time. I want both of you out. He needs my utmost attention. You can come back in a little while." She gently pushed them out the door and closed it before returning to the medicine cabinets.

McNyre looked at Temrane. "She is right. He needs her fully right now. We will visit him later and see if he has improved."

"She was crying, McNyre."

McNyre sighed. He also had seen the tears. "There will be a time later to question her about it."

Rafaela had been unaware of the tears streaming down her face, sure that she had herself in complete control. She gathered her medicines and sat beside Falcon on the bed, not daring yet to look fully into his face, concentrating on the wound in his shoulder.

The punctures were deep, but the edges were clean. A series of white blotches indicated that poison was present. Knowing Crotalus was the perpetrator helped her immensely, as she knew the kinds of poison he used. His poisons were not particularly fast-acting, Crotalus preferring a slow death that tortured the dying with false hope. This poison was no different except that it apparently also had a paralytic effect. She surmised that Falcon had been rendered unconscious almost immediately.

She removed two leeches from a jar on the table beside her and gently laid them over the wounds. Why put him into coma? she wondered. Could Crotalus have pitied Falcon at that moment and decided that killing him was enough, that he did not need to torture his most hated enemy? It hardly seemed likely. Crotalus would have wanted conscious torture. Perhaps he did not know Falcon would lose awareness; perhaps he expected Falcon to be paralyzed and realize until his death that he thirsted and hungered and suffered from the heat, but could do nothing for himself. If that was the case, the unconsciousness was a gift from Menon.

She watched as the leeches became engorged and then detached them gently, noting that the blood flowed more freely from the wounds and the white blotches were gone. She could not be sure she had gotten all the poison, but she knew she had extracted a good portion of it.

She made a poultice with various herbs, including camphor and eucalyptus, and pressed it on his shoulder. She rubbed it around gently for a moment, allowing the salve to work its way into the wounds. She bandaged Falcon and would check his injury later. She then covered him with a light sheet.

Her work being done, she lowered herself to the floor so she could look at his face. Her fingers traced the small wrinkles about his eyes that had not been there before, traveled down the straight nose she remembered so well. She caressed the dark brown beard, noticing the few gray hairs. She entwined her fingers in it, recalling a time when he had been angry with her. As their heated words had silenced and both simply glared at one another, she had reached out and curled her fingers in his beard, tugging it gently. He had tried to keep the fight going, but it was impossible. He had swept her into his arms and buried his face in her hair.

"Falcon, my love, life has touched you lightly. You are more handsome now than ever before, and there is a peace written on your face that speaks of Menon's touch." She longed for him to open his eyes, but knew it was too soon.

The door opened behind her. "Can I come in for a moment?" McNyre asked.

"Of course," she said, wiping the tears from her face and rising from the floor to sit on a stool by the bed.

McNyre sat on another stool. "How is he?"

"It is still too soon to tell. I have bled him, but it may need to be done two or three more times before I have extracted all the poison. But for now, we wait."

McNyre sat silently, staring at his hands, wanting to say so much, but unsure how to begin. He had guessed when he saw her face that the man was Falcon Jaqeth. He knew that Rafaela loved him deeply, understood the sacrifice it had cost to give him up. He wondered what it would be like to see his wife after thirteen years. "I'm sorry," he said at last. "I know this must give ye great pain."

She smiled at him, but the smile contained much sadness. "I thought I would never see him again. I have prayed so hard at times to see him just once more. If he should die, McNyre, I will regret seeing him 'just once more.'"

"Your God wouldn't let that happen. He would not grant your request in order to cause ye pain."

"That is true, but sometimes things that cause me to grow also cause me pain." She looked at McNyre and saw the depth of his compassion. She could see that he longed to comfort her. "You know," she said, "in all the times I've imagined Crotalus and Falcon meeting, I never imagined that Falcon would lose. I always thought he would surely win." She started to cry.

McNyre had never seen her strength so close to breaking. He reached out to her, cradling her head on his chest. "He has not lost yet, Rafaela."

"I feel so helpless . . ."

"You have done all you can. Now let your God do the rest." He let her cry against him a moment. When her tears slowed he looked into her eyes, wishing for half a moment that he was Falcon Jaqeth. "'Tis hard to hold fast to your faith when ye be so tired. Ye did not sleep last night nor today. Go and rest."

"I can't leave him."

"I will watch him. If he even moves, I shall call ye immediately. How long does this bandage stay on?"

"No more than two hours, and then I'll have to change it, and possibly bleed him again."

"Then go rest. I will call ye in two hours unless he needs ye before then." She still looked reluctant. "Ye are not doing him a bit of good by tiring yourself."

"You're right," she said at last. "Call me if he makes any sound or any movement." She looked longingly at the still form on the bed, almost beseeching him to talk to her. She bent low and kissed him gently. "I was angry at you at first," she whispered in his ear. "I thought you had abandoned me. I know it wasn't your choice. But, Falcon, if it is your choice this time to live or die, don't die! I love you." She straightened and with a fond look at McNyre slipped from the room.

McNyre sat in the chair by the bed and looked at the motionless knight. "She is the most wonderful woman I have ever known. If ye do not come back to her, I shall be plenty angry."

• • •

Kreith wiped the sweat from his brow. Although they had battled against Andurin Castle steadily for three days, they seemed no closer to victory. Palmer had sent word to him from Crotalus' castle that the wizard had placed a spell on the warriors to keep them fighting. Kreith wondered if the same spell had been cast on Andurin.

Lord Thomas had led his men into the hills high above the castle to capture Lord Diones' men. The battle between the two armies was bloody. Thomas' men were less experienced than the more established lordship of Diones, but Diones had fewer numbers.

At last the men had been captured, Thomas showing mercy to the ones who swore loyalty to the sword of Prince Kreith. These men, at least, had not been bewitched.

Kreith's troops were seriously depleted, and he cursed his own lack of experience. He felt sure that if Falcon or his father were here, the losses would be much less. The fires Lord Soaje's men threw from the catapults set the forest around them blazing, and it was simply taking too many men to put them out. Water had run out long ago and was being hauled from the Andurin River, but that was time- and man-consuming. Something had to be done about the catapults.

Kreith gathered the lords and their highest knights around him. "As risky as it is, we must invade the castle. I will take five men—I dare not take more, and we will scale the walls of the castle on the north side. Thomas and Ulster will create a diversion to the south of the castle. I know that will put you very close to the river, but try to keep as many men on the south side as possible. Malcolm, Pelaro, and Sipple, attack the front and keep moving forward. Kies, since scaling the castle wall was originally your idea, you will come with me along with four men of your choice."

Kies nodded his understanding, choosing from his remaining men ones he thought capable of scaling a wall. Kreith glanced around at them all, knowing that each lord had lost many knights, many friends. This would be finished soon, he felt, one way or the other. He needed to end it now in order to send troops to Palmer. "Let's go," he said.

Kreith, Kies, and the four knights reached the north side of the castle without being seen, Kreith carrying the grappling hooks and long lengths of rope. From his vantage point on the northern hill, he could see that Thomas and Ulster had constructed their own blazing diversion. They were launching catapults loaded with burning bales of hay and cloth onto the castle. Although some fell short, a few cleared the walls and ignited Soaje's and Tegmen's own ammunition, creating a conflagration that lit up the sky.

Kreith could see men scrambling on top of the walls, trying to put out the flames before the castle and all its weapons were destroyed. "Now!" he said and the six men ran toward the castle, keeping low, alert for any enemy movement.

They rested at the base of the castle, listening to the sounds of the battle going on to the south of them. "We go up one at a time," Kreith said. "Being on the wall is a vulnerable spot. If one is seen, he will most certainly be shot. Go up quickly and quietly, and stay low once you reach the top."

Kreith stepped away from the wall, unwound his rope, and clutched it just below the grappling hook. He looked at the wall rising far above him. He had practiced this with Falcon, but the castle walls of Beren did not seem as high, and there he did not stand on a slope. He swung the hook around a few times, conscious of the men's stares, and threw it skyward. It rang noisily against the castle wall and fell back to the ground.

Kreith immediately started to pull it in and glanced at Kies. He did not smile, as Kreith imagined he might, and Kreith realized that it was not a great failure to not make a hit on his first heave. Or his second and third. This gave him confidence, and his fourth throw did not come back down. "Wait until I reach the top before you start to scale. If my rope comes back down, it means it is a trap and I have been ambushed. Do not then under any circumstances come up, but rather seek out Malcolm. I have placed him in command."

As there was nothing left to say, Kreith tugged on the rope, judged that it would hold, and began climbing. Although he had scaled the wall at Beren a few times, it had not been recently, and his calves began to cramp. But that ache was nothing compared to the pain in his arms and shoulders. He longed to let go just to relax them.

After climbing for what seemed like hours, he glanced up and could see the top ledge. He was tempted to look back down to see how far he had come, but remembered Falcon warning him not to. "There's no good reason to," the knight had said. "The sight of how high you are might paralyze you to where you can't move up or down." Kreith pushed on and grabbed the ledge with his hands. It took a tremendous effort to pull himself over the ledge since he was already exhausted, but he made it.

He relaxed for only a moment before scouting around quickly to make sure he had not been seen. He saw no one, but did see an open window a few feet away. "Thank You, Menon," he uttered. Glancing over the side, he saw one of Kies' men jump on the rope and begin climbing much more quickly than Kreith had done.

Kreith waited until all five of the other men were on the wall with him, then gave them a chance to relax their arms. "I want to find Soaje and Tegmen," he whispered. "If they can be persuaded to give this up, well and good. If not, we shall kill them. There is a good chance the men will surrender their arms if their lords are dead. We shall all enter the castle. There is too much danger of being killed by our own men if we remain on the wall."

He took a deep breath and, keeping low, entered the dark castle through the window.

• • •

Falcon walked through tall reeds in the sand. At last he came to the edge of the beach, water stretching out endlessly in front of him. Wet sand squished between his toes and the waves came in, crashing against his legs, washing away the sand. He turned and walked up the beach. His feet splashed in the water.

Then the water was replaced by wheat, the sand by dark, fertile earth. He was naked, the sun warming him in his purity. He walked and then began running, relishing the feeling of the wheat slapping against his legs. The smell of musky earth and growing things filled his nostrils as his feet crushed the ground, creating a life that surged through him.

He saw the man walking toward him and felt the life within him cry out to the man. He stopped running. He wanted in some ways to turn and run the other way, but he stood still.

The man's hair seemed as gold as the wheat, but Falcon couldn't tell if that was its real color or because the sun shone on him so brightly. He wore a white linen robe that reached to his bare feet. The sun wove its way into every thread of the robe until everything about the man seemed to shine.

He approached and stood before Falcon. Falcon looked into his eyes. They were a dark brown in color, but seemed filled with fire. They burned Falcon with their intensity and made him wish he could hide. Yet, he saw a love in those eyes that far exceeded any expression of love he had before seen. The love wrapped him in its warmness.

He knelt down before the man. He wanted to shout his love to him, but could not speak because of its magnitude. The man touched him on the head. "Rise," he said kindly. Falcon did and felt himself embraced in the man's powerful arms. "Walk with me, my friend."

Tears streamed down Falcon's face—this man had called him *friend*. They walked for miles, enjoying each other's company. Then they raced through the fields, the man relaxing his pace to match Falcon's, although Falcon was not slow. Falcon lay down with the wheat surrounding him, staring at the sky. The man lay next to him, and they contemplated the clouds and a few stars that amazingly Falcon could see even though the sun was shining. They talked of life, of people they both knew, of the man's desires for Falcon. Falcon found himself telling this man things he had never shared with anyone. He felt as though he were disclosing his very soul to an old friend. At last they rose from the ground and stood before a castle, tall and white, in a city of surpassing beauty.

"It is time to go," the man said.

"Where are you going?"

"Not I, but you. You are sleeping in that castle there and must soon awaken. It is in the Forgotten City."

"But where are the Wastelands?"

The man smiled. "You are standing in what you call the Wastelands. You are just seeing things that normally are beyond your vision."

Falcon thought of his walk through these fields with the man and the things of which they had talked. His heart ached at the prospect of leaving. "I would rather stay with you."

"It is not your time yet."

"Am I having a vision?"

"You can call it that if you like."

"Then I will call it a vision. What do I call you?"

The man laughed, his gold hair shaking around him, the sound working its way into Falcon's heart until he too laughed. "I am the Most High . . . I am Menon . . . I am the Redeemer . . . I am the Alpha and Omega . . . I am the Sovereign God."

"And yet You call me friend."

"I do." He held his hand up in a farewell salute. Falcon reached forward and touched the man's fingertips with his own. "I am with you always," the man said.

Then Falcon was in a room, lying in a bed, struggling to open his eyes, but could not.

• • •

Palmer and McIlree were both exhausted. It was no longer anything like a fair battle. McIlree had lost over half his men, as had Palmer, including his second in command. Palmer had taken an arrow in the leg, and though the wound was not bad and he continued in the battle, it was enough of a wound to drain his energy.

Crotalus' men did not fight fiercely. They had been robbed of emotion, yet they fought doggedly, finally being taken down when their heads were severed. But in order for a man to get close enough with his sword to do that, he would have to get shot with arrows numerous times. The men banded together to attack one man and in killing him, lost ten of their own. And still the enemy kept coming.

One of McIlree's men stepped into the tent where McIlree and Palmer were discussing new tactics. "Sir, we have found an opening into the castle at the south end. It was being guarded by a very few men, and they have been subdued. I think we can gain access to the castle now."

McIlree looked at Palmer. "It could be the opportunity we've been waiting for."

"I will take one battalion of men into the castle," Palmer stated. "The rest will continue the frontal attack. I am going to find Crotalus' private rooms and his laboratories and destroy them. Maybe in destroying them, the spell will be broken."

McIlree nodded. "At the very least it will force Crotalus to return. It may be too late to save Falcon, but perhaps it will save the war."

Palmer stood up, deciding which battalion to take with him. He hoped Crotalus *would* return. He longed to put an end to the wizard's miserable life. "If Kreith doesn't come soon," he said as he walked out of the tent, "it may all be too late."

Thirty-Four

After the first day in the Forgotten City, Falcon's health began to steadily improve. He still remained unconscious, but Rafaela could hear that his breathing was less labored and sounded more of sleep. She had bled him three times, and though the white spots did not appear again, she bled him once more to be sure. The wounds were healing, and in a matter of two days she stopped putting the dressing on, allowing the fresh air to work its own cures.

McNyre worried about her health as much as he did Falcon's. She was not sleeping enough and often slept only momentarily in the chair next to Falcon's bed. She went for long periods without food, eating only when McNyre sat in the room with her and forced her to eat. He at last firmly told her to leave.

"I can't leave him. He could wake up at any time."

"And as soon as he does, I will summon ye. Go practice with your sword, or walk in the garden." He pulled on her arm, forcing her to stand, and then propelled her toward the door. "If he awakens and ye are not here, I will get ye before I get anyone else. All right?"

"Agreed. Call me if there is any movement. I'll be in the garden."

He watched her go and settled in the chair. He had called her that first day because there had been movement. It had been a slight gesture with the hand, certainly more than a muscle spasm. He had called Rafaela, and they both watched anxiously. The movement did not come again, but he spoke a single word that sounded distinctly like "wheat." Rafaela talked with him endlessly after that, sure that somewhere in his mind he could hear and understand her.

McNyre had only been in the room for half an hour when Falcon opened his eyes. McNyre smiled and stood up. Falcon's eyes focused on him, and he sat up suddenly, grabbing for a sword that wasn't there.

McNyre rushed over and put a restraining hand on his chest. "Easy," he said, "ye be among friends."

"Who are you?"

"My name is McNyre, from Andurin. You are in the Forgotten City."

"Is Rafaela here?"

McNyre smiled. "She has hardly left your side. She will be very angry with me if I do not leave this instant and get her."

"Wait . . . I was holding a bottle. Do you know where it is?"

"Aye. Ye did not want to relinquish it, but I took it from ye and it is safely in my room."

"Thank you for keeping it for me. It is very important." He looked at McNyre for a moment. "Is there still a war going on?"

"I believe so. We don't receive much news here."

Falcon swung his legs over the side of the bed. McNyre helped him stand. "Do ye think ye should be standing? Ye had a mighty powerful poison in ye."

"I want to find Rafaela."

"I can summon her, and she will come here."

Falcon looked at McNyre and laid a hand on his shoulder that spoke of comradery. "McNyre, have you ever loved a woman?"

"Aye . . . and like ye, one I have not seen in many years."

"Then you will understand. I don't want to wait for her to come here, and I don't want to be lying in bed when I see her for the first time after all these years. I feel wonderful, and I want to pick her up off her feet and swing her around in my arms. I can't do that in bed."

McNyre laughed, liking this knight more than he had thought he would. He helped him dress. "She said she was going to the garden. I'll show ye the way."

As McNyre led him to the garden, Falcon marveled over the beauty of the Forgotten City, made up of shining stone and sparkling glass, leafy green trees and blooming flowers. "And this is only the main castle," McNyre said. "When ye don't have other things on your mind, I'll show ye around the whole city."

They reached the garden, and Falcon stopped before entering it. McNyre looked at him questioningly.

"What is she like, McNyre?"

"She is the most incredible woman I have ever known."

"In what ways?"

"She is tender and at the same time hard as steel. She is independent, fiery, loyal, quick of temper at times. And she handles a sword better than many men."

"She doesn't sound like she has changed much. Does she still worship Menon?"

"Faithfully. Why do ye question these things when ye shall see her in a few moments?"

"I don't know. I haven't seen her in thirteen years. I've wondered at times whether she will still love me or I her."

McNyre laughed. "I have never seen such love as hers as when she was nursing ye back to life. And if ye do not love her, then ye be a great fool."

Falcon smiled. "Lead on."

McNyre wound his way through jungly paths to Rafaela's favorite spot. She had her back to them, watching a waterfall that cascaded down high rocks, spraying the surrounding trees with rainbow droplets.

Falcon watched her a moment, totally entranced. Her hair was short, and he was fascinated by the abundance of curls that danced on her head. She wore a rose-colored dress, and Falcon could see that she had lost none of her talent for dressmaking. The dress flowed around her as though it were a part of her, just brushing the top of her feet. Love burst in him as she knelt gracefully and scooped up water in her hand.

McNyre whispered, "Rafaela, I have brought ye a friend," and then walked from the garden.

Rafaela turned and stood before Falcon, tears shimmering in her eyes. Falcon had imagined this moment for thirteen years. He had dreamed of catching her in his arms with laughter, tears, and kisses. Now she stood in front of him and he felt awkward.

Rafaela too felt shy, finding it much easier to express her love to an unconscious Falcon than one who looked at her with such intensity. She had wondered before if his eyes were still the same, and she looked at them now, seeing the same vibrant blue-green color. But there was depth in them now that before had been lacking. *Experience has taught him much*, she thought.

He saw in her the strength she had possessed before, yet softened by years with Menon. All of his doubts melted like ice in the summer sun. "I remember you saying once," he said softly, "that you could not love anyone who did not win all of his battles."

She smiled slowly, remembering the youthful occasion, liking the way his voice sounded. It had grown older like a rich wine. "I remember."

"I've lost a few. Does it make a difference?"

A tear ran down her cheek. "No."

He crossed over to her and brushed the tear away. "Hello, Rafaela," he whispered and gathered her into his arms.

• • •

Temrane burst into McNyre's room. "Where's Rafaela?"

"She is in the garden . . . but," he said as he grabbed Temrane's hand just as he was about to escape, ". . . I don't think she wants to be interrupted just now."

"But Duncan's back! I saw him from the tower. He has someone with him!"

"I don't doubt it. Duncan picks up people like a horse picks up flies."

"You don't understand, McNyre! I think it's Uncle Candy!"

"Well, let us see."

"Shouldn't I get Rafaela? She would want to see Duncan."

"Let's leave her alone for a few more minutes."

"Why? What's going on?"

"She's with Falcon. He's awake and in the garden with her."

Temrane grew still. "So he's going to be all right?"

"Ye look like ye didn't want him to get well."

Temrane shrugged. "I didn't want him to die, but I didn't want him and Rafaela to be together."

"Why not? She will still have plenty of love for ye, lad."

"I was hoping . . ." His voice trailed off.

"Hoping what?" McNyre prodded.

"I was hoping that you and she would fall in love and marry. We could be a family."

McNyre hugged him. "We are already a family. Nothing can change that. Besides, ye forget that I already have a wife. And ye have an Uncle Candy who I'm sure is anxious to see ye."

They walked downstairs together and went through the main door of the castle. Temrane broke into a run. McNyre watched as the two horses rode up. He saw a man of about sixty jump from the horse and for a moment was fearful of his reception of Temrane. After all, this was the high priest of Hoen, the god who had, for reasons of his own, rejected Temrane. He didn't need to worry. Cand opened his arms.

"Uncle Candy!" Temrane yelled, never doubting Cand's love for him now that he was here. He jumped into Cand's waiting arms and felt himself lifted from the ground in a fierce embrace. McNyre couldn't help but grin, and the grin turned to mirthful laughter as the two hugged and cried and talked at the same time.

He walked over to Duncan, who was dismounting. He clasped the man who had taught him to love and found tears rising in his own eyes. "'Tis truly a day for reunions," he laughed.

"I never thought I would be so glad to see you. I prayed that you would make it here unharmed."

"We had an interesting time of it, but your God has brought us safely here."

"Where is Rafaela? I expected her to be here also."

"She doesn't know yet of your return. She is with Falcon."

"Falcon! You spoke of reunions, but I had no idea . . .!"

"Come, old friend," McNyre said, his arm around Duncan's shoulder. "We have much to tell each other."

• • •

Kreith and Kies led the four men through the castle. They had entered an area that was not in much use. Even the sounds of battle were muffled here. "I would almost bet that Tegmen and Soaje are not fighting," Kreith whispered. "Our best chance of finding them is away from the fighting."

They searched each room in this northern wing, but found nothing. Any weapons they saw they confiscated for their own use. They came to a broad juncture that would lead them to the west wing or the east. Sounds of war were louder here. Kies looked to the west. "If you are correct that they do not fight, I would suggest checking to the west. The fiercest fighting is to the east, and much of the western wing is built into the mountain. It is a very secure arrangement."

Kreith nodded, and they crept down the hall single-file. At the end of the hall the corridor turned left, and Kreith could hear voices coming from that direction. He glanced carefully around the corner and saw four guards at the entrance to the room. The voices came from this room, and he looked questioningly at Kies. Kies nodded. Those were indeed the voices of Soajc and Tegmen.

"If we create enough of a diversion, it will lure the guards away," he whispered. "Kies, you will come with me into the room to face the two wayward lords."

He whispered his instructions to the other knights. Then Kreith and Kies hid themselves in one of the rooms. Jendar, the highest knight, pounded down the hall and turned the corner, surprising the four guards there. "Quick!" he shouted. "The enemy has penetrated the castle! They are in the north wing!" Jendar turned and fled down the hall toward the north wing, along with his three comrades.

Kreith listened and heard one of the lords shout, "Go after them, you fool!" and then heard four guards running in pursuit. Kreith waited until they had passed by. "Now!" he whispered to Kies, and the two hurriedly went into the room.

The two lords sat at a large table, but neither looked surprised when Kreith and Kies burst into the room. Then Kreith noticed the two guards who had been stationed on the inside of the walls. He had foolishly put his and Kies' life in danger.

He swung hard with his sword, connecting instantly with the sword of the guard, hearing Kies do the same. He swung again, not wanting to allow the guard time to go on the offensive. If he could somehow keep him off-balance, he could win.

His youth and lightness were assets that he used to full advantage, knowing that his opponent would tire more readily. He jabbed and cut and swung and speared. Each time the jab was returned, he dodged. He soon discovered that he had the additional advantage of having studied under Falcon Jaqeth. Falcon had taught him strategies used only by the best swordsmen, and this guard was clearly not one of the best.

At last, seeing his foe tire, Kreith stepped closer in a daring maneuver, pulled the man to him with his free hand, and lunged the sword through the joints in the chain mail. Kreith quickly pulled the sword out and turned to the table.

The lords were on their feet, reaching for swords. Kreith almost smiled, for though they had on protective armor it was by no means full armor.

"Surrender your weapons and you shall be treated mercifully."

"Surrender yours, boy! You cannot take on both of us!" Soajc yelled.

Kreith glanced over at Kies and saw what Soaje was talking about. The guard had been killed, but Kies was down. Kreith could hear his heavy breathing, could see the blood seeping from underneath his armor. Death was at hand.

"I am Prince Kreith of Paduan . . . I give you one last warning: Surrender or die!"

Tegmen stepped from around the desk. "Come on, boy . . . Your great military stand is over. Give me the sword and you shall be treated with mercy."

Rather than let them split and be able to get behind him, Kreith attacked. He jumped on the table, and before either could react he leapt on Tegmen, sword in front of him, knocking him to the floor. He stepped hard on Tegmen's right wrist, feeling it crunch under his boot. The fist gave way, and the sword clattered to the ground. The prince then jabbed with his foot and caught Tegmen in the face, breaking his nose. Tegmen fell back, knocked unconscious by the force of the kick.

Kreith turned to Soaje. "I did not kill him. I could have, but I decided to show mercy. Surrender."

Soaje did not answer in words, but in action as he attacked Kreith with his sword. Kreith parried his blows and returned them with a ferocity that Soaje did not expect. But Kreith was tired, sore, guilty over Kies' death, and he wanted to go home. As he thought about leading Kies into this trap, he fought furiously, slashing anything that came into reach, and Soaje was finding it impossible to defend against him.

Soaje would not let himself be backed into the wall, but cleverly turned so he would be pushed out the door. As he got close to it, he turned and fled down the hall. Not to be outdone, Kreith followed. He half-expected Soaje to turn into the north wing, but rather he continued east.

Kreith sped up, knowing that if Soaje reached the eastern wall knights would be notified and Kreith would lose his life in a matter of moments. Soaje ran onto the wall.

Hardly knowing what he did, Kreith took his sword and flung it as though it were a javelin. It traveled swiftly, deadly in its course. It ripped through Soaje's leather vest, spearing him. The impetus of the sword carried him over the edge of the wall.

Knights on the wall rushed to the edge and saw their leader strike the ground a hundred feet below. They turned toward Kreith with wondering eyes.

"Surrender and you shall be shown mercy. Or you can die as your lord did." Kreith said this with as much force as he could muster, but he didn't know what he would do if they rushed at him. He felt movement behind him and turned, expecting another trap, another attack. Kies' four knights stood behind him. He turned to the men on the wall. "Surrender or die."

Swords clattered on the brick flooring, and they were led away by Jendar. Kreith stepped to the edge and looked down on a bloody battlefield. "Knights and people of Andurin and Derrich, Lord Soaje has been killed and Lord Tegmen has surrendered. Surrender yourselves now or die with Lord Soaje."

He saw some men surrendering and some still battling, but Kreith knew the main fighting was over. There would be a few skirmishes still to fight to subdue those who wished to take over Andurin's lordship, but the battle was over.

Kreith looked at Jendar as he returned from delivering the prisoners to Malcolm. Kreith smiled tiredly. "Let's get this over with," he said. "Palmer needs our help."

• • •

Dinner in the Forbidden City that night was a joyous affair. Rafaela and Falcon bantered playfully . . . Duncan enjoyed being with Rafaela again . . . McNyre found many things in common with Falcon . . . Temrane couldn't sit still as he talked first with Cand, then McNyre, then Duncan and Rafaela, and even found that he liked Falcon. The laughter and conversation did not diminish as the evening wore on, but escalated in merriment until Rafaela felt drunk with giddiness.

At last, when the night was well gone, the noise died down and Duncan felt the time was right to talk of serious matters. They all sat in the comfortable Fireplace Room. Rafaela rested on the floor, Falcon's head in her lap. She stroked his hair and his beard. In an odd way she felt they had never been separated. Temrane settled as close to Cand as he could without actually sitting on his lap. McNyre sat across the room from Temrane, so he could watch his face. He enjoyed seeing the life in the boy's countenance and vowed to try and keep it there.

"I have hesitated bringing up certain matters because I felt we needed the joy we experienced tonight. But a new day is dawning, and we must decide what part to play in the unfolding events. Cand and I witnessed many ravages of the war as we crossed the country. We have heard many stories as well. We will only deal with the facts." Duncan looked at Temrane. "The first fact is that your father is dead. McNyre tells me that you suspected his death and feel that it was your fault. In truth, he was killed by his mistress, who has since become a follower of Menon. There was nothing in his death that can be attributed to you."

Cand squeezed Temrane's shoulder, and McNyre winked at him solemnly. Temrane swallowed the lump in his throat, unsure how to feel about his father's death. He grieved, but the bereavement had actually started long before. Fel-hoen had never been as alive to Temrane as Cand was.

"The second thing is that Jerome was seriously injured at Andurin by a traitor."

Falcon bolted upright. "What!"

"The traitor—I believe his name was Diones—shot Jerome, and it was only the quick thinking of Prince Kreith that saved him at all. Jerome resides in Zopel until he is well enough to return home. However, he is out of grave danger. Prince Kreith is leading the armies."

Duncan looked at McNyre. "And I hate to tell you this, but it is only a matter of time before Andurin falls. They joined forces with Crotalus. When I came through the area, they were battling strong against Jerome's armies, but we heard stories that Andurin was already falling. It can only be a short period before it is gone."

McNyre stared at his hands. He thought of friends he had there, the house he had built. He had called Andurin home for twelve years, and now he was homeless. He looked up and caught Temrane's eyes.

"Andurin is not your home," the boy said quietly. "You have another across the water."

McNyre smiled, Temrane's words recalling his own. Perhaps it was time to cut ties with everything that had grown familiar and go home.

"As much as I would like to stay here," Duncan said, "it is my feeling that we must become involved in the war. I want to discuss what we plan on doing."

Rafaela said nothing, but became aware that everyone was looking at her. Obviously her intensity had seized everyone's attention. She took a deep breath and let it out slowly. "I have felt for some time now that I am the only one capable of killing Crotalus. I will leave in the morning and ride to his castle."

Duncan looked at her warily. "How do you intend to kill him?"

"I haven't told you, Duncan, but I've been training with the golden sword of the Menontes. I want to take it with me."

Duncan thought for a moment. "Very well. I can see that you have given this much thought, and you surely know the dangers."

"I do, but there is something else." She looked at Temrane. "I want Temrane to come with me."

"No!" McNyre said. Rafaela looked at him, surprised at the emotion in his voice. "I'm sorry, Rafaela," he said, "but it would be too dangerous. Ye even said yourself that Temrane is still vulnerable to Crotalus' attacks, his lures. He could be lost to us forever!"

"That is why I want him to go with me!" She looked at Temrane. "I cannot force you to go. McNyre is right . . . There is much danger for one who is marked. But by being with me you will be taking the control of your life away from Crotalus."

Temrane looked from Rafaela to McNyre. "Crotalus scares me, but I know I have to go." McNyre sighed, and Temrane looked at him. "She's right. Sometimes I want to go back with him. I don't know why . . . I just do. I must fight him so I will never want to go with him again. I'll go with you, Rafaela."

"All right," McNyre said, "but I'm going with ye."

"It's dangerous," Rafaela said.

"I know! But I'm not letting Temrane go without me."

Falcon looked at Rafaela. "I'm going too."

"Absolutely not! You're not well enough. You are just starting to recover from the large amount of poison he gave you!"

Duncan smiled. "I have to agree with her, Falcon. This is no time for personal vengeance."

"This has nothing to do with vengeance. I have given that up. Crotalus gave me the chance to kill him. I released that to Menon, and He has healed me. But I have other reasons for needing to go. I have a soul in my possession, thanks to Crotalus. And only Crotalus knows where the body is. I also know the location of the children's souls. I have taken this man's soul into my keeping and have an obligation to him, and to the children."

"Very well." Duncan looked at Cand. "It seems as if everyone else is going to Crotalus' castle. Shall we make it unanimous?"

"I think that would be the wise course."

"Then let's get some sleep. We leave early in the morning."

Thirty-Five

Although the ride from the Forgotten City was filled with purpose and some dread, hearts were light, and the six sang songs, talked, and laughed effortlessly. They left the Wastelands as soon as possible, preferring to travel in the cities of Paduan and Corigo. Rafaela noticed a strange look on Falcon's face as they rode through the Wastelands, an intense, searching gaze as though something there was not quite right. She would ask him about it later.

Most of the time they rode two by two, discussing with ease whatever came to mind. Duncan waited until he was with Rafaela to talk about something that had bothered him. "Do you think it is wise for Falcon to come with you?"

"Yes . . . He told me what happened with Crotalus when he was wounded. He won't tell anyone else, but he could not keep it from me. Falcon is right—Crotalus gave him a chance to kill him, and Falcon refused it. I think at that moment Menon grasped that part of Falcon that he has never wanted to let go of, and He has healed Falcon."

"But what about you?"

"I know what you are concerned with, but you needn't be." She told him about burning Falcon's letters. "I let him go at that moment. He had held on to hate and I had held on to love, but both were getting in the way of Menon. When I burned the letters, it was my way of saying I didn't need to depend on Falcon any longer. He rides with us now, and I can and do enjoy his company. But he does not urge me to face Crotalus or to run from him . . . I choose."

Duncan nodded, satisfied. "Then I am glad he comes. The color in your cheeks when he is around is wonderful to behold."

"I also am glad he comes, and I'm glad you and McNyre and

Temrane and Cand have come also. I have never felt so much love before. I feel I have truly found a family."

"When this is over, Rafaela, we should talk long about things. I don't think I can go back to living alone. There is much about Menon which I wish to share with mankind."

"I feel the same way, but I'm not sure I can leave."

"Well, let's finish this battle first before we start another one."

Rafaela smiled at him, love for this man filling her heart. "Very well."

• • •

Palmer and his battalion stormed into the castle as though they already possessed it. They immediately encountered more of Crotalus' men and were engaged for the better part of an hour in dispatching them. Palmer recognized instantly the advantages he had being inside the castle. Crotalus' men could not maneuver as well, and it took much less to bring them down and kill them. Because of this, many of his own men were spared.

He noticed something else as well. None of Crotalus' men went to warn the others. They had seen the enemy and simply turned to fight. *Why didn't I think of that before?* Palmer thought. These men had been robbed of fear, but Crotalus had also taken away their will. They could not plan or strategize – they could only kill.

He sent a messenger to McIlree with this bit of information. Hopefully, he thought, they could defeat this army with cunning. This would be Crotalus' downfall, he felt sure of it. Crotalus could kill Falcon, but in that lustful and greedy act he sealed his own doom. He should never have left his men without his fearful leadership, the only thing that kept them in his army.

"We will divide into groups of four. Go into every room," he told his men. "Set nothing on fire yet, but overturn furniture and break glass, including windows. Any books that you find on wizardry, bring to me. Do not open them. They may be traps that will bewitch you upon opening them. Do not open any bottles that may contain potions. Bring those to me also. When we set our fire, those will be the first things to burn. Keep an eye open for prisoners of Crotalus. Do not kill innocent people in your zeal to destroy the enemy."

He sent the four groups in different directions and could hear them entering into their work with relish. He joined the eastern group and found a vent for his frustration in demolishing the castle.

As they systematically worked their way up the stairs, pausing now and then to fight an enemy that didn't care what they did to the castle, Palmer and his group went on ahead to where Palmer was sure Crotalus' rooms were. As he suspected, he found them on the top floor, facing east. "Wait here," he said.

He slipped into the room and imagined he could feel the evil pressing around him on every side. Here were the books of magic that enslaved men's souls . . . the potions . . . the spells.

He walked over to the window and looked out onto the battlefield. McIlree had received his message and was using strategies that confused the enemy. Although McIlree was still losing men, they were now killing Crotalus' army in greater numbers and with greater ease.

The sound of a trumpet called his attention to the north, where he saw the banner of King Jerome. Kreith had come with reinforcements. The tide had turned.

He turned away from the window and began pulling books from the shelves and heaping them onto the floor. He opened doors and found bottles full of ingredients to make potions. These went on the floor around the books. He attempted to pry open the desk drawers, but found this impossible. He at last settled on pulling the desk into the middle of the floor, next to the fire material.

He went to the door and found the entire battalion waiting for him. "Is this the last room?"

"Yes, sir. We found a few prisoners, all dead but one. He was unconscious. Two men have taken him with the wounded. We also found this." He handed Palmer a bottle with a glass stopper. The word *Merry* was written on it.

"Good. I believe this soul belongs to King Fel-hoen's daughter. We will return it when the war is over. I want everyone to leave the castle. I am going to set fire to this room first and then each descending floor."

The men nodded and left. Palmer turned back to the room and stood in front of the books. His fingers itched to take one up, to know just for a moment what secrets it contained, but he knew this was a lure of the Evil One. He took a torch, lit it, and touched it to the books. Flames roared up, and Palmer ran from the room. He did not know what the potions would do when the fire reached them, and he wanted to be out of the castle.

He touched his torch to a central room on each floor and tossed the torch into the dungeon hole before running from the castle. He embraced Kreith as he saw him, and they turned to view the castle.

Men around them fought, but the sounds gradually died away as each man watched the flames climb higher into the night. An eerie orange glow lit the sky. Suddenly something exploded, and glass shot out at the men. "Down!" Palmer yelled and watched as each battalion fell to the ground before he himself dropped.

An acrid smell filled the air, making Palmer's eyes water and his throat sting. The explosions were coming from Crotalus' study. His potions, spells, books, magic—his various dark arts—were being destroyed and scattered on the wind.

At last the explosions stopped, and there was nothing but the roaring sound of the flames as they ate away the insides of the castle. Palmer stood and looked at Crotalus' men. They stood staring at the burning mass. Though their emotions had not returned, neither had their fight.

"Gather the prisoners!" he shouted to his men. He watched as the rebellious army was led away. Palmer turned to McIlree and Kreith, who watched him with weary eyes, glad the slaughter was finally over. Only the wizard, the leader of this gruesome army, remained.

"That should flush him out," he said confidently. "And then we will have him."

• • •

Crotalus flew over the skies to the Forgotten City, searching in vain for the mythical site. He had been flying for days, still in his falcon transformation, seeking the place where Rafaela's bones resided. He could not find it, and though he was disappointed this did not create in him the anger and frustration it once might have. His hated enemy was dead at his hand. Rafaela, whenever he found her, would be his and his alone.

Crotalus was sure that Falcon had placed a spell on her, bewitching her into loving him. Now that he was dead, there would be no hold on her when he gave her life again. But first he had to find her.

Crotalus almost tumbled from the sky when the first brain-ripping pains shot through him. He pulled up and landed quickly, changing into his human form. Something had gone horribly wrong. His very soul was being destroyed. He cast his mind far ahead of him, to Andurin and beyond. He saw that Andurin had been destroyed.

His psychic sight went to his castle and saw it in flames. He screamed in rage. His men had failed, and he had to get back. Most of the potions and spells he could make up again, and the books he could recreate. But the book *On Raising the Dead* was one he could not lose. It contained all of his experiments up to date. If he lost it, he would have to begin again, and he could not do so, not now when he was so close to discovering Rafaela.

He took to the sky again. His bid for the kingdom of Fel-hoen was lost for a season. He would stay in hiding for a time, concentrate on Rafaela, and when men had forgotten his deeds a little set up a plan, renew his army, and attack. He would not be so kind next time.

The souls . . . He still had the souls. He would hold them for ransom or until they were old enough to serve him. Some of them were close. Perhaps he could find a willing apprentice in one of them.

He flew swiftly, anxious to retrieve his finest work from the fire. Corigo and Paduan were a long way from hearing the last of him . . . A long way.

• • •

As the party of six drew near to Crotalus' castle, Falcon and Rafaela abandoned their horses to the others and walked the remaining distance. Around them they heard the praises of Kreith and proud talk of his glorious exploits.

"He will be a more popular king than Jerome in time," Falcon uttered.

"He has had good teachers. Will you still teach him when the war is over?" Rafaela asked.

Falcon shook his head. "He has no more need for teachers."

"What will you do?"

"I don't know yet . . . I want to be with you."

"Even if I stay in the Forgotten City?"

"I think so."

"Give it much thought, Falcon. Both of us need to be sure of what we want."

He took her in his arms, holding her tight. "I know I don't want to lose you again."

She looked into his eyes and smiled. “You won’t. If you decided against the Forgotten City, I’m not sure I could stay.”

He ran his fingers through her silky curls. “I love you, Rafaela.”

Her answer was to kiss him softly.

“Are you afraid?” he asked as they began walking again.

“Of what might happen today?”

“Yes.”

“No. I have been preparing for it a long time, and I know it is Menon’s will. Crotalus must be stopped, and I alone can do it.”

“Do you need me there?”

“No. I am glad you are here, but I don’t need your presence any longer. I am strong in Menon. How will you feel when I kill Crotalus?”

Falcon paused, uncertain. “I want to rejoice over the destruction of evil, but to grieve because he never knew Menon. Whether or not I will feel that way when the time comes, I don’t know. I don’t want to rejoice because my enemy is lost. I wish you didn’t have to go through this, because I know you loved him at one time. It is possible that you still feel some love for him because he is Menon’s creature, and I know that will cause you pain. I wish it were over.”

She stroked his beard, loving him more at this moment than she ever thought possible. “Soon, my love . . . soon all of this will be over and we can discuss our future together.”

• • •

Falcon popped his head into Palmer’s tent and saw Palmer, Kreith, McIlree, and a few other lords there. “I see you didn’t need my help,” he said as he walked in, enjoying the surprised stares.

“Falcon!” Kreith yelled and jumped up, preparing to give him a life-threatening hug. But then he recalled that the men in this tent were under his command; he was the current leader of Paduan and needed to be worthy of respect. *I don’t care*, he thought, and embraced him.

“I hear you are leading this army.”

“Yes . . . Palmer recruited me from Zopel,” Kreith replied, feeling a little shy under the proud look of Falcon. “Where have you been?”

“In the Forgotten City, recuperating from a snake bite.”

“Did you kill Crotalus?” McIlree asked.

“No . . . He is still alive. I imagine that the destruction of his castle will force him here.”

"That was our plan. We will fall on him as soon as he arrives. We have people watching the skies for a falcon, his last transformation."

Falcon shook his head. "He has too much power and cunning to fight him with normal tactics. Rafaela is here, and she believes she is the only one who can kill Crotalus. I have given it much thought, and have concluded she is right. Rafaela is the only one who could get close enough, the only one he wouldn't try to kill. I suggest putting her in a visible position. That should lure him even faster."

McIlree nodded and prepared to have this carried out. He clapped Falcon on the back before he left the tent. "I can't tell you how relieved I am, Falcon."

"I am also looking for a body," Falcon said. "It could have been in Crotalus' castle. It would have been a man, a knight in Soaje's army. He is soulless. Have you seen him?"

"I have," Palmer said. "We took him with the wounded soldiers. Come . . . I'll take you to him."

Before he left, Falcon stepped over and embraced Kreith again. "Your men outside cannot stop talking about your leadership. I am very proud of you. You are a leader worthy of respect, and I am proud to serve under you, Prince Kreith." Falcon stepped back and offered Kreith the salute given to a warrior-king, the right fist slapped over the chest.

Kreith, more gratified than he could say, returned the salute.

Falcon and Palmer walked from the tent and passed through throngs of soldiers on their way to the tent of the wounded. They were silent for a time, but at last Palmer sighed. "I thought you dead, my friend," he said with much emotion in his voice.

"I should have been, but by Menon's grace I live."

Palmer clasped Falcon to him. "I was in torture after I was told that Crotalus knew where you had gone. I wanted to go after you and warn you. I wanted to abandon my army and the war just to save you. Did he ambush you?"

"No . . . He has hated me far too long to ambush me and let me die quickly. He could have. His insatiable appetite lost him what he truly desired—my death. Tell me of you," he said quickly, not wanting to talk of Crotalus' bargain. "What happened to your leg?"

"I took an arrow in it. It did not go deep, and I was able to remove it myself."

"I am glad this is almost over," Falcon said. "I would not want you killed. You have a wedding to take part in."

Palmer smiled. "It has been on my mind, as has Rafaela. Is she still beautiful?"

"More than ever before. When I am with her, all of life seems joyous. I worried that I might not love her anymore when I finally found her, or that she would not love me. But Menon has given us a love that is strong and will endure much. I know now that no one else could ever fill her place in my heart. Tell me of Kreith."

"He is a good leader, Falcon. You have trained him well."

"Not just me," Falcon said. "We all had a hand in his training, and his father is the noblest man I know. How is Jerome?"

"From the reports I have gotten, he does very well. He is still in Zopel, but I think he shall return home before long. Kreith takes after him. He has a wonderful military mind that he received from you, and a body that takes naturally to the sword and horse. But he has the heart of his father. One of Corigo's lords was killed. Kreith says he mistakenly led them into a trap. His heart grieves that he was the cause of this man's death, although he knows that in war men die. He shall someday make Paduan a king who will be remembered throughout history."

They reached the tent, and Palmer showed him the soldier they had taken. Falcon knelt beside him, studying the face.

"Do you know him?"

"In some strange way, yes. His name is Gilreth. I have his soul in a bottle that Crotalus gave me. I dare not open it yet. His soul could escape, and I have no idea how to put the soul back into the body."

"Is Crotalus the only one who can do that?"

"Yes . . . unless he dies. If he dies, the hold that he has on the soul is dissolved and the soul would return to the body. I want to place the soul as close to the body as possible so the soul doesn't have to travel for many miles."

"Then you will stay here until Crotalus finally comes?"

"I will be here when Crotalus dies. I no longer need to see him destroyed. When he comes, though, I want to stand at the base of the castle, underneath Rafaela. I want him to see that the True God has conquered."

McNyre walked into the room and up to Falcon. "I've been looking for ye. A falcon has been spotted."

• • •

Crotalus could see, even from a distance, the light of his burning castle. He watched as the flames died down, the gutted walls no longer feeding the fire. He swooped closer, searching for a spot to enter without being seen so he could retrieve his book *On Raising the Dead*, easily his most treasured possession.

His sharp eye caught a movement on the castle wall, although now it was just so much rubble. He watched, wondering who would have risked the dying fire and crumbling rock to stand on the wall. His bird's heart thudded inside him, and the pain again tore through his skull.

Standing on the wall, silhouetted against a sky beginning to turn pink and orange with the dawn, was Rafaela.

Thirty-Six

Crotalus circled in the air a few times and then came to rest in front of Rafaela, transforming from the falcon into the man he had been years ago when Rafaela loved him. His hair swept back from a massive forehead and ran down his back to his waist. His golden eyes penetrated whatever they looked at. His chin was firm, his lips thin and cruel.

Rafaela stood before him in a purple tunic and the white wool pants of a sword master. Her eyes too were piercing, but where they had once penetrated a veneer of maliciousness to find the person no one loved underneath, they now pricked his facade of handsomeness to see the venomous evil that lay at his core.

She held a blazing gold sword in front of her.

"You don't intend to use that on me, do you?"

"Yes, I do," she responded softly. "I cannot allow you to go on any longer, hurting people, doing evil."

"Rafaela, everything I have ever done I have done for your love. I thought I had lost you! I believed you dead!"

"I have been living the life of an exile these past thirteen years because of you, Crotalus . . . because of your hate."

"I love you!"

"You hated Falcon more than you ever loved me. Draw your weapon, Crotalus, or I shall have to slay you outright."

He saw the resolution in her eyes. There was no spite, no anger, just a determination to do what had to be done. He unsheathed a sword that he had never had to use, his magic being powerful enough to subdue any enemy.

"Rafaela, you can't be serious about this."

"I am," she said and lunged at him. He parried her blow.

"You know I won't kill you!"

She jabbed again and again was repelled. "Then you had better prepare to die."

"I had every right to hate Falcon!" he screamed. Then abruptly he smiled, everything again right. "I know Falcon bewitched you. I know you would have never left me on your own accord. It was Falcon's doing. But Falcon is dead now, Rafaela. I killed him. And now you are free."

"Falcon is not dead," she said matter-of-factly.

"Of course he is. I killed him myself."

"You tried, but the God of Falcon, who is also my God, restored him." She thrust against the steel of his blade.

"Show him to me!"

"You only postpone the inevitable."

"As you love him and once loved me, show him to me!"

Rafaela sheathed her sword. "Very well . . . He is below us. Walk with me to the castle entrance."

Crotalus followed her through the charred remains of his castle, rage building in him. His life's love was before him, and he could not grasp her. For so many years he had dreamed of her, worshiping her image, conducting experiment after useless experiment to bring her back to life. And now she lived, but he no longer controlled her. Bitterness filled him.

They walked through the door, and the armies surrounding the castle backed away, fear of the wizard evident on many of their faces. Only a few remained immovable, not afraid of any wizard, trusting in their God. Crotalus scanned the faces of these people, searching for one with any real meaning for him. He saw Temrane, and his eyes narrowed. Best to deal with that one later. His eyes again swept over the faces, and at last he found the one he sought.

Falcon Jaqeth stood in that front line of unyielding men. Crotalus threw back his head and howled his pain, a sound that filled the air and made the forest animals run for cover. He screamed, for Falcon had not died. He shrieked also because he had fed on Falcon's hate, and now that food was gone.

"You cannot be alive!" he yelled.

"Your hate could not kill me," Falcon uttered. "My God has conquered."

"Face me then with your sword!"

"I have no desire to. It appears that it is another's task to do so."

Crotalus breathed in and out rapidly, clenching his fists until they reddened, trying to bring himself under control. At last gaining a measure of calm, he turned to Rafaela.

"I failed in bringing about his death. But that doesn't have to be the end of us. I will forget Falcon. We can live together happily. Remember how happy we were in the beginning?"

"Defend yourself," she warned as she attacked. This time it was not one blow that he easily parried, but a series of strikes that backed him toward the castle. But he would not fight.

"Rafaela, remember our happiness."

"It was a happiness, that is true. But I have pure joy now, and you ask me to turn from it?"

"I could kill him now! Where would your joy be then?"

"My joy does not reside in Falcon. He shares it, but my joy would be where it has always been: in the will of Menon." She thrust again and was turned aside.

Crotalus stopped and looked at Temrane. Perhaps another line of reasoning . . . "Why did you bring the boy?"

"Because he has been marked by you and needs to also make his choice against you."

Crotalus smiled at the answer he would have most wished. "He cannot decide against me if I am dead. Cease your opposition long enough to make him choose."

Rafaela cringed inside, knowing that he had set this trap for her and she had fallen into it very easily. *Menon*, she prayed, *make him strong.* She lowered her sword, but did not replace it in the scabbard.

Crotalus turned toward the line. Temrane stood in front of a man about Falcon's age who had his arms crossed protectively around the boy.

"Come to me, Temrane," he said, his voice neutral.

Temrane did not move, but Crotalus noted that the man's arm tightened about him. Something about the man was familiar. "Have we had dealings before?" he asked him.

"Once," said McNyre, "but I promise ye we shall have further dealings if ye harm the lad."

Crotalus smiled. "I don't remember you being so brave before. I need a man like you with me."

McNyre spit on the ground, his only answer. But inside he quaked. *God of Duncan . . .* he thought, unsure how to continue. *God of Rafaela, of Falcon, of Cand, of Paduan . . . Menon*, his spirit cried, *don't make Temrane go through this. Show me what to do and I'll do it.*

"Come here, boy," Crotalus commanded with a voice as sweet as clover. Only Rafaela could hear the power behind it.

Temrane took a few steps toward Crotalus. McNyre, although dying inside, let him go.

"You can have whatever you want, Temrane." Crotalus backed up a few steps, forcing Temrane to step further away from McNyre. "Remember when I first found you in the mountains? You were scared and lonely and angry. Remember? I took you in . . . I cared for you . . . I was going to teach you things." Back a few more steps. "You had been betrayed by your father. I told you that I understood you because I too had been betrayed. No one else is going to understand you, boy . . . not Rafaela or Falcon, because they are betrayers."

He was now close to the entrance of the castle. "McNyre is a betrayer too. They can't appreciate someone like you."

Temrane took one step closer to Crotalus, trying not to listen to the things he said, hearing them anyway. He tried to hold on to McNyre's love for him. Crotalus was saying something else, but he couldn't quite hear it. He took another step closer.

Crotalus suddenly grabbed Temrane around the throat and dragged him through the castle entrance. In seconds they were swallowed by blackness. Rafaela uttered a short cry and leapt after them.

McNyre lunged toward the opening, calling Temrane's name. Falcon grabbed him around the waist and tackled him just before he would have disappeared inside.

"Let him go!"

"I can't! There's no telling what Crotalus will do to him!"

"He won't hurt him."

McNyre looked at Falcon, his sides heaving with effort. "Rafaela is in there too."

"I know. Crotalus will not hurt either of them. It is not their bodies I worry about, but their souls. And that they must face alone."

McNyre nodded his understanding through waves of grief, and the two stood watching the dark castle doorway.

• • •

Rafaela ran through the shell of the castle, pausing occasionally to listen for Crotalus. As soon as she heard him, she began running again, heaviness pressing against her heart, making it hard to keep going. She should not have given in to his desire to see Falcon. She should have killed him on the wall.

Possibly, she thought, she did not because she was having difficulty killing him. He was an evil creature, but he was also someone she had once loved. And throughout all the years in the Forgotten City, without ever forsaking her love for Falcon, she had prayed and hoped that somehow Crotalus would change.

Now he had Temrane. She could not fathom his reasons for wanting him, unless perhaps to hold Temrane hostage so she wouldn't kill him. She remembered hearing McNyre calling Temrane's name as he disappeared into the castle and the burden of anguish in his voice.

She stopped running and sank to the ground. She would not be able to bear it if something happened to Temrane. She could not go to McNyre and tell him she was sorry and watch the life in his eyes die. Should she give up, allow Crotalus to win, and return to him? At least then the boy would be free.

"Menon, what should I do? Don't let him be harmed because of my foolishness. I can't go with Crotalus, for that would be denying You and that I will not do."

She stood up and walked to the castle wall where she had first stood. The crowds below watched her anxiously. She yelled in a voice loud enough to resonate through the entire castle, "Crotalus! In the name of Menon, I command you to face me!"

• • •

Crotalus ran with Temrane, hearing Rafaela's footsteps pound after him. He felt that she would most likely go upward, so he headed toward the dungeon. The only thing he could think to do was to turn Temrane against Rafaela. If he could force his mark further on Temrane and control him, they could face Rafaela with her love for the two of them rather than just one.

He sat on the floor, dragging Temrane down with him. The footsteps had stopped, and he wondered if Rafaela was resting. He fixed his eyes on Temrane, forcing the boy to look at him. His eyes bore into his soul, reading what was there.

"Temrane, tell me what it is that you want most in the world."

"I want to be with Rafaela."

"We will. The three of us, very soon, will be together. What else?"

"McNyre."

"What about him?"

"I want to be with him."

"You want a family, don't you?"

"Yes."

"But McNyre already has a family."

"But they are a long way away. I am his family now."

"That is true, but perhaps he plans on leaving you to find his real family."

Temrane didn't reply, Crotalus' answer striking close to what his heart had feared.

"Temrane, look deep into my eyes. I can give you that family. You and I will be as one. We will be with Rafaela. With my power in you, we can make sure McNyre will never leave you. That's what you want, isn't it?"

"It wouldn't be the same."

Crotalus practically howled with frustration. "What do you mean it wouldn't be the same?"

"I want him to stay with me because he loves me, not because I use some spell to keep him. That's why you should let Rafaela go, because she doesn't love you anymore. Forcing her to love you isn't real love."

"You little fool!" he spat. "What do you know of real love? Your mother was a whore who sold herself for your father, and your father gave you life simply to gain a kingdom! Where is love in that, you miserable worm!"

"I don't know," Temrane admitted softly. "But I know I will never find love with you because you can't give love. I would rather die right now than go with you because I've at least felt love in my lifetime."

Crotalus screamed in rage at the impudence of this boy, angered that his mark could penetrate no further. Temrane had been too long in the presence of Falcon and Rafaela. Though this boy did not yet confess Menon as God, the stink of that decision lay full about him. Their prayers for him covered him like a sheet of steel, and Crotalus could not pierce it.

"Come on," he hissed, yanking Temrane to his feet. "If it is death you want, then death you shall receive." He stopped suddenly, a sound reaching his acute ears: footsteps on the wall. Rafaela had not given up yet.

He heard her voice resounding through the ruins: "Crotalus! In the name of Menon, I command you to face me!" He struggled against her command, but the authority in the Name was too great to be denied. Still clutching Temrane, he moved reluctantly up to the wall and stood before Rafaela.

• • •

She held the sword in front of her, ready to use it against Crotalus, no matter what the cost. She wished she could command Crotalus to release Temrane, but she knew this was Temrane's decision and one she could not interfere with. "Temrane," she said, "you must choose now."

"I have decided," he answered. "I want to come with you."

"Crotalus, release him. You have no right and no power to cling to him who has denied you. Let him go."

Temrane walked free of Crotalus and stood to one side, wanting to run down into McNyre's arms and yet wanting to see the final outcome.

"Rafaela, listen to me," Crotalus begged, using every power in his voice to convince her, "if you love the boy so much, then we will be together as a family . . . the three of us."

"Lift your sword."

He did as she commanded, but continued to reason. "Rafaela, look at me! I used to look this way because of your love. I have let anger and lust change my countenance into something fearful. I enjoyed the terror that my looks bred in men's hearts. But you can change me! Do not leave me—I will be who you want me to be!"

Rafaela paused, her weakness exposed.

Crotalus saw the pause and pressed his advantage. He threw down the sword and took a step toward her. "We can be happy together! Change me!"

Her sword wavered. *Menon, show me what is truth. If he is truly changing, then I cannot kill him. Or is this a lie so I will not kill him?*

"I cannot change you," she said cautiously. "Only Menon can change a person's heart."

"Very well then," Crotalus said, "I give in to you."

"Don't give in to me—give in to Menon. Kneel on the ground before me and confess that Menon is Supreme and Sovereign Lord over all, that he is the One True God, the Everlasting."

Crotalus stood for a moment, bile rising in his throat, the thought of uttering those words burning his mouth. But if he would thus gain Rafaela by mouthing the words . . . But he also had to bend his knee, and that he would not do, not for any mythical god, not even for Rafaela.

Hate spilled out of him, and he snatched his sword from the ground and lunged at Temrane. It had been his fault from the very beginning. He would feed on Temrane and then deal with Rafaela.

Rafaela saw the hunger in his eyes as he grabbed the blade. She raised the gold sword and ran it through Crotalus' heart before he could use his own against Temrane. She grabbed Temrane and clasped him tightly to her chest, so he could not see the evil face blacken with rage, nor hear the vile and filthy vituperations that came flooding from the wizard's mouth as he spewed forth his hatred of Falcon, Temrane, Rafaela, and most of all Menon.

Rafaela watched as his body shriveled into a small, blackened mass, ages old, and then was scattered by a cool and purifying wind.

• • •

McNyre and Falcon watched the confrontation from the ground, and although they could not hear the words, they saw the movements and saw Crotalus finally go down by Rafaela's sword. Both held their breath until they saw Rafaela holding Temrane and knew that both were safe.

They hugged each other and cried with happiness, laughing and talking at the same time. Then Temrane and Rafaela came out of the castle, and Temrane ran straight for McNyre, who caught him up and swung him around as though he were a little boy and not thirteen years old. They were joined by Kreith, Palmer, Duncan, and Cand, all delirious at the end of the terrible war. Loud laughter and song from the armies filled the air.

Joy overflowed in all their hearts, and a supernatural wind touched their cheeks, drying their tears.

Thirty-Seven

One week after Gilreth's soul was restored to him, Falcon and a contingent of others arrived in Melram. The children had found themselves liberated from the abandoned building upon the death of Crotalus, but remained inside awaiting Falcon's return even though he had been gone longer than the promised ten days. They greeted him with song and hilarity, as if he were a pied piper who had freed them from chains.

Falcon did not want to recapture them, but saw no other way of getting them to Zopel. So he brought bottles in a wagon and asked each child to fly into the bottle. He then wrote the child's name on the bottle. This achieved, they rode back to Zopel and to parents who looked for their children's return with eager anticipation.

Falcon remained on his horse as each family grabbed the bottles, and he reveled in the sound of laughter and weeping as the children returned to their own bodies. Doors then burst open all around him, and children flooded into the streets, jumping on him, pulling him from his horse, smothering him with their love.

Falcon stayed in Zopel for two days visiting each family, not able to get his fill of the children. He cried over Lis when he saw her mangled legs and wished he could restore to her the joy of flight. Her parents, Farni and Freyda, were overjoyed to have Lis and Anne back, even though they were frail. Farni had become a follower of the Redeemer God, and that changed everything.

Falcon watched as Niccola became the mother she wanted to be and played ball with Caldon, rolling with him on the ground even though she was the queen.

He spent time with each family, getting to know the adults as well as their children. The only people he wasn't able to see were Winni and Drucker. They had reclaimed Jasper, but were still bitter over the wasted sacrifice of Kalei. In time Falcon heard they had found a new god, the god of ice, son of Velad the sea goddess, and had moved high into the Amil Mountains to build a temple to him, with Drucker installed as the high priest.

• • •

"Hold still!" Falcon ordered as he helped Palmer lace up a silk shirt in preparation for his wedding.

"Why do I have to wear this shirt anyway? I would be more comfortable in the shirt Ivy made."

"This shirt is traditional . . . So be quiet and hold still." At last the lacing was done, and Falcon looked at Palmer critically. He wore the dark blue pants that signified loyalty, the white shirt that symbolized purity, and the laces that represented the many ties not only to God but to family and friends. Each friend of Palmer's had sewn a thong onto the shirt, Niccola representing the first woman to be allowed such an honor due to Palmer's insistence.

"You look good," he said at last. "Not as good as I'll look in a week's time, but passable."

"Such high praise!"

"You know, you haven't told me yet where you are taking my sister to live."

"I waited because I wanted to be sure."

"And are you sure now?"

"Yes."

"Then tell me!"

"We are going to live in Zopel."

"Zopel! I expected someplace a little closer."

Palmer laughed. "I did too, but Jerome asked me to go. Malcolm was killed in the war, and they need a knight to lead the army. I agreed to be that knight."

"How much does this have to do with Niccola?"

"Quite a bit," he admitted. "Niccola and Lomeli are still so young in the ways of Menon, and I desire to help them grow."

"I'm not trying to cast doubt on your friendship with her, but does Ivy understand all this? Does she like Niccola?"

"She didn't at first. Let's face it, Falcon . . . For all our talk of women working alongside men and serving on our councils, how many men do you know who have women as close friends? I think that's a mistake . . . Maybe not in all cases, but certainly in mine. I explained that to Ivy, and she has spent some time with Niccola. Niccola has tried so hard to become friends with Ivy; also, Ivy couldn't help but be won over. And Niccola is not that much older than Ivy, just a couple of years. It will be good for both of them."

"Then, my friend, I wish you every happiness. I could not want anything more for you."

"And what of you, Falcon? Are you going to the Forgotten City?"

"I don't know yet. I know I am getting married next week, and that is enough right now. Maybe I'll become a farmer."

"And farm what?"

Falcon got a faraway look in his eyes. "Maybe wheat." He shook his head. "No matter. Today is not the day to make decisions about my future. I'm going to see Ivy for a few minutes."

They looked at each other a moment, both feeling that winds of change were sweeping into their lives. Falcon crossed the room and embraced Palmer, wondering if something had been lost for the things they had gained.

Palmer read his thoughts and clapped him on the back. "My friend, we shall never part. Though we live in different places in the world, Menon will always keep us together."

"We are brothers of the soul," Falcon said as he walked from the room. "You are right. Like it or not, we cannot be parted."

Ivy was waiting for him when he entered her room. He stood in the doorway and looked at her, love filling his heart. She wore the white wedding garment of her mother, her hair piled on her head and pressed down with pearls. "I have never seen you so beautiful," he said sincerely.

She crossed the room and pecked him on the cheek. "Rafaela helped me dress. I like her, Falcon! I was so young when she left. I'm glad I had the chance to get to know her again before we go our various ways."

"We will try and see you often. I don't want to lose my family."

Ivy knew he referred in part to their father, and her eyes misted as she hugged Falcon. "I miss him too. I wish he could be here to see my wedding."

"He would have loved seeing you in that dress. Come on," he said, offering her his arm, "your groom is waiting."

• • •

Falcon and Kreith walked across a field of high grass in The Fertile Valley. Within weeks the grasses would be harvested and the trees robbed of Fall fruit, and in months the ground would lie fallow under piles of snow.

"I don't know why we can't get married now," Kreith said to Falcon. "What difference is a few years going to make?"

"All the difference in the world," Falcon said solemnly.

"My mother was a young bride. Almost all women are married young."

"These are different circumstances. For one thing, Merry has lost her father and needs time to grieve. For another, she is just beginning to learn the ways of Menon from Niccola. She needs time to grow and for that relationship to mature. Also, you are not running off and marrying a peasant. This union will unite two countries. It should be firmly grounded in Menon. You also need time to develop into the kind of king who will command the respect of his people."

"You have made your point. I understand and will wait the three years. And you will be here to help me become a ruler."

Falcon paused and took a deep breath. He had not wanted to tell Kreith, and yet would not allow anyone else to do so. "No, I won't be, Kreith."

"What do you mean?"

"It is time for me to give up the knighthood. I intend to seek peace, as my father once said. Rafaela and I have decided to live in the Forgotten City."

"But you can't! I still need you!"

Falcon smiled. "No . . . You have fought your first battle and came through victorious. You did not need me then and did not often seek the counsel of advisors. Palmer is right . . . You are a natural leader—you were born to it."

"But my mistakes cost a man his life."

"There are things you cannot learn anywhere but on the battlefield, and that is one of them. Things may not have been different even with years of training. Examine all your decisions, and don't be afraid to go to Jerome if you doubt your abilities."

"Kreith!"

They both turned and watched as Merry came running across the fields, dark hair flying behind her, delight written on her face. She ran to him and fell into his arms. He lifted her from the ground, and Falcon beamed at them as they kissed and laughed.

They began running toward a shady grove, and Kreith slowed enough to yell to Falcon, "Don't leave without saying good-bye."

• • •

McNyre carefully applied another coat to the boat. Duncan had found it for him, and McNyre had spent the last week repairing it and then coating it with strong resin to resist the water.

Temrane sat next to him, stubbornly refusing to cry although the tears clouded his eyes, making it impossible for him to paint the boat.

"Are ye going to sit there all day and not say anything?"

"There's nothing to say," Temrane answered. He and McNyre had not spoken since McNyre told him he was leaving. Temrane had not even asked why, unable to bear the thought.

"Are ye even going to say good-bye when the time comes?"

He looked at McNyre, his eyes pools of misery. "Please don't go," he whispered.

McNyre laid his brush down and faced Temrane, their knees barely touching as they sat on the ground. "I have to go. I should never have left, and now it's time to return."

"Why do you have to go?"

McNyre sighed. At last they would discuss it. "I told ye at one time that it was my destiny. I ran from it, and now it's time to set things right."

"But things may have changed since then! Your country might not even be in slavery anymore."

"Aye, that's true, but I don't know that."

"Then take me with you."

"I can't do that. I plan on returning and freeing my people. Ye have just been through one war. Did ye like it so well that ye want to be involved in another? I couldn't take ye into that."

Temrane sat silently, staring at his feet. "Is that the real reason?"

"What other reason would there be, lad?" he said gently.

"That you are looking for your family."

"I *am* going to look for my family. I thought ye knew that."

"But is that the reason you won't take me?"

McNyre stared hard at Temrane, failing to understand the import of his question. "I'm confused," he said at last.

Temrane boldly looked into McNyre's face. "Because you already have two children, you don't need me anymore. You have your family!"

McNyre gathered Temrane into his arms, holding him close, his own tears threateningly close. "Do ye really believe that, lad? Ye are my life! Ye are like my own son, and it hurts me more than I can say to have to leave."

"Will you at least come back when you're finished?"

"As soon as my people are free, I will return for ye. If my wife has not been wed to someone else, then ye shall live with us as our son. My other son and daughter will be as your brother and sister." A thought suddenly struck him. "Temrane, what about your mother and sister? Ye can't leave them. Maybe ye should go back to Zopel and live with them."

"No. If I can't go with you, I'll stay with Uncle Candy. Merry is going to get married soon to Prince Kreith . . . He told me so. And Mother doesn't wish to see me."

"Why not?" he asked incredulously.

"She knows I didn't pass the Calli-kor, that I have been banned from Corigo in disgrace. Candy said that when he saw her, she didn't do anything but stay in her rooms. She doesn't even have any use for Merry. She believes Candy was banished because of his lack of loyalty to the gods. I can't go home."

Indignation filled McNyre. "That is nonsense! What does Cand say?"

"That we are better off without their laws and sacrifices and lifeless gods."

"I agree. Stay, then, with Cand and Duncan until I return." He picked up Temrane's brush and handed it to him. "Come on now . . . Help me finish this boat. It is going to have to be very sturdy to take me across the ocean and back again."

Temrane smiled and dipped his brush into the resin.

• • •

"The boat is coming along nicely," Cand said as he watched McNyre work. Temrane had gone back to the main castle to get something to eat.

"The wood was still good . . . That helped. I think I'll be ready to sail in two days' time."

"I wanted to talk with you about that."

"All right." McNyre replaced the brush and wiped off his hands, hoping Temrane would bring him something as well.

"Temrane seems easier about your decision to leave him here."

"There was never any question of him going," he said simply.

"I think there was. Tell me what reason you gave him."

"That it was too dangerous, and it is. I'm going into a country that will very soon be at war."

"Is that your real reason?"

McNyre laughed. "That is the exact question he asked me."

"McNyre, I haven't known you long, just a couple of weeks. But I have watched you and Temrane during that time. The two of you have something very special. He told me he didn't like you at first. Sometimes it happens that way. People don't like each other, and then something happens that draws them together. That was what happened with you and Temrane, wasn't it?"

"Aye. We have come through a lot together, and I guess the little differences we had just didn't seem to matter after that."

"I can tell that you love him, and he thinks the sun rises and sets on you."

McNyre closed one eye and focused the other on Cand as though he watched a strange animal. "As ye say, I haven't known ye long, but ye are usually more direct than ye be right now."

Cand laughed. "All right, I will be direct. I know the reason you won't take Temrane, and it has nothing to do with the danger in your country. My love for him stands in your way."

McNyre looked away, anguish wringing his heart. "I can't deny that."

"Then take him with you."

"Take him with me? He is your nephew. I could not deprive ye of his companionship."

Cand smiled. "I have thought about this a long while. When Temrane first disappeared, I thought I would die. He was my life. Well, I have found him again, and if he leaves with you, I will still have a part of him. He will not be taken from me." He sighed and sat down on the ground, motioning to McNyre to join him. "McNyre, I am an old man. Because my brother was so much younger than I, people naturally assumed that I was younger than my age. But I am sixty, and though I could live many years yet, and hope that Menon gives me many, I do not know that I will live long enough to see Temrane to full maturity. He needs a father, McNyre, and though you are a little young to be his father, certainly younger than Fel-hoen, Temrane still looks to you for guidance."

"What are ye going to do?"

"Duncan has decided that he likes traveling, so we shall travel. He wants to talk about Menon in every town in both countries. I want to go with him."

McNyre stared at Cand until Cand laughed. "Smile, McNyre," he said. "I am giving you my permission to take Temrane with you."

As the words sank into his understanding, McNyre smiled, then beamed and began laughing as tears rolled down his cheeks. His laughter was contagious, and soon both were filling the air with their hilarity.

Temrane came over the hill, bringing McNyre some bread and cheese. "What's going on?" he asked, the corners of his mouth lifting slightly as the men's mirth rolled over him.

"We need to finish the boat, lad!" McNyre hollered. "We leave in two days' time!"

• • •

Falcon and Rafaela walked over the endless expanse of sand. "Someday," Falcon said, "this won't be called the Wastelands. Close your eyes, Rafaela. Can you see the wheat? We will plant wheat and grasses and oats. People will stand where we are standing and see nothing but green and yellow growing things. Can you see it?"

She laughed at him. "No. As hard as I try, I can only see sand and more sand. Do you see it?"

"Yes. When I close my eyes I can see it more clearly than I can see the sand with my eyes open. It will be that way someday. And these roads will be traveled. The Forgotten City will be opened up again. People will come here to learn about Menon and His people of old. They will read the books and look at the paintings. They will meet Menon here in a way they cannot in other places. This will be a place of learning."

Rafaela rested her head on his shoulder as they walked, loving the sound of his voice, wanting nothing more from life than to fulfill these dreams of Falcon's. They were her dreams too, visions she had longed to achieve, but could not because of her fear of Crotalus. That was all over now.

And as the newly married couple talked about their desires and plans for the future, so did Cand and Duncan. They had packed their horses and were setting off for Amick. They jogged along the road until they met Falcon and Rafaela and then dismounted.

"I thought you weren't leaving until later tonight," Rafaela said.

"We have had a change of plans," Duncan answered. "McNyre and Temrane are loading the boat; they are ready to leave. My friend did not want to watch Temrane sail away. I think he was afraid of begging Temrane to stay, so we said good-bye and are on our way."

Rafaela put her arms around Duncan. "I shall miss you."

"And I you. You have been a daughter to me, and it is not easy to leave."

"I could not have asked for anything more from you. Come and see us often."

"We will try to come at least once a month."

Rafaela watched them go with tears coursing down her face. Falcon wisely was silent and let her grieve. He knew her emotions; he had felt the same when he said good-bye to Beren. *Changes*, he thought, *everywhere changes.* Would life ever settle down again?

They walked quietly to the dock and saw that McNyre and Temrane were indeed ready to sail. Rafaela hugged Temrane hard, wishing she didn't have to let him go. Temrane returned the embrace. Though he was sad at leaving her, he did not wish to stay. He was going with McNyre, and to him that was everything in the world.

Rafaela then hugged McNyre. "Go with Menon. Turn to Him for counsel and for guidance. I pray that He will protect you and Temrane. Come back to us soon."

"I love ye, Rafaela. Ye and Duncan are the ones who have given me the strength to go back." He clasped her again and then Falcon. He entered the boat with Temrane, singing a song he had learned when he was a boy.

Rafaela turned from the water as the boat set off, the wind catching eagerly at the sail. Falcon gathered her close, trying to tell her with his body that he would never leave her. He gently kissed her nose.

"Falcon, let's go for another walk. Tell me about the wheat."

• • •

Devona walked along the road from Beren to Zopel, her services again in demand. She turned at the sound of jingling behind her.

"Devona, why do you walk?" Batakis asked.

"My wagon needs fixing again. I think I will sell it and the old horses and buy a young horse I can ride."

Batakis helped her up onto the seat. "If we were married, we could sell your team and wagon and not buy anything else. We would make a tidy profit."

"There you go talking about marriage again! You had better be careful, Batakis. I might take you up on that one of these days, and then where will your teasing have got you?"

"I'm not teasing, Devona."

She looked at him, his face more serious than normal, his voice soft.

"Devona, I love you. I have loved you for a long time. I am asking you to marry me." He smiled a little. "I could stop the wagon and get down on my knees."

"There is no need for that. Batakis, I am thirty years older than you."

"That doesn't matter to me! If I love you and you love me, what difference does it make how old we are?"

"A lot of difference. We have nothing in common."

"We have the children in common. They are the most important thing in your life and in mine. You are past the age of having children, and I will never marry if you don't marry me. We both have Menon and a love for Him that surpasses everything, even the children. What more do we need in common?"

She smiled lightly. "Perhaps you are right."

"Does that mean you'll marry me?"

Her eyes twinkled at the eagerness in his voice. "I think I will."

His eyes showed her how much happiness she had brought into his life. "We will have the children at the wedding," he said. "All of them, dressed in flowers and big bouquets . . . and music, lots of music . . ."